Questions & Answers

Public Law

Questions & Answers Series

Series Editors: Rosalind Malcolm and Margaret Wilkie

The ideal revision aid to keep you afloat through your exams

- advice on exam technique
- summary of each topic
- bullet-pointed answer plans
- model answers
- diagrams and flowcharts
- further reading

Q&A Company Law
Stephen Judge

Q&A Criminal Law
Mike Molan and Geoff Douglas

Q&A Employment Law
Richard Benny, Malcolm Sargeant,
and Michael Jefferson

Q&A English Legal System
S.Kunalen and Susan McKenzie

Q&A Equity and Trusts
Margaret Wilkie, Rosalind Malcolm,
and Peter Luxton

Q&A EU Law
Nigel Foster

Q&A Evidence
Maureen Spencer and John Spencer

Q&A Family Law
Penny Booth with Chris Barton
and Mary Hibbs

Q&A Human Rights and Civil Liberties
Steve Foster

Q&A International Law
Susan Breau

Q&A Land Law
Margaret Wilkie, Peter Luxton,
and Rosalind Malcolm

Q&A Landlord and Tenant
Mark Pawlowski and James Brown

Q&A Law of Contract
Adrian Chandler and Ian Brown

Q&A Law of Torts
David Oughton, Barbara Harvey,
and John Marston

Q&A Public Law
Richard Clements and Philip Jones

Questions & Answers

Public Law

FIFTH EDITION

Richard Clements
*Principal Lecturer in Law, Bristol Law School,
University of the West of England*

Philip Jones
*Senior Lecturer in Law, Bristol Law School,
University of the West of England*

2009 and 2010

OXFORD
UNIVERSITY PRESS

OXFORD

UNIVERSITY PRESS

Great Clarendon Street, Oxford OX2 6DP

Oxford University Press is a department of the University of Oxford.
It furthers the University's objective of excellence in research, scholarship,
and education by publishing worldwide in

Oxford New York

Auckland Cape Town Dar es Salaam Hong Kong Karachi
Kuala Lumpur Madrid Melbourne Mexico City Nairobi
New Delhi Shanghani Taipei Toronto

With offices in

Argentina Austria Brazil Chile Czech Republic France Greece
Guatemala Hungary Italy Japan South Korea Poland Portugal
Singapore Switzerland Thailand Turkey Ukraine Vietnam

Oxford is a registered trade mark of Oxford University Press
in the UK and in certain other countries

Published in the United States
by Oxford University Press Inc., New York

First published 1997
Second edition 2001
Reprinted 2002
Third edition 2004
Fourth edition 2007
Fifth edition 2009

British Library Cataloguing in Publication Data

Data available

Library of Congress Cataloging in Publication Data

Data available

Typeset by Laserwords Private Limited, Chennai, India
Printed in Great Britain
on acid-free paper by
Ashford Colour Press Limited, Gosport, Hampshire

ISBN 978–0–19–956075–2

10 9 8 7 6 5 4 3 2 1

Contents

The Q&A Series

Key features

The Q&A series provides full coverage of key subjects in a clear and logical way.

The book contains the following features:

- Questions
- Commentary
- Bullet-pointed answer plans
- Diagrams
- Suggested answers

 online resource centre
www.oxfordtextbooks.co.uk/orc/qanda/

Every book in the Q&A series is accompanied by an Online Resource Centre, hosted at the URL above, which is open-access and free to use.

The online resources for this title include revision and exam advice, a subject-specific glossary, and links to websites useful for the study of public law.

Preface

When this book was first published, in 1997, the current Labour government had just come to power, with many promises of constitutional reform in its election manifesto. The Human Rights Act was swiftly enacted in 1998 and, having been in force since 2000, it has begun to change public law. This can be seen in the chapter on Human Rights but it is also evident in increased challenges to the law on Public Order and changes in the law on Freedom of Expression. A new right of Privacy seems to be developing, as a direct response to the rights guaranteed in the European Convention on Human Rights. The 'War on Terror' was, presumably, not expected in 1997, but this has produced a large amount of anti-terrorist legislation and led to some conflict between the Executive and the Judiciary, with the judges having to interpret that legislation, and sometimes object to that legislation, so that it conforms to human rights. The Human Rights Act has also heightened an awareness of already existing rights and led to more applications for judicial review. It has also increased interest in the previously moribund area of public authority proceedings, dealt with here in the final chapter. Not only have human rights proceedings been brought against the Crown and other public authorities, but there have also been repeated attempts to widen their liability in tort. In 1997, the Labour government also promised to reform the House of Lords. The House of Lords Act 1999 swiftly reduced the number of hereditary peers to 92, but further reform has stalled. The same could be said for rather vague, non-manifesto pledges, to reform the procedures of the House of Commons. There have been changes, but they are not great and the matter of voting reform is still under study, even though all political parties are concerned by the low voter turnout at elections. A Constitutional Reform Act was enacted in 2005. This was not promised in 1997, but its effects are not as sweeping as its title might suggest. The office of Lord Chancellor, which contravened the strict theory of the separation of powers, has been much changed, although the title remains. Many of the functions have been transferred to the new Ministry of Justice, headed by the Secretary of State for Justice. The Lord Chancellor no longer has to be a Lord and so both posts may now be accountable to the Commons. The Judiciary now governs itself and the system for appointing judges has been reformed to reduce Executive influence.

In 2007, the new Prime Minister, Gordon Brown, consulted on whether reform should go further and a written constitution be adopted, together with a UK Bill of Rights and Responsibilities, which would add to the existing rights in the European Convention. Apart from having published proposals (*The Governance of Britain* (2007)), nothing has happened yet but maybe there will be changes to report in the next edition of this book.

We have tried to give flavour to this book by giving views and getting under the skin of how aspects of the constitution really work. You may disagree with a given 'slant' here or there: in a democracy, that is your entitlement!

Our thanks are due to Jane Kay, one of the original authors of this book, who has now retired. Much of the structure of the book and its contents are still the product of her hard work and insight into the workings of the UK constitution. Any errors in the book remain the responsibility of the current authors alone.

Richard Clements
Philip Jones
December 2008

Table of Cases

Table of Statutes

Articles of the ECHR are tabled under Sch 1 of the Human Rights Act 1998

1

Introduction

The two authors have considerable experience in teaching constitutional and administrative law and related subjects. We think that this enables us to give some guidance and advice on how to approach this subject and tackle typical coursework and exam assessment questions. What we do not claim to do is to give you the answer to every possible question that might be asked.

One initial point of clarification. On your course, and in this book, some topics, such as Devolution, specifically consider England, Northern Ireland, Scotland and Wales. Some historical reference may be made to 'Great Britain', 'Britain' or 'England'. This apart, we are considering the constitution of the United Kingdom.

Public law is different from the other compulsory law subjects in that it is very wide ranging. Much of it is not really law at all and therefore calls for different skills in the student. To understand public law properly it helps to have some knowledge of current affairs and politics. Students often think that it is unfair to expect them to know things that are not in the textbook or were not in the lecture but there is a reason for this. Public law is a compulsory subject because of the vital importance of having an understanding of the constitution of the country the laws of which you are studying, for itself and for its significance in terms of the values it rests upon and the historical and cultural context it provides in your further study. Politics is all about governance, so an understanding of who exercises political power, how and why is of immense importance in your study of laws that bind us all in everyday life. You will find your study of constitutional and administrative law very much easier, and probably more engaging, if you keep up with current affairs, even if you never let it darken your door again once the course is over!

With this subject there is often no single, right answer; be it a problem or essay question with which you are faced. There is no constitutional rulebook set in stone and covering every eventuality. For instance a problem question about police powers carries with it the factor that a police officer always has discretion, just as the Prime Minister is constantly faced with decisions requiring him to exercise his judgement, and any essay question concerning constitutional reform is all about argument of options and opinions. It is all about studying in depth and detail, reading enough to encounter 'all' sides of an issue, as well as honing key skills including effective research, critical analysis and evaluation.

As the United Kingdom does not have a 'written constitution', the syllabus is accordingly very wide ranging. Different public law courses will include some different topics and syllabuses may emphasise different themes, although there is a universal core of content. In this book we have tried to tackle the most typical subjects. If you study past examination papers at your institution you will see that there is no magic in what comes up. Rote learning of set answers to set questions is absolutely not what to do. What does assist, however, is that within the parameters of your course, there are only so many topics that can be tested, only so many themes and issues to be examined and only so many styles of problem or essay questions that may be put. This presents an opportunity not for 'question spotting' but to marshal pertinent common material and arguments. Plan in advance by thinking roughly what you would do when faced with several varieties of the same sort of question. The examples we give in the book are meant to help here, embracing many 'typical' questions, demonstrating common lines of argument and emphasising key features of the UK constitution that crop up time and again. You do not have to agree with our arguments or conclusions and they are not designed for regurgitation anyhow. Consider how we have used material and constructed argument.

One particular aspect of constitutional and administrative law is the considerable overlap of topics. In reality no country's constitution operates in conveniently separated boxes. So, you must approach your study and assessments in the same way. You must think across topics and make the links in your answers. It will make all of the difference to your understanding of and success in the subject.

In answering essay questions, objective, coherent, cogent, corroborated argument of all sides is key. Preparation and planning are crucial. You must make effective use of appropriate, referenced sources. Use primary sources wherever possible. Read essay questions carefully, they can often be misunderstood. Identify the main topic first. Do not, as one author once did, mistake a question on Crown privilege for one on the royal prerogative! They are not at all the same thing. Often rather dense and obscure quotations are used, putting propositions and quandaries, followed by 'Discuss'. Do not worry if you have never seen the quotation before or have never heard of the author. In fact the quotation may contain useful information and help to focus your answer. Refer back to and use the quotation as appropriate. Above all, provided you understand what is being said and are clear about the topic area, do not be put off. For example, a question like the following might seem intimidating, but in reality it is not hard.

> The short explanation of the constitutional conventions is that they provide the flesh which clothes the dry bones of the law; they make the legal constitution work; they keep it in touch with the growth of ideas.
> (Sir Ivor Jennings)
> Discuss.

It is obviously about constitutional conventions! It indicates that only a small part of the constitution is law, 'the dry bones'— much of it is convention. They are 'dry bones', because if we only looked at the laws we would get a very misleading impression of the constitution. Without conventions the constitution would be unworkable. Give examples. The 'growth of ideas' bit indicates that conventions are flexible and change as politics and society change. Again, give examples.

To some students, problem questions seem more tangible and clear in public law. The essence is to apply the law to the facts. The facts can be very helpful, provided you make full use of them. Again the first thing to do is to identify the main topics upon which the problem focuses; be warned: it is possible to 'disguise' areas quite easily in this subject. Then you identify the main legal points raised. They should often trigger cases in your memory. Do not worry if you cannot remember the exact name, still make full use of them in your answer. Make sure that you answer the exact question set, fully. For example, if it says 'Advise the police', don't advise the person arrested. If you have two clients to advise concerning three incidents in which both were involved, then your answer structure must have six sub-answers. The advice to both clients may or may not be the same or very similar upon each matter, but the important thing is that you answer the question comprehensively by addressing each element.

Whether you are writing an essay or a problem answer it is always best to do a rough plan first, listing the main points that you intend to cover. For a problem you might also include a list of the main cases. For an essay you would need not just cases, but authors' opinions and examples.

If you have done some work and have some basic knowledge, there is nothing of which to be frightened. Constitutional and administrative law is not about mathematical formulas; you will not get 100% or 0% depending upon your final conclusion (essay question) or advice (problem). What matters is how you get there: identifying the right topic, issues and arguments; effective, substantiated argument; and effective application to the focus of the nub of the question set. Remember, again, that there is rarely a single, right answer.

If you are asked for your view, give it, but ensure that it is given in addition to and not instead of substantiated, objective argument. Reform of the UK constitution seems ever to gather pace, as the government proposals set out in *The Governance of Britain* (2007) illustrate. Hence, questions upon reform may crop up more and more. Even if the entire question is devoted to 'what would you do' in reforming the constitution or an aspect of it, you must still give a full account of what is supposed currently to happen, critical analysis and evaluation of how and why practices have changed, and of what actually happens now, then turning to an informed, corroborated argument for (and model of) reform. Having put forward a proper argument supported by evidence, may you then give your own *political* viewpoint? If the terms and nature of the question make it necessary or appropriate, yes. A problem question upon public disorder will very likely require strict application of law to facts only, but a discursive essay question upon the same topic may well seek your view. If you think that the Public Order Act 1986 is draconian in its impact upon freedom of expression and protest, or, to give a different illustration, that the UK's membership of the European Union is vital to prevent the growth of nationalism and xenophobia, so be it: provided, as with everything, what you write or say is relevant and material. If you are asked for an opinion on the way in which European Union law has affected the traditional doctrine of the sovereignty of Parliament, do not express the view that you hate all things European and that you dislike the way 'foreigners' are taking over this country! Irrespective of the marker's opinion of such a opinion, it fails the test of relevance and materiality. It has no bearing upon the legal and political issues concerning the question posed. Instead, what you should do is show that you are aware of the domestic and European Court of Justice case law on this subject, and, in a really good answer, are aware of why the law has evolved in that way.

As in all legal subjects, there are not any real short cuts to success but we hope that this book can convince you that public law is not quite as intimidating as you thought.

Constitutions; the Nature and Sources of the United Kingdom Constitution

Introduction

For many, this is the most difficult area of the whole subject. It is rather theoretical and seems to have no beginning and no end. Different lecturers have very different approaches in this area. Some like to include a lot of political theory and others do not. We hope that the Questions and Suggested Answers in this chapter help your understanding of the key ideas and issues.

There is a fairly traditional set of issues that have been considered relevant to 'the nature of the UK constitution'. For reasons of space this book has restricted itself to them. However, the techniques indicated in the Suggested Answers may be applied to other constitutional questions. These questions might be general, such as 'What is democracy?', 'Is the UK democratic?', 'What is the nature of the State?', or 'Explain limited government and the concept of legitimacy'. More specific issues such as federation or the lack of a written constitution might also be investigated. In some respects these are just more modern ways of asking the old questions like, 'what is the Rule of Law?' or 'does a separation of powers control the Executive?' Often the same sort of material, such as cases, past political incidents or academic opinion crops up whatever the question being asked. For example, a famous case like *Council of Civil Service Unions v Minister for the Civil Service* [1985] AC 374 could be used to illustrate arguments relating to Convention, the Rule of Law, the Separation of Powers, the lack of a written Bill of Rights as well as the attitudes of the courts to the State and the unlimited power of the government.

A good starting point is, why does any country have a constitution at all? The obvious answers are: first, to limit the power of the government so that it cannot do whatever it likes; secondly, to protect the rights or liberties of the individual not just from the government but also from other powerful groups; and a third less obvious reason is legitimacy. Why does 'the people' accept that a particular small group of individuals is entitled to govern and set the laws of the land? This is often a function of a written constitution: such documents often say that the people of the country have decided upon these particular constitutional arrangements. For example, 'We the People of the United States do ordain and establish this constitution for the United States of America.'

The UK is different: it is one of the few countries in the world without a 'written constitution'. Most constitutional writing concerning the UK would claim that, despite this, the UK does have a constitution. Some critics, however, dating back to Thomas Paine in the eighteenth century (*The Rights of Man* (1792)) and continuing into modern times (for instance F. F. Ridley 'There is no British Constitution: A Dangerous Case of the Emperor's Clothes' (1988) 41 Parliamentary Affairs) claim that the UK's arrangements are so defective that there is no constitution at all as none of the key aims (granting legitimacy, limiting government and safeguarding liberties) is achieved. Many countries with a written constitution have specialist courts to deal with public law issues, separate from the private law courts. This system is not known in the UK because, without a written constitution, there is not a clear-cut distinction between public law and private law.

The conventional view, as put in for example A. V. Dicey's *Introduction to the Study of the Law of the Constitution* (1885), Sir Ivor Jennings' *The Law and the Constitution* (1959), is that the UK does have a constitution, but in contrast with a written constitution, which is set out in one or a limited series of documents, it is 'unwritten', namely coming from many different sources, such as statutes, cases and Crown prerogative, and not being protected from change. The inherent flexibility and evolution is supposed to be the advantage of the UK constitution.

Much of the UK constitution is now written down, in a whole swathe of statute law. However, a significant element is unwritten and indeed not law, being the Conventions of the constitution, which oil the wheels and plug the gaps. Vitally important matters like the existence of the Prime Minister and the real powers of the Queen are governed by convention.

Some consider 'restraining principles' such as the Rule of Law and the Separation of Powers as sources; we consider these topics later, in the context of restraining the power of the State.

Question 1

A written constitution would make a great improvement to the United Kingdom system of government.
   Discuss.

Commentary

A constitutional law course will often start by considering what a constitution is, including a comparison between so called 'written' and 'unwritten' constitutions. Many students will be hoping for a question like this to turn up in an examination, but it is not quite as straightforward as it seems to write a *good* answer to a question like this.

The phrase 'written constitution' is really a misnomer. A written constitution need not be contained in one document and the constitution could be a few pages long or hundreds of pages long. Some unwritten constitutional conventions will also operate. By the same token, an 'unwritten constitution' will include some elements that are written down somewhere. A written constitution is one that is largely codified in one document or a limited series of documents and, invariably, has legal status. A particular country's written constitution may be short and vague or long and detailed, and it may or may not have special, higher legal status than the ordinary laws of the land. An unwritten constitution is not codified as described above, instead having many different sources.

The question poses a proposition. The student should not take it for granted as being right and indeed does not have to agree with it. Typical of many public law questions, there is no single, right answer to this kind of question. What is required in answer is cogently to argue all sides of the issue, in essence discuss the arguments for and against a change to a written constitution for the UK discuss coming to a substantiated conclusion. An effective answer will proffer sufficient examples of points made, including up-to-date examples.

Answer plan

- What a constitution is for
- Written constitutions are adopted following major upheaval such as independence or revolution
- Written constitutions have legal status, sometimes as higher law with a special amendment procedure
- Written constitutions often contain a Bill of Rights
- The UK constitution comprises many sources including statutes, cases and conventions
- An unwritten constitution is flexible, whereas written constitutions may be rigid
- A written constitution cannot contain or provide for everything.

Suggested answer

Every organised state has a constitution, but it does not necessarily have to be a written one. Even clubs and societies have a constitution, as there have to be some rules and the members need to know who has the power to make decisions or take actions. So what is the purpose of a constitution? A constitution grants legitimacy to the State and its governance, provides for how the State is to be governed, limits the power of those who govern and (in a liberal democracy) protects the individual citizen from them. It is there to ensure that those who run the State do not behave in an *arbitrary* manner. They must act according to the rules and procedures and not just persecute a citizen for no good reason. For example, a government official could not just say to someone 'I do not like you, you cannot live in this country.' Instead there must be laws about nationality, immigration and fair trial. A constitution provides for these things, but just as importantly it would also state who has the power to do what. Who can make laws, is there a Head of State, is there a Prime Minister and who has the real power to decide?

Nearly every country in the world, apart from the UK, New Zealand and Israel, has a written constitution. Generally, countries adopt a written constitution when there is a dramatic break with the past and there is a need to make a fresh start with a new system of governance. For example, the end of the eighteenth century saw the United States of America obtaining its independence (from the UK) and the French Revolution overthrowing the rule of King Louis XVI, each country consciously embracing a new beginning with a new, written constitution. England was, in fact, one of the first countries to have a written constitution, with Oliver Cromwell's 'Instrument of Government' in 1653, after he had overthrown and executed Charles I. It only lasted, however, until 1660, when the old system of royal government was restored. Since then the UK system of government has changed out of all recognition, but it has changed gradually and there has never been such a drastic break with the past that required or engendered a general desire from politicians or the people for a written constitution.

The constitution of the United States is generally considered a 'classic model' written constitution starting as it does with a clear statement of the 'values':

> We the people of the United States, in order to form a more perfect union, establish justice, insure domestic tranquility, provide for the common defense, promote the general welfare, and secure the blessings of liberty to ourselves and our posterity, do ordain and establish this Constitution for the United States of America.
>
> We hold these truths to be self-evident, that all men are created equal, that they are endowed by their Creator with certain unalienable Rights, that among these are Life, Liberty and the pursuit of Happiness.

The UK has no such statement so we have to rely on writers like the nineteenth century Dicey, for statements of constitutional values.

A written constitution often lays down a special procedure under which the constitution can be changed. For example, Article V of the US Constitution stipulates that two-thirds of both Houses of the Congress or two-thirds of the legislatures of the States can propose amendments to the Constitution. This has to be ratified by the legislatures of three-quarters of the States. In the Republic of Ireland, a Bill passed by both Houses of Parliament, together with a majority of the votes in a referendum and the assent of the President amends the Constitution. In contrast, there is no special procedure to change any part of the UK constitution.

The written constitution of a federal country will tend to detail the federal structure, providing for (in whatever degree of detail) the powers of the regions (often called ' states' or 'provinces') and the powers of the central or federal government. The unification of once independent 'countries' to form a federal state is often the reason for adopting a written constitution and occurred in the United States of America, Canada, Australia, Nigeria, Malaysia and Germany, to give just a few examples. The UK, as the name suggests, is a union of once separate countries, but it is not federal. Instead, the Parliament of the UK, which sits at Westminster, retains full legislative supremacy. It has recently granted varying degrees of self-government to Scotland, in the Scotland Act 1998, to Northern Ireland in the Northern Ireland Act 1998 and to Wales in the Government of Wales Acts of 1998 and 2006. The UK Parliament can, however, repeal those Acts and regain full powers to govern Scotland, Northern Ireland and Wales. There is no written constitution to stop the sovereign Parliament of the UK doing this. The question is whether Westminster would do this, which comes down to political acceptability and consequences.

Many written constitutions contain a list of 'Rights', to which the citizen is entitled. Often, as in the United States and Germany, they are constitutionally protected and cannot easily be taken away by the Executive or Legislature. The UK has a Bill of Rights from 1689, but that was designed more to reduce the power of the King rather than to grant individual rights. The Human Rights Act 1998 now gives domestic force to most of the European Convention on Human Rights. Section 3 of this Act, however, carefully preserves the supremacy of Parliament. UK courts cannot 'strike down' (judicially review) primary legislation even if it is incompatible with human rights, and Act of Parliament can still restrict human rights.

Most written constitutions contain some sort of 'organisation chart' of government and explain whether there was a President or Prime Minister, or both, and what their powers are, who has the power to legislate, who appoints the judges, and so on. There is no equivalent in the UK, as the system of governance has just evolved over the centuries. The Head of State is the Monarch, which is a matter of ancient common law, and there is no law that says that there has to be a Prime Minister. The existence of a Prime Minister is down to 'convention' or non-legal custom (below).

As seen, the UK constitution can be found in many sources. Acts of Parliament are important and many are of constitutional significance such as the Act of Settlement 1700 and the European Communities Act 1972. More and more of the UK constitution is now developed by passage of Acts of Parliament. These can be very important changes, for example the Human Rights Act 1998, making positive human rights directly enforceable in UK courts for the first time or the Constitutional Reform Act 2005 in strengthening the separation of powers. This indicates that nothing is permanent in the UK constitution, everything may change.

Cases also form important sources of the UK constitution. For example, the House of Lords reaffirmed the principle of the supremacy of Parliament in *Pickin v BRB* [1974] AC 765, but a few years later had to moderate it, to take account of membership of the European Union in *Factortame (No. 2)* [1991] 1 AC 603. Unlike many of the countries with a written constitution, the UK does not have a Constitutional Court that rules on constitutional issues; it should be noted that the new Supreme Court to be established under the Constitutional Reform Act 2005 in no way mirrors that of the United States for example. All legal cases, constitutional or not, go through the same court system

Historic documents, such as the Magna Carta 1215 and the Bill of Rights 1689 are important for establishing constitutional principles, such as the idea that the King or Executive does not have unlimited power, but these documents do not have the special, formal legal status of a written constitution; indeed all law in the UK is ordinary law, be it concerning the constitution or any other matter.

A lot of the UK constitution is not legal at all and consists of constitutional conventions, which were defined by Dicey in his *The Law of the Constitution* as: 'understandings, habits or practices which, although they may regulate the conduct of the several members of the sovereign power are not in reality laws at all since they are not enforced by the courts.' (p. 24 10th edn 1959). Much of the most important parts of the constitution can be found in convention, such as the existence of the Prime Minister, the Cabinet, ministerial responsibility, accountability to Parliament and how the considerable legal powers of the Queen are exercised by ministers in her name. Constitutional conventions are not legally enforceable (*Attorney-General v Jonathan Cape Ltd* [1976] QB 752) and whilst in one sense are constant, may be said to be constantly changing. For example, whereas in the 1950s a minister would have had to resign for having an extra-marital affair or for being homosexual, neither of itself commands resignation today.

This is supposed to be the major advantage of an unwritten constitution, its flexibility and its ability to change. By contrast, it can be difficult to change a written constitution. On the other hand, if everything can change, as it can with the UK constitution, then the protection of individual liberties is arguably less strong. Also, without the relative certainty of a rigid written constitution, the citizen and even the politician may find it more difficult to know just where he stands in terms of the true constitutional position.

Some think that Prime Ministers and the governments that they lead have too much power and can take away any right by just using Parliament to pass an Act or by merely changing a convention. However, even in countries with written constitutions, that document is unlikely to reveal the full constitutional position. For instance in the United States, the power of the Supreme Court to strike down legislation for 'unconstitutionality' is not found in the written constitution but in a case, *Marbury v Madison* 1803 1 Cranch 137. Under Article II of the US

Constitution, the President needs the consent of the Senate to agree treaties, but a practice or convention has grown up of making 'Executive Agreements' with other countries without Senate approval.

The difference between a written and unwritten constitution is not as great as some suppose, because it is not possible to write down everything in a document that will be valid for all time. Much of the UK constitution is in Acts of Parliament anyway and that is increasingly the position today. Every country has different constitutional arrangements and those of the UK just reflect its individual history of being one of the oldest unified states in the world.

Question 2

The main purpose of constitutional conventions is to ensure that the legal framework of the Constitution will be operated in accordance with the prevailing constitutional values or principles of the period.

(*Re Amendment of the Constitution of Canada* [1982] 125 DLR (3d) 1)

Discuss.

Commentary

Nineteenth century writers like A. V. Dicey and early twentieth century ones like Sir Ivor Jennings stressed the importance of conventions in the UK constitution. Probably they over-stressed their importance and constitutional writers looked for conventions that did not really exist, for instance in the area of ministerial responsibility. There was a reaction in the 1960s and some writers asserted that there were no such things as conventions. Opinion has now swung back again, as in *Re Canada* (1982). Conventions definitely exist and are of significance in the UK constitution. Questions on conventions usually demand familiar territory to be considered: what are conventions, how do they operate, how do they change and how are they enforced? The student is usually expected to be critical, often done most effectively by using specific examples of operation, breach and sanction.

Answer plan

- Habits or practices, or mandatory conduct of those involved in the day-to-day workings of the constitution
- Conventions are not laws and thus not legally enforceable
- Conventions are enforced by peer pressure, public opinion or personal morality
- Conventions evolve over time.

Suggested answer

In all constitutions, even those that are written, like that of Canada, various practices or ways of doing things that are not strictly provided for in the constitution grow up over the years. These practices can harden and become the accepted way of doing things. Then they may be called conventions. In *Re Canada* (1982), although the written Canadian constitution did not require it, it was the convention that the consent of the Canadian provinces be obtained before changes were made to the constitution.

In the UK, a country without a written constitution, conventions are particularly important. In the late nineteenth century, Dicey drew attention to the role of conventions in the UK. He believed that most of the UK constitution and many of its most important parts consisted of conventions. This did not mean that there were no rules, merely that a lot of the rules were not legal ones. As he put it in *Introduction to the Study of the Law of the Constitution* (1885):

> The other set of rules consist of conventions, understandings, habits or practices which, though they may regulate the conduct of several members of the sovereign power, of the Ministers, or of other officials, are not in reality laws at all since they are not enforced by the courts. This portion of constitutional law may, for the sake of distinction, be termed 'the conventions of the constitution', or constitutional morality.

If one looks only at the legal rules of the constitution, this gives a seriously misleading impression. Legally, the Queen may refuse the Royal Assent to a parliamentary Bill. However, by convention she always agrees, taking the advice of Her Majesty's government. Legally, the Queen chooses the Prime Minister, but by convention it is always the person who can command a majority in the House of Commons. By law the Queen chooses her own ministers, but by convention they are chosen by the Prime Minister.

Conventions are clearly not the law because, as in the above examples, they sometimes contradict the strict legal position. The courts take judicial notice of the existence of conventions and in considering them where relevant to the case decision, they may influence that decision, but the courts cannot enforce conventions because they are not law. In *Attorney-General v Jonathan Cape* [1976] QB 752 there is an interesting discussion of the various conventions relating to Cabinet secrecy, but the court could not enforce them, only the material law, breach of confidence. In *Madzimbamuto v Lardner-Burke* [1969] AC 645 the court observed that there was a convention that the UK would not legislate for (the then) Rhodesia without that colony's consent. This however did not stop the UK Parliament from legislating in breach of the convention if it chose.

There are many examples of convention. It is probably impossible to make a complete list. The office of Prime Minister and the existence of the Cabinet are conventional only. Ministers are accountable to Parliament and responsible for the actions of their civil servants. Significant parts of the Ministerial Code reflect conventional behaviour; although the Code is written down, it is not of legally status and merely reproduces convention. Parliament meets every year, but the Bill of Rights 1689 only says that it should meet 'frequently'.

Conventions do not just affect politicians and the Monarch, they apply also to the judges, to councillors, to all involved in the workings of the constitution. So, for example, it is by convention that Law Lords usually do not participate in the legislative work of the House of Lords.

One of the difficulties with conventions is identifying a convention. It can be hard to differentiate between what is convention and what merely everyday behaviour, or more specifically day-to-day politics. Whereas some such as Dicey (above) saw conventions as describing what happens (habit, practice) (above), others consider conventions to prescribe acceptable conduct. In *The Law and the Constitution* (1959) Sir Ivor Jennings recommended a three-stage test. First, what are the precedents; how often and how consistently has this practice been observed before? Secondly, did the actors in the precedent believe themselves to be bound by the rule, obliged to follow the precedent? Thirdly, there must be a reason for the rule. In other words, the convention must fit in with the perceived notion of what should be done and how, according to the accepted principles or values of the constitution like democracy, accountability. This test works well with some of the major conventions, for example, the convention that the Royal Assent always be given. The precedents are very strong, no Monarch having refused since 1708. It seems clear that the present Queen considers herself bound by the convention, having strictly followed the precedent throughout her reign of more than 50 years. The principal reason for the rule is that an hereditary Monarch should abide by the wishes of the democratic government; it would be unacceptable for an unelected Monarch to interfere. Whilst the convention regulating Royal Assent is a strong, well-established example on the Jennings test, it is not so clear-cut with some others, such as when a minister should resign, and this to some gives rise to doubts about conventions generally.

Conventions are continually changing. Up until 1902 a Prime Minister could come from the House of Lords or Commons. Since then they have always come from the Commons. From the 1960s a convention was established that no new hereditary peerages would be created, yet in the 1980s Mrs Thatcher created one (and this was followed by her own ennoblement). So, is there a convention here and, if so, what is it; it certainly is not strongly established on the Jennings test, being questionable if not falling down on precedent. How conventional behaviour evolves may either add to or lessen stability and certainty in assessing what will or should happen next time, in essence will the convention be followed. Also, of course, new conventions may be established. For example, Tony Blair was the first Prime Minister to attend the Liaison Committee comprising the 'Chairs' of the various select committees and set up to question the incumbent Prime Minister monthly. Gordon Brown has followed Mr Blair's precedent and so, whilst there is no legal requirement for attendance, there is now the expectation of this and perhaps an ever-strengthening sense of obligation. As an editorial in *Public Law* in 1963, pp. 401–2, put it: 'so let us delete those pages in constitutional textbooks headed conventions, and talk about what happens and why what happened yesterday may not happen tomorrow'.

Conventions are called rules but they do not look much like rules. They are often vague and imprecise. In contrast with laws, there is no body or designated procedure for making a convention. In many cases, despite the efforts of writers like Jennings, it is hard to say whether a convention exists or not.

Even if existence and breach of convention is established in a given situation, there may still be difficulty in enforcement. If a law is broken, a binding court order and penalty will follow. But what if, for example, a minister is revealed to have lied to Parliament in clear breach of convention? Whereas the minister may choose to resign or be forced by the Prime Minister to resign, this is not necessarily the case. Whilst Foreign Secretary Lord Carrington and his ministerial team resigned as a matter of honour in 1982 following the Argentinean invasion of the Falklands, such proactive conduct is rare. If one traces through the many ministerial 'lapses in conduct' of the 1980s and 1990s, most were seen to cling to office and try to ride out the very public media scrutiny and political pressure, usually supported by the Prime Minster of the time. Even leaving aside the lack of independence of the Prime Minister and his motivation (from principle to pragmatism to expediency), is it satisfactory that some resign and others do not? Whilst the inherent flexibility may better suit what is more naturally a political rather than legal realm of constitutional activity, this leaves those unhappy with the outcome with no recourse, with principles, values and even morals at stake. The major apologists for conventions had their solutions. Dicey states that if a convention was broken then legal problems would eventuate. His example was that if Parliament did not meet every year, the Budget could not be authorised nor could a standing army, both legal necessities. It is hard to see how this could apply to some conventions like, for instance, ministerial responsibility. Jennings believed that conventions had to be obeyed because 'the system' would break down if they were not and 'political difficulties' would arise. If the Queen refused her Assent there would be a crisis as indeed there could be if the Prime Minister tried to govern without a majority. Again this can only apply to some conventions. When Mrs Thatcher refused Opposition nominations for life peerages hardly anyone noticed.

Re Canada (1982) considered the sanctions available. In extreme cases of unconventional behaviour a constitutional superior can dismiss the guilty person. In 1975 the Prime Minister of Australia was dismissed by the Governor-General for trying to govern without an approved Budget. Prime Ministers sometimes dismiss erring ministers. The real enforcement though is reflected in the quotation in the question. Conventions merely reflect 'the prevailing constitutional values or principles of the period'. This recognises that conventions change over time; indeed it may be argued that, far from being the rock of constancy, conventions are constantly changing. It would now be utterly unacceptable for the Queen actively to rule the UK or an unelected Lord to lead the government. It also means that constitutional 'rules' are not like 'legal rules'. As Dicey suggested years ago they are more like moral rules. Politicians, judges and others refrain from breaking constitutional rules because they accept the rule in terms of right and wrong behaviour or perhaps because they fear the disapproval of their peers or the public. As with any moral rule, there are genuine disagreements as to what the rules are and some rules are considered more important than others. There are strong or normative conventions such as those that surround the role of the Queen. These will seldom, if ever, be broken. In contrast there are weak or simple conventions, for example that judges must abstain from party politics, perhaps more honoured in the breach than the observance.

The UK system, which is based on conventions, can accommodate enormous constitutional change without the need for a revolution or new constitution. That the Queen no longer governs is just one example. The weakness is that the evolution of the constitution cannot be halted and government may be tempted by the lack of legal restraint to take more power for itself. For example, local government was considered a counter-balance to central government but since the Second World War central government has removed much of its powers. This may or may not be 'unconventional' but it is not illegal.

Question 3

The UK is becoming a more federal country.
 Discuss.

Commentary

The structure of the UK is dealt with in the early chapters of most public law textbooks. Many students read this quickly and dismiss it as raising no constitutional issues worth discussing. Indeed, most English-based students probably think that the undoubted fact that Scotland and Northern Ireland have different legal systems from that of England is of no great interest, because they have already been told that they are only studying English law. This is reminiscent of earlier constitutional writers, such as Dicey, who wrote of the constitution of 'England', which usually included Scotland and sometimes Ireland as well! We should not, however, take the structure of the UK for granted, as it is a product of history and has changed over the centuries. Since the Labour government came to power in 1997, the UK constitution has changed, with devolution for Wales and Northern Ireland and the re-establishment of a Scottish Parliament after an absence of nearly three centuries. The key to answering this question is an understanding of the structure of the UK, which is nothing like as uniform as is sometimes imagined, and an attempt to define the word 'federal'. Anyone can look it up in the dictionary, but, like many words of constitutional significance, its exact meaning remains elusive, with different writers defining it differently.

Answer plan

- The difference between a unitary and a federal state
- The structure of the UK
- Devolution of administration
- The primary legislative powers of the Scottish Parliament
- The delegated legislative powers of the Welsh Assembly
- The restoration of self-government to the Northern Ireland Assembly
- A written constitution for the UK. The conundrum of parliamentary sovereignty
- The definition of a federal state.

Suggested answer

It is usually assumed, without too much discussion, that the UK is a unitary state. Like many other basic ideas in the UK constitution it can be traced back to the nineteenth century writings of A. V. Dicey, where he stated in his *The Law of Constitution* that:

> Unitarianism, in short, means the concentration of the strength of the State in the hands of one visible sovereign power be that Parliament or Czar.

By contrast:

> Federalism means the distribution of the force of the State among a number of co-ordinate bodies each originating in and controlled by the constitution.

Crudely then, unitarianism means a concentration of power at the centre, whilst federalism means a distribution of power between the central authority and, say, regional governments. Some would be satisfied with this rough and ready distinction, but Dicey is saying that there is more to it than that. The sovereignty of Parliament meant that the UK had to be a unitary state because Parliament did not share its supreme legislative authority with any other person or body. Conversely, in a federal state, supreme authority would lie in a written constitutional document, which would divide power between the central authority and the regions, provinces, states or whatever they might be called. So it depends upon what one means by federalism. It is therefore necessary to consider the structure of the UK to establish whether any divisions of authority between different governmental spheres may be identified.

The structure of the UK is not as uniform as is sometimes supposed, because it is a union of several countries that were once separate. Wales was conquered by England in the middle ages, but the two countries were not formally united until an Act of Parliament in 1536. The same legal system operates in both England and Wales, but some of the administration of government was devolved to Wales as long ago as 1964 with the establishment of the Welsh Office, headed by the Secretary of State for Wales, a minister in the UK 'Whitehall' government.

Scotland was never conquered by England, but instead the two countries voluntarily united. From 1603 they were ruled by the same king and by the Treaty of Union 1707, the two countries merged to form Great Britain. Their two separate Parliaments became (or were replaced by) one, but, in the Treaty, care was taken to preserve some distinctly different Scottish institutions. Private law, the courts, the church and universities were all protected from change by the new Parliament of Great Britain. To this day Scottish law, the church, education and local government remain different from their English equivalents. As with Wales, some of the administration of government was restored to Scotland with the establishment of a Scottish Office and a Secretary of State for Scotland in 1928.

Ireland presents a far more complicated picture. The kings of England had been trying to conquer and subdue that country since the twelfth century. For a short period from 1782 an Irish Parliament, with legislative independence, existed, until 1800 when there was an attempt to emulate the 1707 union of England and Scotland. The Union with Ireland Act formed the United Kingdom of Great Britain and Ireland and established one Parliament for the new country. This arrangement has not proved as enduring as the union of England and Scotland, because of the growth of a 'Home Rule' movement in nineteenth century Ireland, which turned into demands for outright independence in the early twentieth century. The southern part of Ireland broke away in 1920 to form an independent country, which was formally recognised by the UK Parliament by the Ireland Act 1949.

Northern Ireland remained part of the United Kingdom and under the Government of Ireland Act 1920 had its own Parliament, Prime Minister, Cabinet and Civil Service. This Parliament, however, only had limited powers to legislate, no power to raise taxes and it was clear that the Westminster Parliament retained supremacy. Due to the upsurge of nationalist feeling in the late 1960s and 1970s, 'direct rule' from London replaced the Unionist-dominated 'Stormont Parliament', itself suspended in 1972 and never restored.

The 'British Islands' present an interesting constitutional anomaly. The Channel Islands are not part of the UK, but instead are possessions of the Monarch. These islands retain their ancient legislatures, governments, courts and legal systems.

They have considerable autonomy to make their own laws, even those relating to taxation. It is generally thought that the Westminster Parliament retains legislative supremacy and could override the wishes of the islands, but, by convention, it does not do this and instead seeks the agreement of the island governments. The Isle of Man is another ancient kingdom and it, too, retains its own legislature, Tynwald, its own government and legal system. It is clear that the UK Parliament still has ultimate legislative authority, but again, in practice it is not exercised.

So, it can be seen that a number of separate legislatures and governments already exist or have existed within the UK. Because of an increase in support for nationalist political parties in Scotland and Wales, a Royal Commission on the Constitution was established in 1969, reporting in 1973. This 'Kilbrandon Report' came up with the idea of 'devolution':

> the delegation of central government powers without the relinquishment of sovereignty.

The Labour government tried to implement this for Scotland and Wales in 1978, but there was insufficient support expressed in the referendums held in each country.

In the Scotland Act 1998, a Scottish Parliament, elected by the voters of Scotland, was re-established with full legislative power, except for those matters specifically reserved to the Westminster Parliament. The Scots Parliament also has the power to vary the basic rate of income tax by up to 3% and to determine spending priorities. A Scottish government has been established with ministers and its own 'First Minister'. Indeed, the Scotland Act could almost be regarded as a kind of 'written constitution' for Scotland for it defines many things that are left to convention in the Westminster arrangements. It specifies how the First Minister is to be chosen and requires 'special majorities' of two-thirds, to do things like call an early election or dismiss a Scottish judge.

Since 1998, the Scottish Parliament has grown in influence. Under the 'Sewel convention' the UK government has agreed that it will not legislate on matters devolved to Scotland, unless the Scottish Parliament consents. This Parliament is now controlled by the Scottish National Party and it has suggested replacing the council tax with a local income tax and, more importantly, holding a referendum on independence for Scotland.

Under the Government of Wales Act 1998, Wales now has an elected Assembly. The Assembly only has the power to enact delegated legislation, although it too has the equivalent of a First Minister (the 'Leader of the Assembly') and a government (the Executive Committee'), which is accountable to the Assembly.

The powers of the Welsh Assembly have been extended by the Government of Wales Act 2006, extending the matters upon which the Assembly may legislate. There is also the possibility of the Welsh Assembly gaining full legislative powers, if the people of Wales agree in a referendum. Yet the 2006 Act clearly states the UK Parliament retains the ultimate power to legislate for Wales.

The Northern Ireland Act 1998 restored devolved government to that country and established an elected Assembly with legislative powers. It, however, has considerably less power than the Scottish Parliament, as it is unable to legislate on a number of matters reserved or excepted to the Westminster Parliament. Unlike the Scotland Act, the Northern Ireland Act makes clear that it does not affect the power of the UK Parliament to make laws for Northern Ireland on any subject. There is a Northern Irish government, however, with ministers accountable to the Assembly. As in the Scotland and Wales Acts, there are provisions distinctly resembling a 'written constitution'. For instance, 'special majorities' are required to elect the First Minister and Deputy First Minister. This caused problems with the first elected Assembly of 1999, when the republican Sinn Fein and the Unionist parties could not agree over who should be First Minister. Accordingly the Westminster Parliament resumed control under the Northern Ireland Act 2000. Devolved government was restored by another Act of the UK Parliament, the Northern Ireland (St. Andrews Agreement) Act 2006. Also, in 2006, control over policing was ceded to the Northern Ireland Assembly and now an agreement to implement this has been reached by the key parties, supposedly the last piece in the 'jigsaw' of 'home rule' by the mandatory coalition representing both communities.

So has the UK become a federal state? According to Bradley and Ewings' *Constitutional and Administrative Law* a federal state would need a written constitution to guarantee that the autonomy granted to Northern Ireland, Scotland and Wales could not legally be removed again by the Westminster Parliament. It has been argued (above) that Scotland, Wales and Northern Ireland already have written constitutions in the form of the Acts of Parliament establishing their localised governance. All that is lacking is something similar for England. There still remains the obstacle that the Westminster Parliament remains supreme, even if there might be slight doubts in Scotland and the Channel Islands. The power that it has given can be taken away or as Munro puts it in *Studies in Constitutional Law*:

> ... the United Kingdom is classed as a unitary, not a federal state. The Parliament at Westminster is omnicompetent.

Not all definitions of federalism are quite so legalistic. For instance, de Smith and Brazier (*Constitutional and Administrative Law*) define it in more practical, political terms:

> The difference between a federal and non-federal constitution will often be clear-cut; sometimes it will only be one of degree; sometimes it will be positively misleading.

So in reality is the UK a federal state? Even though Northern Ireland, Wales and, particularly, Scotland have been granted increasing rights to legislate on their own affairs, how much independence do Wales, Ireland, Scotland, the Channel Islands and the Isle of Man really have? What has been granted can be taken away, as the experience of Northern Ireland indicates. The more powerful Westminster Parliament and government usually have the means to ensure that their wishes are respected, even without legislation. For instance, Westminster decides how great a share of tax revenue each part of the UK receives. However, the Scottish Parliament is the most powerful of the devolved structures and, if the people of Scotland actually voted for full independence, that might call into question how powerful the UK Parliament ultimately is; as a matter of law, it could still abolish the Scottish Parliament, but, as a political reality, this seems highly unlikely.

Further reading

Barnett, H. *Constitutional and Administrative Law*, 7th edn (Cavendish, 2008), chs 1, 2, 4 and 5.

Bradley, A. and Ewing, K. *Constitutional and Administrative Law*, 14th edn (Longman, 2006), chs 1, 2, 5 and 6.

Loveland, I. *Constitutional Law, Administrative Law and Human Rights*, 4th edn (OUP, 2006), chs 1, 3 and 9.

Prime Minister and Cabinet

Introduction

This topic will be included in any constitutional law course. Assessment questions in this area are common and often concern the same territory, classically for example the relationship between Prime Minister and Cabinet.

The working of the constitution here is governed largely by convention rather than law. At the risk of stating the obvious, it is all about politics.

For both problem and essay questions, strong answers will be distinguished by effective use of examples. It is important to show familiarity with current political developments, showing the reader/marker that you are aware of the significance of the subject you are studying.

Question 1

To what extent is it true to say that the UK has moved from a system of Cabinet government to a system of Prime Ministerial government?

Commentary

This is one of the classic subjects for debate in constitutional law, and there are as many opinions on it as there are commentators. The conclusion you may reach is less important than the quality of the arguments displayed. Because the question addresses change in the constitution, you must show an awareness of change over time, that is, how the situation has developed historically. It will also be desirable to make comparisons between specific Prime Ministers. Any reference to contemporary developments will impress, though the core of the answer should include the classic examples of Prime Ministers using their powers, or being prevented from doing so by Cabinet. A distinguished answer will 'bring alive' the practical working of the senior reaches of government, peppered with reference to styles of leadership of key individuals and the influence of key circumstances and events. In essence, government boils down the 'human factor', behaviour and interactions.

Answer plan

- PM's powers derive from convention
- Choosing members of government
- Control of Cabinet and its committees
- Downing Street staff
- Style, circumstances, events.

Suggested answer

When Bagehot wrote his classic study of the UK constitution in 1867, he identified the Cabinet as the central controlling institution and the principal today of the 'efficient' parts of the system. When, however, in 1963 Richard Crossman (a Shadow Cabinet member at the time) provided a new introduction to Bagehot's work, he wrote:

> The post-war epoch has seen the final transformation of Cabinet Government into Prime Ministerial Government.

Many commentators have agreed with Crossman, especially concerning the prime ministerships of Margaret Thatcher (1979–90) and of Tony Blair (1997–2007). In the case of Mrs Thatcher, arguably Cabinet government was ultimately reinforced, as a key factor in her being forced from office was that she no longer really had the confidence of her cabinet.

In the UK constitution, both Cabinet and Prime Minister are creatures of convention. Their functions and powers are not defined by law, but have developed gradually in order to provide a form of government answerable to Parliament rather than to the Monarch. The Cabinet developed from the practice of government ministers meeting in private, in the absence of the Monarch, to agree upon policies to be presented to Parliament. No legal rules defined which minister was to be regarded as most important. The position of First Lord of the Treasury, with responsibility for government finance, inevitably made the holder first, or Prime, Minister.

Initially, the Prime Minister was described as 'primus inter pares' or first among equals. Although by the nineteenth century some Prime Ministers, such as Gladstone, were exercising a dominant influence, others, particularly if they sat in the

House of Lords, were little more than chairmen of the Cabinet. In the twentieth century it became an established convention that the Prime Minister must sit in the House of Commons, giving democratic accountability to the elected House and thence to the people. Since 1945, political practice has come to concentrate intense attention upon the position of Prime Minister, and with the growth of the media in more recent times, ever more upon the individual person.

The Prime Minister's powers derive almost exclusively from convention and the Royal Prerogative, not from statute. Whether such powers are exercised by the Prime Minister alone, or by the Cabinet collectively, may be determined by established convention, but will often be a matter of political practice or expediency. Conventions may change over time. The decision to ask the Monarch to dissolve Parliament and call a general election was at one time taken by the Cabinet, but since 1918 the Prime Minister has made that decision, after such consultation with colleagues as appears desirable, in the Prime Minister's judgement, at the time.

The initial creation of a new government provides the first illustration of the inter-relationship between the Prime Minister's powers and political practice. By convention, the Monarch calls on the leader of the party that can command a majority in the House of Commons to form a government. The new Prime Minister then has the power to select all of the members of the new administration. The Cabinet is therefore of the Prime Minister's own choosing and could be expected to reflect his or her ideas. But in practice, the Prime Minister's choice will be constrained. For example, leading members of the party will expect important posts, preferably those that they shadowed while in Opposition; former political favours may need to be repaid, and an inexperienced office-holder may be 'advised and expected' to form a cabinet embracing the wide spectrum of political leanings within the party umbrella. The longer a Prime Minister remains in office, however, the more opportunity there is for the Cabinet to be reshaped according to the Prime Minister's real preferences. When first Prime Minister, inexperienced and lacking a power-base, Mrs Thatcher was obliged to include in her 1979 cabinet many of the 'old guard' from the previous Tory administration, many of whom did not share her brand of Conservatism. By 1983, however, she had around her a hand-picked complement of like-minded colleagues.

It is now accepted political practice for there to be cabinet reshuffles at least annually; ministers whose performance is seen as inadequate, or who are not fully in sympathy with the Prime Minister's policies may be removed and promising talents of like mind to the Prime Minister will be brought in to key posts. The dismissal of ministers can, however, weaken a Prime Minister by making enemies, providing a focus for party discontent. The very act of leadership in radical change of personnel, invariably carried out with great speed, may backfire and be perceived as weakness or panic. For example, Harold Macmillan's so-called 'Night of the Long Knives' in 1962, when he sacked seven cabinet colleagues including the Chancellor of the Exchequer and Lord Chancellor, intended to appear strong and giving new direction and vitality to a tired government besmirched with scandal and problems, was actually perceived—at least as portrayed by the press—as ruthless and desperate.

Once the government is formed, the Prime Minister has a decisive voice in the processes by which it operates. Because of the increasing complexity of modern government, meetings of the full Cabinet deal with only a fraction of government business. The Prime Minister controls the content and order of the agenda. He may keep controversial items off the agenda, though this will be subject to political constraints. In 1986, Michael Heseltine resigned from the Cabinet—in session—when prevented from raising the 'Westland affair' in the particular meeting.

The Prime Minister, in chairing Cabinet, can lead and order the discussion. Cabinet usually decides policy by consensus rather than by vote. The Prime Minister normally concludes discussion by summing up the sense of the meeting, which will be entered in the 'minutes' (general summary notes). It is a matter of personal style whether the Prime Minister allows a genuine consensus to develop or attempts to dominate the debate. Mrs Thatcher tended to dominate, although vigorous arguments were still had. Perhaps in part as an 'antidote', her successor John Major was particularly collegiate.

A 'presidential' style was Mr Blair, who conducted most business by sub-committee or one-to-one ministerial discussion, merely reporting matters (post facto) to a cabinet meeting, which often lasted well under an hour.

Sometimes pratice varies according to situation, for example in James Callaghan's Administration of 1976–79, cabinet would sometimes take a day, occasionally more, shaped in no small part by the government having no majority in the Commons as well as party in-fighting between 'left' and 'right' political factions.

One constraint is that a Prime Minister may not be able to control how the debate develops (assuming he allows one), and in any event he cannot insist upon the adoption of a policy against the wishes of the rest of the Cabinet. Ultimately, convention dictates that his position depends upon having the confidence of cabinet and so if the policy is key then he may not survive in office: some might say that Mr Blair side-stepped the problem by not involving cabinet in the decision to go to war with Iraq; the Butler Report 2004 investigates the workings of government in this matter.

The Cabinet forms the apex of a hierarchy of cabinet committees, sub-committees and working groups, and most government business will be dealt with outside the full Cabinet. The Prime Minister now has considerable freedom in establishing and staffing such committees, and may, by careful selection, ensure that only those likely to favour his opinion are involved in the taking of the decision. Decisions made in a cabinet committee are generally as final as those made in the full Cabinet, and all ministers remain bound by collective responsibility even if they were not party to the making of the decision, however significant, illustrated again by the Iraq war decision. The existence of cabinet committees used not to be publicly admitted, but since 1992 the identity and membership of several have been officially revealed. A Prime Minister may even avoid the use of such formal bodies and use wholly informal working groups to take sensitive decisions. Tony Blair is said to have met ministers individually to persuade them to support the invasion of Iraq, before any collective discussion; the Butler Report refers to his 'kitchen cabinet' and 'sofa government' style. This clearly shows how the Prime Minister can exercise a dominating influence over the decision-making process. This may, however, lead ultimately to discontentment and political problems. Robin Cook, for example, resigned over the invasion of Iraq and subsequently voiced frequent criticisms of Tony Blair's style of leadership.

Against the back-drop of exponential growth in the volume and complexity of matters of governance, some delegation is unavoidable. That said, the Prime Minister has a general responsibility for government policy and is therefore entitled to intervene in almost any aspect of the work of any department, subject only to the limits imposed by energy and enthusiasm. All Prime Ministers are expected to take a particular interest in economic and foreign affairs. Diplomacy is now conducted to a great extent by summit meetings, and the regular meetings of the European Council of Ministers are the main focus for developments in the European Union. In other matters, a Prime Minister may allow departmental ministers to develop their own policies within an overall strategy, or may insist on involvement in all developments.

The Prime Minister has the assistance of a range of support services, including a Private Office, staffed by the most promising young civil servants, a Press Office, led by so-called 'spin doctors', and a Political Office staffed by party workers. All recent Prime Ministers have engaged policy advisers from outside the Civil Service, though problems have arisen where these advisers are thought to have had too much influence and have arguably harmed the position of civil servants by at least trying to politicise their role. Some commentators argue that, under Tony Blair, these support services expanded to the point where they could be described as a Prime Minister's Department. It may be that Mr Brown has lessened involvement somewhat. That said the Cabinet Office, the government department that works most closely with the Prime Minister, now has ministers including a cabinet minister and has sprouted specialist units such as the Prime Minister's Strategy Unit and the Social Exclusion Unit. Perhaps the only reason why a Prime Minister's Department has not been created on an official basis is that it would be taken as ultimate proof that a system of Prime Ministerial government had been established.

There can be no doubt that recent years have seen an increasing concentration of media attention on the Prime Minister. The high-profile feature of the television broadcasting of Parliament is the weekly Prime Minister's Question Time, perhaps creating a perception that the Prime Minister is the government, whatever may be the reality. Elections are described as if they were a contest between party leaders, and it can be argued that elections give the Prime Minister a personal, not just a party, mandate. This strengthens the hand of a successful Prime Minister, but also increases the likelihood that a party's response to unpopularity will be to replace its leader.

Determining ministerial career paths, ministerial breach of convention and sanction and with a Commons majority, the Prime Minister has enormous power. It is very difficult to envisage a return to the days when the Prime Minister was only first among equals. Even a Prime Minister who does not wish to dominate the government would find it impossible to reverse the popular perception of the dominant leader. There are very considerable powers available to a Prime Minister who wishes to make full use of them, and such a Prime Minister will overshadow the rest of the government. However, the Cabinet remains the forum in which fundamental issues have ultimately to be decided, and no Prime Minister can ignore or evade the objections of the majority there to the policies he wishes to pursue and in difficult times, the Prime Minister needs his cabinet. The picture drawn by Bagehot is still recognisable.

Question 2

Estella Remington (ER) became Prime Minister last year when her party won a general election with a majority of 30 seats. She promised, during the election campaign, to provide a massive expansion of higher education. She has now decided that this can only be achieved if a special tax is imposed on graduates. She has discussed this privately with the Chancellor of the Exchequer, who agrees with the scheme. No other ministers have yet been informed, and several of them are likely to be critical of the plan.

What steps may ER take to try to ensure that:

(a) the scheme is adopted as government policy;

(b) the necessary legislation is passed through Parliament; and

(c) the public accepts the need for the new tax?

 ## Commentary

This question is principally concerned with the powers of the Prime Minister, but related topics come into play. The extent to which material on pressure group activity and policy formation would need to be included would depend on whether your course takes such a political slant. You will be expected to demonstrate a clear understanding of the conventions governing the Cabinet and the legal rules governing the passage of legislation by Parliament. The answer will be greatly enhanced by an awareness of political realities. Too often students' answers read as if this was an abstract theoretical problem, whereas this scenario could quite easily arise in practice. Obviously, being a problem question, it must be answered as such and not as if it were an essay question.

Answer plan

- Policy adopted by Cabinet or cabinet committee
- Whips' control of party in Commons
- Disputes between Lords and Commons
- Influencing the media: 'spin'.

Suggested answer

ER has a considerable range of powers and means of influence available to ensure the adoption of her policies. Indeed, it is arguable that the UK system of government has become one of Prime Ministerial government. There are, however, constraints on the Prime Minister's powers, and even determined Prime Ministers may find that they fail to ensure the adoption of at least some of their preferred policies, even with a clear mandate and Commons' majority.

(a) The scheme should be formally proposed as policy in a meeting of the Cabinet. It will be discussed and if agreed, usually by consensus, then it becomes policy and, by the convention of cabinet collective responsibility, all cabinet and junior ministers are bound by it and to support it in public, specifically in Parliament, irrespective of any dissent in cabinet or private misgivings. If an individual minister cannot accept and support the policy, then by conventions he must resign. It would be most unlikely in practice that any such matter would be raised in cabinet without extensive prior consultations with the cabinet ministers directly affected, specifically the Secretaries of State for Children, Schools and Families (CSF) and for Innovation, Universities and Skills (IUS). To avoid the possibility of an embarrassing defeat, the Prime Minister is sure to take soundings generally among her colleagues, so that she can take the matter to Cabinet having already satisfied herself of a majority there.

Most issues are not, however, dealt with by the full Cabinet, because of pressure of business, but are instead referred to cabinet committees. There are both permanent and temporary committees and sub-committees. As Prime Minister, ER selects the membership and remit of all of these bodies. It would therefore be possible for her to refer this scheme to a committee, the membership of which she has carefully selected to provide a majority in favour of it. The Chancellor of the Exchequer and the above Secretaries of State would have to be members, but ER has a fairly free hand in selecting the other members. It would be to ER's advantage to chair the committee herself, giving extra power to guide the discussion.

It is accepted practice that matters decided by a cabinet committee are not discussed again by the full Cabinet. Only if there is disagreement within the committee, or the matter proves to be one of extreme sensitivity, will it be referred up to a Cabinet meeting. It is therefore quite likely that this scheme could be adopted as government policy without the involvement of some members of the Cabinet, who will nonetheless remain bound by collective responsibility. This gives rise to the possibility that a minister who considers himself to have been bypassed, may resign, thereby revealing splits in the government that the Opposition can exploit. The resignation of Michael Heseltine over the 'Westland affair' is an example of this. For many senior ministers this is, however, a reluctant path as it may mean an extended period of political oblivion.

Once adopted as government policy, the civil servants in the Treasury and the Department for IUS will be instructed to prepare the necessary legislation and administrative procedures. Normally such a major proposal would be announced in the Queen's Speech at the opening of the next session of Parliament, but the Government may propose legislation at any time.

(b) Assuming ER succeeds in having the scheme adopted as policy, the next hurdle is the passage of the necessary legislation through Parliament. As a measure affecting taxation, it will be introduced in the House of Commons. The government has a comfortable Commons majority so ER need not be particularly concerned about the attitude of the opposition parties; indeed, vehement criticism of the Bill by them may well encourage the loyal support of her own backbench MPs.

The task of getting the legislation through lies with the sponsoring minister and the whips. The whips must ensure a disciplined turnout of MPs to vote on the measure. After the formal introduction and First Reading, the Second Reading provides the opportunity for the House of Commons to debate and vote on the principle of the Bill. Defeat at second reading will force the withdrawal of the Bill, but this is a rare occurrence. The whips will inform ER in advance of potential revolts, and any measure likely to be defeated will be withdrawn for amendment before the government suffers the embarrassment of defeat. After second reading, the Bill will be referred to a Standing Committee for detailed examination. The government will have a majority on this committee proportionate to its overall majority, thus it should have no difficulty in getting the Bill safely through this stage, even if forced to accept amendments from its own side. If the opposition parties attempt to delay the bill by filibustering, the government can ask the House to pass a Programme Motion restricting the time allowed for discussion. Once the Committee Stage has been completed, the government will have to decide whether to accept any amendments made in committee, or to have them reversed by a vote of the whole House. The vote on Third Reading will complete the Bill's passage through the House of Commons.

The whips' careful use of persuasion, cajolery and coercion will normally ensure the passage of all legislation to which the government is committed. Backbench revolts have, however, become more common as it is no longer the convention that any defeat will force the government to resign. Only defeat on a formal Vote of Confidence will force a resignation and general election, as in 1979. It is possible for a Prime Minister to turn a vote on a particular piece of legislation into a matter of confidence in order to demand his party's support, but this may be regarded as a sign of weakness rather than of strength, forcing backbench MPs to choose between their beliefs and their political survival.

The Bill will then be sent to the House of Lords, where a similar pattern of readings will be followed. Voting in the House of Lords is somewhat unpredictable because the Upper House is less shackled by party discipline and there are many cross-bench Lords without a fixed party allegiance. This Bill is likely to arouse the keen interest of those peers interested in higher education, and the final result of the votes cannot be foreseen.

The House of Lords has shown itself more willing in recent years to reject government legislation and, since the removal of the hereditary peers, has announced that it will no longer observe the Salisbury convention, under which it would not obstruct legislation intended to fulfil government manifesto commitments. It is therefore possible that the government may have to resort to the Parliament Acts procedure, as was done for the European Parliamentary Elections Act 1999 and the Hunting Act 2004.

If the Bill were to contain no provisions except for the tax, it would be classified as a Money Bill and the Lords could delay it for only one month. If, as is more likely, it also contains other provisions then the Lords may delay it for one session. On the other hand, the Lords may be satisfied with amending the Bill, which will then have to return to the Commons. The government will then have to decide whether to accept the amendments or to try to persuade the Lords to concede. Only if the Bill has been passed by both Houses in identical form can it proceed to Royal Assent, which by convention presents no challenge, and become law within one session.

(c) In persuading the general public of the scheme, ER's greatest asset is the opportunity to make effective use of the media including trying to influence the opinion of the press. The Prime Minister has a Press Office, which holds regular lobby briefings with journalists. All of the arguments in favour of the scheme will be advanced and opposing arguments rebutted. The press will then report, likely giving a range of slants overall. It is vital for any Prime Minister to cultivate good relations with the media so far as possible, but attempts to manipulate it have been subject to considerable criticism in recent years and may prove counter-productive. Some newspapers are traditionally—but not always—supportive of a party of its chosen political leaning so ER might reasonably expect some favourable coverage, giving momentum and leverage with the public mood. However, as the community charge ('poll tax') of 1989–90 illustrated, a policy imposing a new tax and perceived as unjust may do lasting damage to a government.

It is likely that this scheme will provoke many individuals to write to their MPs, especially as its effects will likely impact particularly upon the articulate and educated. It will therefore be desirable for all MPs of the government party to be supplied with material suitable for explaining and justifying the scheme to their constituents, thereby perhaps keeping both the MPs and their constituents on-board.

It may be that the scheme will provoke protest and demonstrations from students, but these may most wisely be 'ignored' by government as they are as likely to turn public opinion in favour of the scheme as against it, especially if protestors break laws and become violent. When this happened in the poll tax demonstrations, it inflamed opinion on both sides of the argument. In the last resort, it must be remembered that there are as many as four years to go before the next general election. Even if the tax is unpopular, ER may reasonably believe that it will have ceased to be a matter of major concern by then.

Once a measure has been adopted as government policy, its chances of becoming law are very high. Very little government-sponsored legislation is rejected by Parliament, and public opinion can rarely be mobilised so as to prevent the government pursuing its policies. The greatest problems for the Prime Minister lie in getting the initial agreement of cabinet colleagues, but even here the influence of a determined Prime Minister may be hard to resist.

Question 3

How does the convention of individual ministerial responsibility operate in relation to departmental error? How has this been affected by recent developments in Parliament and government?

 Commentary

The first part of this requires not just a statement of the traditional doctrine but also analysis identifying the difficulty in establishing how ministers are supposed to behave. Once again, examples should be used including some drawn from recent practice; the stuff of conventions concerning politicians is politics, political behaviour and happenings. The second part of the question gives the student useful hints as to where to look for changes. In Parliament, the reform of select committees has made an impact. In government, changes to the structure and organisation of departments are making it increasingly difficult to apply the established doctrine.

Note, as ever, the parameters of the question set: it is specifically confined to departmental ministerial responsibility. Its answer should not drift into detail of the responsibility of civil servants, nor digress into ministerial responsibility for personal conduct, such as financial impropriety or sexual scandal. Finally, detail from the Ministerial Code, whilst likely to be pertinent in answering a problem question, is unnecessary here as the Code essentially reflects the spirit and prevailing values of the convention under consideration.

 ## Answer plan

- Government accountable to Commons
- Questioning ministers
- Questioning civil servants
- Questioning Next Steps agencies.

Suggested answer

Ministerial departments are subject to some legal accountability (for example, *Carltona v Works Commissioners* [1943] 2 All ER 560). Albeit not legally enforceable, the Ministerial Code and Civil Service Code set out in written detail much of what is required or expected in the dealings of departments and of their personnel. However, it is convention, unwritten and non-legal, which still governs much of what may or must be done and thus it is political enforceability and sanctions that regulate departmental and ministerial conduct. Traditional constitutional doctrine states that each minister is responsible to Parliament for the work of her department. This is intended to ensure that government departments are ultimately accountable, through Parliament, and via the Commons to the electorate. Such accountability is essential in a democracy, and is an elaboration of the general accountability of the government as a whole to Parliament. It is well established that the ultimate sanction to enforce this is the power of the House of Commons to force a government to resign by passing a vote of no confidence in it. Similarly, a minister who loses the confidence of the House of Commons has to resign, though in practice, a Prime Minister who knew that a minister was facing defeat in such a vote would require an immediate resignation before any vote occurred. How the doctrine operates in less extreme circumstances is, however, more difficult to ascertain.

The classic instance used to describe the doctrine of ministerial responsibility is the 1954 'Crichel Down affair'. Civil servants in the Ministry of Agriculture refused to honour a promise made to a landowner, when his land was compulsorily purchased for military use, that he or his heirs would be given the opportunity to repurchase the land when it was no longer needed. There was no suggestion of corruption or other gross impropriety; rather it was a plain case of maladministration. The minister was not directly involved, but when a critical report was published, he considered himself obliged to resign, being the person ultimately responsible. This course of action was praised as particularly honourable.

In the 40 years since then, it has become clear that this was not a typical example of the doctrine of ministerial responsibility in operation. Rather, it was the unpopularity of the government's whole agricultural policy that led to the loss of backbench support for the minister in question. The only other example since then of a ministerial resignation for departmental, rather than personal fault is the resignation of Foreign and Commonwealth Secretary Lord Carrington and his junior ministers in 1982 when Argentina invaded the Falkland Islands. The stance taken, as subsequently explained by Lord Carrington was that, even though with hindsight he would not have acted differently in the conduct of matters preceding the invasion, the invasion represented a national humiliation (with very serious consequence) for which he had to take responsibility. He did not engage in line-by-line analysis of the Ministerial Code to assess whether he might survive by the letter of the convention; he resigned on principle and in honour.

What then does the doctrine of ministerial responsibility amount to in 'normal', less extreme circumstances? Its starting point is the right of MPs to question each minister about the activities of the department and the corresponding duty of the minister to answer. Since all Crown servants other than ministers were excluded from the House of Commons at the beginning of the eighteenth century, the minister was the only person available for questioning. When government activity was much less, it was reasonable to expect ministers to know what was going on in their departments. As government activity has increased, it remained the expectation that the minister should be able and willing, given reasonable notice, to answer questions on any aspect of the department's work. This provided one of the principal means by which an individual could seek redress for grievances, as the complainant in the Crichel Down affair eventually did. Many such grievances would be dealt with without publicity, and even those that did reach the floor of the House of Commons would conclude with an explanation, an apology and a promise of redress from the minister, without the issue of resignation even being raised.

From the 1960s onwards, other means of redress were developed, to supplement or even replace the traditional method. In 1967, the office of Parliamentary Commissioner for Administration, now the Parliamentary and Health Service Ombudsman, was introduced, providing an alternative course of action for an MP whose constituent was aggrieved by an act of maladministration. As the Ombudsman's reports and recommendations are almost always accepted in full by government, and appropriate redress offered, there is no need to invoke the doctrine of ministerial responsibility, and no question of resignation is raised.

The other development has been the immense growth in use of judicial review, providing legal redress, wholly outside the political process. A finding by the High Court that a government department had acted ultra vires may provoke the Opposition to derision, but is not taken as a ground for threatening the minister's political survival. It is possible to imagine that in extreme circumstances, a judicial ruling could bring the minister's future into question. In the case of *Re M* [1994] 1 AC 377, it was held that government ministers could be held in contempt of court; arguably such a finding should place considerable pressure upon the minister to resign.

It remains one of the bases for the doctrine of ministerial responsibility that only the minister was present in Parliament to be questioned. However, beyond the floor of the House, select committees have the right to call civil servants to give evidence, and the departmental select committees use this right extensively. There can be problems; although the committee can in theory insist on the civil servant's presence, the minister may refuse permission and attend in person instead. In practice, the committee would have to be satisfied with that. Civil servants who do attend are expected to obey a memorandum of guidance from the Cabinet Office that restricts the answers they can give on sensitive issues. If they refuse to answer particular questions, the committee cannot force them to do so. In spite of these limitations, it has become common to see civil servants appearing before select committees, and MPs are finding this form of scrutiny in some ways more effective than questioning the minister in the traditional way. No longer is the minister the only person who can be called to account by Parliament.

The development that is likely to have the greatest impact on the traditional doctrine of ministerial responsibility is the reorganisation of the government under the Next Steps programme. This was intended to improve the management and efficiency of the government, by converting those parts of the Civil Service that provide services to the public into separate agencies, each under the control of a Chief Executive. Ministers, assisted by a central core of civil servants, would lay down the general policy for each agency, leaving the agency to put that policy into operation.

Concern was expressed as to how these new arrangements could be reconciled with the traditional understanding of ministerial responsibility, especially as no institutional provision was made for any new form of parliamentary accountability. But some new procedures have developed. As agencies were established, ministers developed the practice of replying to parliamentary questions about the work of agencies by simply informing MPs that they had passed the matter to the Chief Executive, who would answer the MP by letter. MPs were concerned that this procedure provided inadequate scrutiny, in particular because such replies would be private. After a long campaign by MPs, such replies are published in Hansard, like written answers from ministers, making them matters of formal record. This however, carries the implication that the minister is not responsible or accountable for the operations conducted by the agency, as he would have been before the reorganisation.

To follow up a complaint relating to an agency, the MP has limited scope for raising the matter on the floor of the House. It is, however, possible for the Chief Executive of an agency to be called before a select committee, and this has become the normal practice where a large number of complaints are giving cause for concern (and 'hit' the media). The relevant select committee conducted a thorough investigation into the former Child Support Agency, for example. If there is direct accountability of the agency to Parliament by means of the detailed scrutiny by a select committee, the responsibility of the minister becomes almost irrelevant.

Major difficulties remain, however, in establishing accountability where matters fall between day-to-day operational matters, with which the minister is not concerned, and matters of high policy for which the minister alone remains accountable.

In conclusion, it is clear that the shouts of 'Resign!' which greet a minister whose department has been at fault are little more than a ritual. Crichel Down, far from setting the precedent of expected behaviour, is in fact unique. It is difficult to imagine any circumstances in which a minister—given Prime Ministerial backing—would heed and act upon an obligation to follow that precedent in the absence of personal fault. It would perhaps be better to improve the means by which Parliament scrutinises the Executive directly, rather than trying to revive a doctrine that took shape in a more leisured age, when the minister read and even wrote his own despatches. The arrival of Executive Agencies may yet provide the opportunity for the development of new means of scrutiny, if Parliament wishes to perform this function more effectively.

Question 4

Consider the following situations in relation to the convention of ministerial responsibility.

(a) In her Budget speech, the Chancellor of the Exchequer announced her intention to impose Value Added Tax (VAT) on books and newspapers. Twenty government backbench MPs have told the whips that they will vote against this proposal, and if necessary against the whole Budget. The government has an overall Commons majority of 15 seats;

(b) Sirah, the Secretary of State for Transport, proposed to the Cabinet that extra safety barriers be erected along all elevated sections of motorways, but her proposal was rejected on grounds of cost. Last week, 40 people died in a motorway crash that the safety barriers would have prevented. Sirah told Jenner, a journalist, about the rejection of her proposal, and he has published an article blaming the rest of the Cabinet for the loss of life;

(c) Lesley, the Foreign and Commonwealth Secretary, informed the House of Commons two years ago that he would be adopting a new, morally sustainable foreign policy. It has now been discovered that the Foreign Office has being negotiating for a year to surrender a small UK colony to a neighbouring dictatorship. No information about this has ever been given to the House of Commons;

(d) Smith, a junior minister in the Department for Transport, crashed his car on the M4 motorway. PCs Ford and Austin attended the accident. Smith was breathalysed, the result negative. Smith was slightly injured as was his passenger Jones, a financier, the financial dealings of whom are currently under investigation by the Department for Business, Enterprise and Regulatory Reform. PCs Ford and Austin completed reports on the accident, but were then told by their superiors that instructions 'from on high' were to remove all records of it.

Commentary

This problem covers various aspects of ministerial responsibility. The student's first task will be to identify and explain the particular facet of the convention that may apply in each case, being careful to describe and illustrate how the convention actually operates in practice. Use of examples (including recent ones), an awareness of political realities, and even a familiarity with the attitudes of the press, will be most useful.

Note that it is only the convention that is to be applied, not any laws that may also be relevant.

Answer plan

- Loss of vote of confidence
- Collective responsibility; 'all saying the same thing'
- Individual responsibility for self and department
- Personal misconduct.

Suggested answer

(a) The convention of ministerial responsibility requires above all that the government must have the confidence of the House of Commons. If it loses that confidence it must resign, either to be replaced by another government in which the House of Commons does have confidence or, more usually, to cause a general election. The issue raised in this problem is to identify the circumstances in which a government defeat in the Commons will be taken as an indication of such a fatal loss of confidence. It was thought at one time that any defeat on a major issue would demonstrate a loss of confidence and force the government's resignation, but over the last 20 years or so this has changed. It is clear, however, that any defeat on a formal vote of confidence, moved as such by government or Opposition, will make the government resign. This occurred in 1979, when the Labour government lost a vote of confidence (by one vote) and immediately called a general election. Here, this government could adopt the high-risk strategy of making the vote on VAT a vote of confidence, if it judges that this would make the 20 (or at least 6) rebel backbenchers rally to support it. But if the 20 were to persist in their rebellion, then the government would, if defeated, have no choice but to resign.

Defeat on one aspect of the Budget would not in itself force the government to resign; it would merely cause political embarrassment. In recent years, a government has been forced to rescind an increase in fuel tax, without any threat to its survival in office. Defeat on the entire Budget, however, presents a more complex problem. Traditionally, the votes on the Queen's Speech and the Budget were seen as being tantamount to votes of confidence, but it is not clear whether this is still the case. However, it can be argued that it is both a political and a legal necessity for a government to have its financial proposals accepted by the House of Commons. A Finance Act must be passed each year. Were the Budget to be rejected, the only way the government could survive would be to propose, and have passed, a vote of confidence, and then to introduce a new and acceptable Budget. This would be a political humiliation for the Chancellor of the Exchequer that she could hardly survive, but it would be possible for the government as a whole to claim that it retained the confidence of the House of Commons just enough to enable it to continue in office. In this sense, unlike the formal vote of confidence itself, holding the confidence of the House becomes a question of degree (of sufficiency). From the facts, it appears that all of the 20 rebels have taken a principled stance upon the particular matter, challenging and presumably expecting its front bench to compromise. However, the high stakes are clear to all concerned and it may be that more than 15 from its own side may trouble the government again in the future, especially if it the government does 'back-down' to win them back in this instance.

(b) As well as the relevant laws (official secrets legislation, Public Records Acts and confidentiality), the convention of collective ministerial responsibility require all ministers (cabinet and below) to support government policy once decided and to refrain from revealing discussion had in Cabinet. If a minister has a fundamental disagreement with the rest of the Cabinet, and is not prepared to accept government policy, that minister must resign. Foreign Secretary Robin Cook was considered to have acted in a principled way when, in 2003, he resigned because he could not support the invasion of Iraq without United Nations approval. There was criticism of Clare Short's failure to resign from the Cabinet when expressing similar opinions.

In reality, in most governments, differences of opinion between ministers will be publicly known and discussed in the media. This may be tolerated for a time, but eventually the Prime Minister's patience with dissent will be exhausted. Revealing the story to Jenner is in breach of collective responsibility. Journalists jealously guard the identity of their sources. Jenner will also wish other revelations to follow in the future. Accordingly, Jenner is very likely to maintain the confidentiality of his conversation with Sirah and so, on the face of it, Sirah will not be found out as the source of the disclosure.

It can be argued that it is not justifiable to describe collective ministerial responsibility as a convention, given that ministers do not always adhere strictly to it, whether speaking off the record or expressing their views in carefully coded language. There is nonetheless a recognition of the political reality that an openly divided Cabinet cannot hope to survive and few ministers will take a disagreement so far as to resign, or to express dissent so openly that the Prime Minister has no option but to dismiss them.

(c) According to the convention of individual ministerial responsibility, a minister is accountable to Parliament for the activities of his department. This gives Parliament the right to question him and imposes on him an obligation to answer; the Ministerial Code gives specific requirements as to the nature of answers. The minister is the only person available for Parliament to question, at least on the floor of the House of Commons. If the minister cannot satisfy MPs, particularly those from his own party, he may lose the confidence of the House of Commons. In extreme circumstances, the House of Commons could force the resignation of a minister by passing a vote of censure against him.

The Ministerial Code and a Resolution of the House of Commons specify that a minister must give truthful and accurate information and must not knowingly mislead Parliament. If it were to be shown that Lesley had knowingly misinformed Parliament by, for example, denying that any such negotiations were taking place, that would be regarded as a grave offence and it is almost certain that he would have to resign. Giving Parliament misleading information by mistake may, however, be forgiven, if the minister admits the error as soon as it is discovered and apologises. For example, in the 1980s a junior Home Office minister assured the House of Commons that pregnant female prisoners were not kept fettered while in labour, having been given that assurance by civil servants. When it was discovered that the civil servants had been wrong, she apologised immediately to the House and the apology was accepted.

It is now considered acceptable for a minister to deny personal knowledge of and responsibility for purely operational matters within his department. Successive Home Secretaries, for example, have successfully used this stance to avoid responsibility for prison escapes. Could Lesley deny all knowledge of the negotiations? They were of such importance and sensitivity that the Foreign Secretary either must have known or should have known if he were running his department effectively. His defence in these circumstances may be to assert that he has not actively misled Parliament, but has merely failed to keep MPs informed. The 1996 Scott Inquiry into 'Arms to Iraq' revealed the widespread attitude in government that information should not be disclosed if at all possible, in spite of the implications for parliamentary scrutiny of the Executive. What is particularly interesting about that affair is that those ministers who were found to have misled Parliament were protected by their Prime Minister and the government side of the House. The vote on the Scott Inquiry was treated as a vote of confidence in the whole government. Backbench MPs as usual fell into line behind the three-line whip and the government survived by one vote.

Lesley may claim that he has not really misled Parliament or that his failure to keep MPs informed was due to the delicacy of the negotiations, or that there is no real contradiction with the morally sustainable foreign policy. Whether these arguments will win the day will be determined in practice by the attitude of the Prime Minister and the government side of the House. If the government has a loyal majority in the House of Commons that is prepared to back Lesley, then he may ignore calls for his resignation from the Opposition. If, however, the government considers that public opinion is strong and requires a 'scalp', then whether or not Lesley is merely the scapegoat, he may find himself sacrificed.

(d) Although personal misconduct by government ministers will generally lead to public and media criticism, it is unlikely that the mere fact that Smith has crashed his car would endanger his position, although there is the safety perspective given his Transport portfolio. On the facts, he was not over the drink-drive limit, there is no other suggestion that he is particularly culpable and no one has been seriously injured. Much more serious, however, is the question of why Jones was a passenger in his car. Any suggestion of financial impropriety, perhaps even apparently inappropriate association, is likely to be regarded by the public and media as very reprehensible, and various ministers have been forced to resign for such reasons. Peter Mandelson and George Osborne have survived, so far, following the revelation that each had been in the company of controversial Russian billionaire oligarch Oleg Deripaska; both have been harmed, whatever the truth of the allegations against each of them in their dealings with Deripaska.

In this problem there is the further suggestion that someone in authority is attempting to conceal what happened. If it were merely shown that the police and the Crown Prosecution Service had decided, in the proper exercise of their lawful discretion, not to prosecute Smith for any offence, there would be no problem. Removing police records, however, is a serious matter and any suggestion that there has been political interference in the legal process breaches the separation of powers, would be constitutionally unacceptable and would provoke public outrage. If this were to become known, Smith, and any other minister involved, would be forced to resign, and such a scandal might endanger the whole government. A cover-up is always regarded as unforgivable, however minor the initial offence.

Further reading

Bradley, A. and Ewing, K. *Constitutional and Administrative Law*, 14th edn (Longman, 2007), chs 7, 13.

Hennessy, P. *The Hidden Wiring* (INDIGO, 1996), chs 3 and 4.

Loveland, I. *Constitutional Law*, 3rd edn (Butterworths, 2003), ch 9.

Turpin, C. *British Government and Constitution*, 5th edn (Butterworths, 2002), ch 7.

Woodhouse, D. *Ministers and Parliament* (OUP, 1994).

4

The Royal Prerogative

Introduction

The title 'royal prerogative' seems rather quaint, ancient and irrelevant to the modern constitution. If the ordinary person has heard of it at all it summons up images of the Queen, ceremonials and obscure customs like the Queen's right to whales, sturgeons and swans on the river Thames. This gives an extremely misleading impression. The royal prerogative in fact contains some of the most important powers of government: foreign affairs, defence and justice. Munro defined it as: 'those attributes peculiar to the Crown which are derived from common law, not statute and which still survive' (*Studies in Constitutional Law* (1999) 159).

Despite the 'royal' reference, the Queen is not in fact the person who takes the decisions. Although, legally, powers under the prerogative belong to the Queen, by convention they are actually exercised by Her Majesty's government, often by the Prime Minister personally. The main concerns for the constitutional lawyer are control of and accountability for exercise of this power, reflected in the preponderance of (usually essay type) questions on this subject.

Commonly questions focus upon judicial control, specifically judicial review of the exercise of prerogative power. The most important case is *Council of Civil Service Unions v Minister for the Civil Service* [1985] AC 374. Students often make the mistake of just learning this one case and then are stumped for anything else to talk about. There are other cases! There are not many of them, but it is important to know them well in order to answer questions on this area. They would include *Attorney-General v De Keyser* [1920] AC 508, *Burmah Oil v Lord Advocate* [1965] AC 75, *R v Home Secretary ex parte Northumbria Police Authority* [1987] 2 WLR 998, *Blackburn v Attorney-General* [1971] 2 All ER 1380, *R v Home Secretary ex parte Bentley* [1993] 4 All ER 442 and *R v Home Secretary ex parte Fire Brigades Union* [1995] 2 All ER 244.

More broadly framed questions may also embrace parliamentary accountability and control over prerogative acts (**Chapter 5**).

An interesting constitutional quandary is, in what if any circumstances might the Queen resume her legal powers and take prerogative decisions? This can also be seen as an issue of control. If a government was behaving 'unconstitutionally' by abusing the

Queen's prerogative powers, it is thought that the Queen might be able to, or even have a duty to dismiss that government. More topic overlap is thus illustrated (Conventions, **Chapter 2** and the position of the Prime Minister, **Chapter 3**).

One of the widest prerogatives, and arguably the most significant, is the Crown's power to conduct foreign affairs, including committing the UK to war. The Crown's decisions in this area are usually unchallengeable as are some of its actions. Whilst there was a parliamentary debate and vote upon whether the UK should go to war with Iraq in 2003, prerogative decision of the government or even of the Prime Minister is legally sufficient. Arguably a convention of involvement of—if not approving vote by—the House of Commons is being established. In any event, reform if not removal of this specific prerogative power is now actively being considered, the government having tabled reform proposals (*Governance of Britain* (2007)).

Question 1

As De Keyser's case shows, the courts will enquire into whether a particular prerogative power exists or not, and, if it does exist, into its extent. But once the existence and the extent of a power are established to the satisfaction of the court, the court cannot enquire into the propriety of its exercise.

(Lord Fraser in *Council of Civil Service Unions v Minister for the Civil Service* [1985] AC 374)

Discuss.

Commentary

This is the most common question on the royal prerogative and a quite well-used quotation. Note, in particular, that the question does not confine itself to *Council of Civil Service Unions* (the '*GCHQ*' case). The 'twist' in the quotation is that Lord Fraser is explaining what the law was *before* the *GCHQ* case. A good knowledge of this key case would make this apparent but even if you do not recognise this, adequate study of the topic should produce an accurate answer in any event.

Answer plan

- Prerogative is the common law power of the Crown
- The courts may decide the existence and the extent of a prerogative power
- The exercise of some prerogative powers may be judicially reviewed: *GCHQ*
- High policy is not judicially reviewable
- Exercise of prerogative power affecting the rights of the individual subject may be reviewable.

Suggested answer

The royal prerogative is the remains of royal power. Munro describes it as:

> those attributes peculiar to the Crown which are derived from common law, not statute, and which still survive. . .
> (*Studies in Constitutional Law* (1999) 159)

Because they are the powers of the Crown it was thought for a long time that they enjoyed the same legal immunities as the Queen and could not be reviewed by the courts. The House of Lords had made this clear in cases like *Chandler v DPP* [1964] AC 763 and *Gouriet v UPW* [1978] AC 435. This was despite trail-blazing dissents by Lord Denning, notably in *Laker Airways v Department of Trade* [1977] QB 643 and even Lord Devlin in *Chandler* had expressed some doubt. To Lord Denning, prerogative powers were government powers just like statutory powers and if they were abused they should be controlled.

The courts had always been able to exercise some sort of control over preroga-tive. Since as early as the *Case of Proclamations* (1611) 12 Co Rep 74, the courts have asserted entitlement to decide whether there was adequate precedent for the prerogative claimed to exist. This gives the courts more power than is commonly realised because the precedents are often unclear. For instance in both *A-G v De Keyser's Hotel* [1920] AC 508 and *Burmah Oil v Lord Advocate* [1965] AC 75 the court decided that, although the government could seize and even destroy a person's property in order to defend the realm, compensation must be paid. This had not been clearly established in earlier cases. As late as 1987, the courts recognised that there was a prerogative of maintaining the peace of the realm; *R v Home Secretary ex parte Northumbria Police Authority* [1987] 1 WLR 998. In 2001 the Australian courts established in *Ruddock v Vadarlis* (2001) 66 ALD 252001 that there was still a prerogative power to expel aliens. What is certain, however, is that the courts will not recognise a 'new' prerogative for which there is no historic precedent. As Diplock LJ said in *BBC v Johns* [1965] Ch 32 at 79:

> It is 350 years and a civil war too late for the Queen's courts to broaden the prerogative.

A-G v De Keyser's Hotel [1920] AC 508 recognised that if the government had a prerogative power and a statutory power to do the same thing, the government should act under the statutory power, thus giving the citizen greater protection and respecting the wishes of Parliament. This principle also applies to an Act of Parliament that has not been brought into force; the prerogative must not be used in preference to the statute, *R v Home Secretary ex parte Fire Brigades Union* [1995] 2 All ER 244.

Judicial review of the prerogative was finally allowed in the *GCHQ* case. Lord Fraser gave a number of reasons for this significant change of tack, chiefly that the

Queen was not personally involved in the use of the prerogative and so the court would not be involved in questioning her legal immunity. He also noted that there had already been a judicially review of decisions of a Tribunal and of a Coroner's Court (in *R v Criminal Injuries Compensation Board ex parte Lain* [1967] 2 QB 864 and in *A-G of Duchy of Lancaster v Overton Farms Ltd* [1982] Ch 277 respectively). With the development of judicial review in the last 30 years there was no longer any reason to distinguish between statutory and prerogative powers.

All five House of Lords judges agreed that *some* prerogative powers could be judicially reviewed. It is unclear though *which* prerogative powers would be subject to judicial review. All their lordships agreed that a 'minor' use of the prerogative, here concerning the conditions of service of civil servants, could be reviewed. Lords Fraser and Brightman thought that this was possible because it was only a delegated use of the prerogative. An Order in Council gave the minister for the Civil Service power to alter civil servants' conditions of service. The Order in Council itself could not be reviewed but the minister's decision under it could be. Prerogatives like control of the Armed Forces and foreign policy 'were unsuitable for discussion or review in the law courts' (Lord Fraser, 398).

The other three judges, Lords Scarman, Diplock and Roskill were of the opinion that whether a prerogative could be reviewed depended upon its 'subject matter'. Only the lower level, non-political uses of the prerogative could be considered by the courts. Decisions upon matters like national security, also involved in this case, had to be left to the government. Only it had the information upon which to make a decision. Lord Roskill supplied a handy list of prerogatives that were unreviewable and had to be left to government: entering into treaties, defence, grant of mercy, award of honours, the dissolution of Parliament and the appointment of government ministers. Lord Diplock thought that the prerogative should also be reviewable when its exercise affected private rights and expectations of citizens.

Judicial reviews of the prerogative resulting in success for the applicant are still rare, notwithstanding the *GCHQ* case. *R v Foreign Secretary ex parte Everett* [1989] AC 1014 concerned the refusal to renew Everett's passport. The court followed the reasoning of Scarman, Diplock and Roskill in *GCHQ* and stated that they could not review the prerogative when it concerned matters of 'high policy'. This case did not concern weighty questions of foreign policy and also affected the rights of the individual. It was therefore susceptible to judicial review, but on the facts the court concluded that there had not been a breach of natural justice.

In *R v Home Secretary ex parte Bentley* [1993] 4 All ER 442 the court was prepared to ignore the previous case law, including the obiter dicta of Lord Roskill in *GCHQ*, and permit judicial review of the prerogative of mercy. The Home Secretary had misunderstood his legal powers when taking his decision and, although no formal order was made, he was asked to reconsider. In contrast the Privy Council declined to follow *Bentley* in *Reckley v Minister of Public Safety (No. 2)* [1996] 1 All ER 562.

The court looked at foreign affairs in *R (on the application of Abbasi and Another v Secretary of State for Foreign Affairs and Secretary of State for the Home Department* [2002] WL 3145052. Abbasi, a UK national held at Guantanamo Bay post '9/11', argued that the Foreign Office had a duty to intervene on his behalf with the US government. The court declined to interfere, but conceded that judicial review would be available if the Foreign Office decision was irrational or defeated legitimate expectations.

Residents of the UK, who do not hold UK nationality, also detained at Guantanamo Bay, have also sought similar judicial review. The claim in *R (Al Rawi) v Secretary of State for Foreign and Commonwealth Affairs* [2006] All ER (D) 46 met with even less success, the courts refusing to intervene in whether the UK government made representations on their behalf or not.

Legislation for the UK's overseas territories is made under the authority of Orders in Council. In *R (Bancoult) v Secretary of State for Foreign and Commonwealth Affairs (No. 2)* [2001] 1 QB 1067, the court ruled that a law ordering islanders to leave Diego Garcia was ultra vires the relevant Order in Council. This is similar to the *GCHQ* case itself, where a delegated power under the prerogative could be reviewed. The courts went further in *R (Bancoult) v Secretary of State for Foreign and Commonwealth Affairs (No. 2)* [2006] All ER (D) 149 where a new Order in Council had been issued, refusing to allow the Diego Garcians to return. It was held that the Crown had no prerogative power to exclude UK subjects from the territory and that this new Order was irrational.

It does seem, therefore, that the courts have become more willing judicially to review prerogative acts when they affect individual rights, embracing matters once considered out of bounds, 'non-justiciable'. *Bancoult*, for example, touched upon important foreign policy considerations. Diego Garcia was emptied in order to make it available as a military base for the United States.

Question 2

The principal convention of the UK constitution is that the Queen shall exercise her formal legal powers only upon and in accordance with the advice of her ministers, save in a few exceptional situations.

(de Smith and Brazier *Constitutional and Administrative Law*)

Discuss.

Commentary

This is the sort of question that many students of constitutional law dislike! At first glance it is unclear what area(s) of the syllabus it concerns. The student who looks a little longer might think that it is about convention. It is, in a way, only about a very specific group of conventions: those that surround the role of the Queen and her perogative powers. The nub is that the Queen nearly always acts on the advice of her ministers, but it is thought that there are some exceptional situations when the Queen could exercise power and say 'No' to her ministers. In answering this question it is essential to use actual examples. The other aspect of the question is the issue of constitutional control: should the Queen take a more active role in controlling the excesses of 'her' government?

Answer plan

- Does the Queen still have the right to make a personal choice
- The Queen has the right to be consulted, the right to encourage and the right to warn
- In a 'hung Parliament' the Queen can become involved in establishing who is to govern
- If the Prime Minister acts unconstitutionally, the Queen may dismiss him.

Suggested answer

Old cases like *The Case of Proclamations* (1611) 12 Co Rep 74 made a distinction between the ordinary and absolute prerogatives. The ordinary prerogatives were areas in which the Queen had no personal discretion. Nowadays she would merely act on the advice of her ministers. The absolute prerogative covers areas where the Queen has a choice. Usually this is thought to involve only the award of some honours such as the Order of the Garter. It is possible, though, that in some other, more substantively important, constitutional situations the Queen still might have a choice.

It is accepted that the Queen does have the right to express a view to her ministers upon how her prerogatives are used. Bagehot put it that the Queen has 'the right to be consulted, the right to encourage, the right to warn' (*The Law of the Constitution* (1867)).

More recently, these principles were restated in a letter to *The Times* on 27 July 1986 by the Queen's Press Secretary, Sir William Heseltine. There had been press coverage claiming that the Queen disapproved of some of the policies of the then Prime Minister, Margaret Thatcher. The letter said that the Queen 'was entitled to have opinions on government policy and to express them to her chief Minister'. However, the Queen was 'bound to accept and act on the advice of her Ministers'. Importantly the letter concluded with the constitutional reminder that discussions between the Queen and her ministers are confidential. It is difficult therefore to know for certain whether the Queen, or any previous Monarch, has ever gone beyond expressing a forceful opinion. That is allowed as long as the government has the final say.

Some examples are clear. The Sovereign has not refused assent to an Act of Parliament since 1708. Even that was on the advice of Queen Anne's ministers who did not like what Parliament was proposing. George V expressed the view that he could refuse assent to an Irish Home Rule Bill in 1914. He said that he would do this to 'avert a national disaster' but that there was 'no such evidence'.

Conventionally, the Prime Minister chooses his or her government. In 1945, George VI is recorded as having expressed a preference in who was appointed to certain ministerial positions. He also expressed opinion on matters such as whether the prerogative of mercy should be extended to persons sentenced to death. There is nothing 'unconstitutional' about such 'advice'. However, when the Callaghan government (1976–79) made proposals for devolution, the Queen's public 'warning' that she could not forget that she had been crowned Queen of the United Kingdom was met with some controversy and criticism for being an interference or attempt to influence the elected decision-makers (there also then being political disagreement between the government and Opposition upon the issue).

If the Queen actually made a personal choice as to who should become Prime Minister it would be very controversial. She would be accused of political favouritism. Usually there is no decision for the Queen to make. There is a clear result from a general election and the leader of the majority party is called upon to form a government. If there is a 'hung Parliament', where no single party has an overall majority in the Commons, as was quite common early in the twentieth century, matters are by no means so clear.

In 1916 the country was ruled by a coalition of parties led by the Liberal leader, Asquith. The war was going badly and he resigned. The King sent for Bonar Law, leader of the second largest party, the Conservatives. Bonar Law could not form a government. This put the King in a difficult position. Would he have to make a personal choice? Instead George V hosted a conference of the party leaders and Lloyd George, another Liberal, emerged as the Prime Minister.

In 1974, amidst considerable economic difficulty and industrial strife, there were two general elections. The first, February 1974, resulted in a hung Parliament. The incumbent governing party, the Conservatives led by Prime Minister Edward Heath, polled the most votes of any single party; Labour won the most seats but, crucially, not an overall majority of seats. Heath did not offer his resignation as Prime Minister and instead tried to form a new government by coalition with the Liberals. After several days the talks broke down without agreement, Heath resigned and the Queen was advised to send for the Labour leader, Harold Wilson, to form the next Administration. So, for some days it was not clear which party would govern and the Queen might have had to become involved. It is generally accepted that Heath did not act 'unconstitutionally', the unwritten constitution and the nature of convention affording him some flexibility in a less than clear-cut situation.

A somewhat similar process used to occur when the Conservative Party was in office and the party leader resigned as Prime Minister. Before 1965 that party had no system for electing a leader. The Monarch would consult party notables and a new Prime Minister would 'emerge'. This last occurred in 1963 with the selection of Sir Alec Douglas-Home. It is thought that the Monarch would sometimes express an opinion on the merits of a particular candidate. For instance it is understood that George VI leaned toward Lord Halifax rather than Winston Churchill in 1940, but there is no suggestion that the Monarch took the final decision (which favoured Churchill).

The most controversial incident of this type occurred in 1931. Ramsay Macdonald was Prime Minister in the first Labour government. He was convinced that it was in the national interest to reduce public expenditure, in particular unemployment benefit. His own party could not accept this. The leaders of the other parties agreed with Macdonald. Macdonald offered to resign but the King did not accept his resignation. Instead George V consulted the leaders of the other parties. They advised that Macdonald should stay and form a 'National government'. Macdonald took this advice and won a resounding victory at a general election later in the year. Ironically he ended up as the Labour Prime Minister of a largely Conservative government. Subsequently George V has been criticised for playing too active a part in the choice of Prime Minister. Presumably the King did what he did on the advice of the other party leaders and because he thought that it was in the national interest. The electorate seems to have approved.

It is similarly thought that the Sovereign could refuse the Prime Minister's request for a general election. In a letter to *The Times* on 2 May 1950 the King's Private Secretary said that refusal could be justified if three conditions are satisfied. First the existing Parliament was able to carry on, secondly a general election would be detrimental to the national economy and thirdly another Prime Minister with a working majority could be found. Following on from the latter condition, the position of the Monarch would be aided if supported by some ministers. Although there are Commonwealth examples, in Canada in 1926 and South Africa in 1939, there are no modern UK examples. The crucial element which might justify the Monarch's refusal would seem, again, to be the national interest.

The most spectacular example of the Sovereign resuming an active role would be the dismissal of the Prime Minister. This last occurred in 1834 when William IV dismissed Lord Melbourne. In 1975, however, the Governor-General of Australia (the Queen's representative as Head of State) dismissed the Australian Prime Minister, Gough Whitlam. The Senate was refusing to agree to his budget because of illegal ministerial misbehaviour in procuring overseas loans. The Prime Minister recommended that there should be an election for seats in the Senate only. The Governor-General refused and dismissed him from office. A Governor-General acts in the name of the Queen and exercises her powers. It is not thought that the Governor-General consulted the Queen in this incident. The Governor-General was criticised and there was political 'fall-out', but he had acted within his constitutional powers.

The Gough Whitlam affair shows that the Queen has the power to dismiss a Prime Minister if he or she is behaving 'unconstitutionally'. The problem in the UK, with its unwritten constitution, is: what is unconstitutional? Trying to evade the correct parliamentary procedure and to continue governing without a majority to pass legislation were the apparent 'crimes' of Whitlam.

In conclusion, there is a rather varied series of incidents, in the UK and the Commonwealth. It does seem that the Monarch claims the right to protect the 'national interest' even if it is against the wishes of the majority party. A difficulty with this, however, is that opinions as to what best serves the national interest may vary. The rarity of incidents of royal interference indicates that Kings and Queens have, rightly, been very cautious about when it is appropriate to interfere. Perhaps it is the *possibility* of this reserve position being invoked that is the key in, for example, deterring inappropriate behaviour and in maintaining responsible governance by those entrusted, by election, to wield political power.

Question 3

The UK and the Republic of Fantasia (Fantasia) are in dispute about possession of an island called Lackland, which has been sovereign UK territory for the last 200 years. Fantasian troops invade and take control of Lackland. UK Armed Forces are deployed to remove them. No formal declaration of war is made, but the Crown takes a number of actions. It withdraws the passports of some UK citizens resident in Fantasia thought to be helping the Fantasian invasion forces. Further, Fantasian citizens resident in UK are arrested and expelled. A number of UK-owned and registered ships are requisitioned, without compensation, for military use. UK troops occupy and also destroy properties belonging to both Fantasian and UK citizens.

The UK action is successful and a peace treaty is concluded between the UK and Fantasia. Among other provisions, it stipulates that neither country accepts liability for loss or damage inflicted during the hostilities. No UK legislation is enacted to give effect to the treaty within the UK, as it is not thought necessary.

A number of UK and Fantasian citizens are aggrieved by the actions taken against them by the UK during the hostilities and each seeks a legal remedy.

Advise them.

 ## Commentary

The actions in question were taken by the UK government by exercise of royal prerogative powers concerning foreign affairs. The Crown has wide powers at its disposal, which in the older cases tended to be challenged without success in the courts. In more recent cases, the courts have been more inclined to intervene to protect the rights of the individual.

Close attention to the facts of the question reveals the prerogatives, and thus the related cases, to be considered: war and the deployment of troops, the issue of passports, the expulsion of aliens and the confiscation of property at home and abroad. The relationship between treaties and domestic law as demonstrated by the **Human Rights Act 1998** giving effect to the **European Convention on Human Rights**. Act of State is lurking in there somewhere. To most students it is a nightmare, but it is important to realise that it is not at all clear from the cases what it is.

Depending upon the nature of the particular problem question, it may be best to tackle it line-by-line as the scenario unfolds. This tactic is certainly best in this example.

Answer plan

- The war prerogative is unchallengeable in the courts
- The prerogative to issue passports is reviewable
- Aliens may be expelled under the prerogative
- The prerogative allows the requisition of property, with compensation
- Act of State is unchallengeable in the courts
- So too the treaty-making prerogative.

Suggested answer

The declaration and conduct of war is one of the established royal prerogatives. Whilst there is no formal declaration here, such conflict and troop deployment is covered. It is most unlikely that a court would entertain any challenge as to whether war was justified or troops should be sent: *Chandler v DPP* [1964] AC 763. This was confirmed by *CCSU v Minister for the Civil Service* [1985] AC 374 (the *GCHQ* case) where, in particular, Lord Roskill included war as one of the pre-rogatives that was beyond the control of judicial review. An indirect challenge to the legality to the 2003 Iraq war was also not allowed in *R v Jones* [2006] 2 WLR 772. This does not, however, mean that the Crown can do as it pleases (below).

It was once thought that the prerogative to grant, replace or withdraw passports was unchallengeable. After the *GCHQ* case this changed. In *R v Foreign Secretary ex parte Everett* [1989] AC 1014 the Court of Appeal held that the Foreign Secretary's refusal to renew a passport was subject to judicial review for Everett had a right to natural justice. Here, however, the facts may be distinguished. Taylor LJ stated that matters of high policy were not justiciable. War is a matter of high policy, so it is possible that the courts might refuse to intervene here. In *GCHQ* itself, a similar matter of high policy, namely national security, overrode the requirement of natural justice. Also, as in *Everett*, whilst the court might find the Applicants' cases reviewable, it might, in its discretion, award no remedy.

The expulsion of enemy aliens has been held to be an unchallengeable prerogative matter; *Netz v Chuter Ede* [1946] Ch 224. In the famous case of *R v Bottrill ex parte Kuechenmeister* [1947] KB 41 it was held that the Home Secretary could intern an enemy alien. What is more, only the Home Secretary could decide when the war was over, that too being a matter of royal prerogative. Even in peace-time the courts of Australia upheld a prerogative power to expel aliens in *Ruddock v Vadarlis* (2001) 66 ALD 25. In the problem presented, war is not formally declared and the Home Secretary would probably act under related (immigration) legislation rather than the royal prerogative. At the time of the first (1991) Gulf War some Iraqi nationals were threatened with deportation. The courts were at least willing to look at their cases, although they decided that they could not investigate an issue of national security; *R v Home Secretary ex parte Cheblak* [1991] 2 All ER 319. Subsequently, the European Court of Human Rights ruled in *Chahal v UK* (1997) 23 EHRR 413 that the courts should be able to review such government decisions based on national security. However, in *Rehman v SSHD* [2001] 3 WLR 877 the House of Lords kept to the view that they were unwilling to question the Secretary of State decision to report a foreign national on grounds of national security.

The requisitioning of a UK subject's property is certainly allowed in wartime. Compensation, however, must be paid: *Attorney-General v De Keyser's Royal Hotel* [1920] AC 508.

According to *Burmah Oil v Lord Advocate* [1965] AC 75, when UK-owned property abroad is destroyed for wartime purposes, compensation must be paid. This seems to be confirmed by *Nissan v Attorney-General* [1970] AC 179, when UK forces requisitioned and damaged an hotel in Cyprus. The House of Lords confirmed that this action did not qualify as an Act of State and therefore Nissan might have a remedy. Act of State was here defined as an action of government policy that should not be considered by the courts ('non-justiciable'). The case law seems to make a distinction based upon the nationality of the victim. Act of State cannot be committed against a UK citizen. Nissan was a UK subject and so had his remedy in a UK court. Actions in Fantasia which harm Fantasian citizens almost certainly qualify as Acts of the State, as held in *Buron v Denman* [1848] 2 Ex 167, where the Royal Navy destroyed Spanish property in Africa, acting upon clear government policy to stamp out the slave trade. This can be contrasted with *Johnstone v Pedlar* [1921] 2 AC 262 where the property of a US citizen was confiscated within the UK. This was not an Act of State. The true ratio of this case is hard to define. May an Act of State be committed in the UK? It seems that it cannot be committed against the citizen of a friendly country, here the USA. However *Johnstone* is interpreted, it certainly does not apply to the citizens of a country with which the UK is at war and against which the UK commits acts in that foreign country.

It is clear that the conclusion of a treaty is an unchallengeable act in the UK courts; *Blackburn v Attorney-General* [1971] 2 All ER 1780 confirmed in *R v Foreign Secretary ex parte Rees-Mogg* [1994] 1 All ER 457. It is also clear, though, that the treaty cannot affect legal rights within the UK unless it is given statutory force. Statutory rights are unaffected; *Laker Airways v Department of Trade* [1977] QB 643. So too are common law rights, such as trespass and negligence: *The Parlement Belge* [1879] 4 PD 129, confirmed in *Littrell v USA (No. 2)* [1994] 3 All ER 203.

In conclusion, the UK citizen affected by these 'wartime actions' has a fairly good chance of some kind of legal remedy. The removal of passports may, however, be more difficult to challenge. *Rehman* suggests that the Human Rights Act 1998 has not made a significant difference to how the prerogative is interpreted by the courts. Assuming, as would be likely, the government to have extended the territorial coverage of the Human Rights Act to include Lackland (*R (Quark) v Secretary of State for Foreign and Commonwealth Affairs* [2006] 3 All ER 111), the difficult issue then becomes whether the Act would apply to UK troops deployed there: *R (Al-Skeini) v Secretary of State for Defence* [2008] 1 AC 153, concerning the claim that UK forces deployed in Iraq had killed civilians without justification. In this case the court decided that the Act did not apply as the UK forces were not in effective control of the country. Instead, Iraqi law applied, as did the First Geneva Convention 1949 on the protection of civilian persons in time of war. It is probable that the Geneva Conventions apply to what happened in Lackland but not the Human Rights Act 1998, the latter being intended for time of peace.

Question 4

Behind the phrase 'royal prerogative' lie hidden some issues of great constitutional importance which are insufficiently recognised.
(Munro *Studies in Constitutional Law*)

Consider whether you agree with this statement.

Commentary

Many students tend not to warm to this sort of question, hence we have included it! It is obviously about the royal prerogative but to answer it properly requires, as is common, knowledge and application of other public law topics including the nature of the constitution (**Chapter 2**) and accountability to Parliament (**Chapters 3** and **5**). Be warned, it is extremely dangerous to revise for a constitutional examination just by looking at, say, four topics and hoping that they will come up. Many constitutional questions spread across several areas.

This particular question draws upon elements of Questions 1 and 2 in this chapter and is really about the large amount of government power hidden behind the prerogative and the lack of adequate legal and political controls over it. The answer is an example of a fairly one-sided argument. The 'lack of recognition' aspect is perhaps of more significance than may at first appear: arguably the very 'mystique' of these ancient powers is a part of the problems of transparency, accountability and control.

Answer plan

- Prerogative powers are used by the government of the day
- These include some of the most important powers of government
- Many of these powers are ill-defined
- Judicial review of some prerogative powers is now possible: *GCHQ* case
- Judicial review of matters of high policy is not possible
- Parliament has limited control over the use of prerogative powers.

Suggested answer

The royal prerogative concerns 'those inherent legal attributes which are unique to the Crown' (De Smith *Constitutional and Administrative Law* (1998)). Whilst some of these do still remain vested in the Monarch in person, by convention most (in volume and significance) are now exercisable only by Ministers of the Crown. It is true that, by convention again, the Queen must be consulted and, as Bagehot put it, she has 'the right to be consulted, the right to encourage, the right to warn' (*The Law of the Constitution* (1867)), but in reality the royal prerogative now amounts to powers of the Her Majesty's elected government.

Many of the central and most important government powers lie within the royal prerogative. They include the conduct of foreign affairs, defence and national security, claims to territory, maintaining the peace, the running of the Civil Service, mercy and pardon, some aspects of immigration and the grant of honours.

A problem with these ancient powers is that it is often unclear what exactly they allow the government to do. Occasional legal challenges require the courts to attempt to clarify which powers still exist. For instance, in *Attorney-General v De Keyser* [1920] AC 508 historical research was needed to discover the circumstances in which the Crown could requisition property in wartime. No really clear answer was obtained, so that when a similar point came up again in *Burmah Oil v Lord Advocate* [1965] AC 75 there was still doubt. As late as 1987 a 'new' prerogative power emerged in *R v Home Secretary ex parte Northumbria Police Authority* [1987] 2 All ER 282, which stated that the government has the power to maintain peace in the kingdom, this amounting to a tool of significance, and a very wide and vague tool at that, in addition to the extensive statutory Executive powers effectively at the disposal of the police. The '*Northumbria*' case related to policing of the miners' strike (1984–85), a long-running industrial dispute of considerable controversy including criticism of the conduct of miners and of the police. In the context of such a 'battle' of high stakes and much violence, could a government, for example, imprison people without trial if it claimed that it was keeping the peace of the realm? To take a roughly similar example, the government has a duty to uphold and maintain national security, as recognised in the *GCHQ* case [1985] AC 374. What exactly is national security and what is government allowed to do to preserve it? There are no clear answers to these two questions. The attitude of the courts has always been to leave judgments upon what constitutes a perceived or actual threat to national security to government and it is therefore perhaps no surprise that in cases such as *Chandler v DPP* [1964] AC 763, and *Rehman v SSHD* [2001] 3 WLR 877 courts have been satisfied upon very little evidence and refuse to 'second guess' government when it invokes national security as its reason for what it does.

In the *GCHQ* case the House of Lords declared that it could control how the royal prerogative was used, by means of judicial review. Arguably, the grounds for doing so, such as illegality, irrationality and procedural impropriety are quite limited but, leaving that aside, all their lordships agreed that some government prerogative powers lay outside the control of the courts. Lords Fraser and Brightman considered that only delegated use of the prerogative could be reviewed, that is the decision of the minister but not the Order in Council itself. The politically controversial prerogatives had to be left to government. Lord Roskill identified these as treaties, defence, mercy, honours, the dissolution of Parliament and the appointment of government ministers.

Cases before and after *GCHQ* show that the courts are in fact very reluctant to interfere with government prerogative decisions. In *Chandler* [1964] the deployment and armament of troops was outside the control of the courts. A decision by the Attorney-General to take legal action or not was unchallengeable, *Gouriet v UPW* [1977] 2 WLR 310. The decision not to renew a passport was, in theory, reviewable *R v Foreign Secretary ex parte Everett* [1989] AC 1014, but in reality the courts agreed with the government's policy not to renew the passports of wanted criminals. Taylor LJ considered that the courts should not look at 'high policy' Executive decisions, but could review lower level decisions affecting the rights of individuals. The court continued this approach in *R (Abbasi) v Foreign Secretary* (2002) WL 31452052. Abbasi, detained by the USA at Guantanamo Bay, wished the UK government to intervene on his behalf. The court refused to tell the government what to do, but maintained that such decisions were potentially reviewable. Somewhat of a contrast is *R v Home Secretary ex parte Bentley* [1994] 4 All ER 442. Here the court, whilst considering itself unable to tell the

Home Secretary what to do, and not making an Order, did find the manner of exercise of the grant of pardon reviewable and invited the Home Secretary to reconsider the decision not to grant Bentley a posthumous pardon. This, however, was not followed in *Reckley v Minister of Public Safety (No. 2)* [1996] 1 All ER 562. The two *Bancoult* cases, *R (Bancoult) v Secretary of State for Foreign and Commonwealth Affairs (No. 1)* [2001] QB 1067 and *(No. 2)* [2006] All ER (D) 149, may be signs of a new direction: the courts refused to accept the removal of the right of the inhabitants of Diego Garcia to return to their island. Individual rights are becoming more important since the Human Rights Act 1998.

The courts have often justified their approach by saying, in cases like *Chandler* and *Gouriet*, that the proper body to control the use of these highly political powers is Parliament. It is true that Parliament may remove prerogatives as in the Bill of Rights 1689 and the Treasure Act 1996. Where both statutory provision and prerogative apply, government must use the statutory power rather than the prerogative one; *De Keyser*. The courts have also held that the government must not ignore the will of Parliament when statutory powers have replaced a prerogative but have not yet been brought into force; *R v Home Secretary ex parte Fire Brigade Union* [1995] 2 All ER 244. However the government (through its Commons' majority) usually controls what Parliament does and it is inconceivable that the Legislature would be allowed to remove or restrict an important prerogative power against the government's wishes.

By convention, ministers are accountable for their actions to Parliament. This would include actions under the prerogative. However, by long standing practices many prerogative areas are hidden from the view of Parliament. Since 1955 successive governments have refused to answer MPs' questions on the Prime Minister's advice to the Queen, the grant of honours, mercy in death sentences and senior appointments such as to the Privy Council. Similarly, governments may refuse to answer questions on many defence issues such as arms sales, issues of national security and confidential relations with foreign states. The Parliamentary Commissioner for Administration is also prevented from investigating many of the same areas and also personnel matters concerning the Civil Service.

Legally, the Queen decides upon military action, using her prerogative. By convention, the Prime Minister actually takes the decision, perhaps first consulting cabinet or selected senior ministers. The government has proposed (*Governance of Britain* (2007)) reform concerning the prerogative to declare war, partly on the back of the controversy surrounding the basis of the decision to go to war with Iraq in 2003 (Butler Report) and how matters subsequently turned out. Opposition parties have indicated similar thinking. In the meantime, perhaps a convention is becoming established that (where practicable) Parliament is at least involved by debate if not given power of sanction by vote. In 1982 Mrs Thatcher sought the support of the Commons by emergency debate. Mr Blair committed the troops to the Iraqi border but action only went ahead after the Parliamentary debate and a resulting vote in favour; Mr Blair has stated that he would have resigned had the government lost the vote. Another sign of change is that in 2007 the government allowed Parliament to vote upon whether to retain and update the UK's nuclear deterrent, whereas previously such decisions have been taken by a small sub-committee of the Cabinet.

The House of Commons has tried unsuccessfully to remove the government's prerogative powers and to replace them with more clearly defined and controllable statutory powers: Labour MP Tony Benn's Private Member's Bill in 1988 for example.

It can be seen that the royal prerogative gives the government of the day great power. This power is subject only to limited accountability, not amounting to control. However, change is now a distinct possibility, despite the temptation for those in power jealously to guard that power.

Further reading

Barnett, H. *Constitutional and Administrative Law*, 7th edn (Cavendish, 2008), ch 5.

Bradley, A. and Ewing, K. *Constitutional and Administrative Law*, 14th edn (Longman, 2007), ch 12.

Loveland, I. *Constitutional Law, Administrative Law and Human Rights*, 4th edn (OUP, 2006), ch 4.

Munro, C. *Studies in Constitutional Law*, 2nd edn (Butterworths, 1998), ch 8.

5

Parliament

Introduction

In any constitutional law course, the subject of Parliament is likely to be central. Courses vary, however, in the balance struck between the political and legal aspects. In a course where political issues are given prominence, one would expect to find examination questions on the likes of the defects of the electoral system, the powers of backbench MPs and reform of the House of Lords. More strictly legal topics would cover parliamentary privilege or the legislative process for example. This chapter includes questions of both types.

Questions addressing possible reforms will be popular with examiners. To answer such questions well, the student who has already formed strong opinions must be careful to marshal the arguments in favour of their opinion and counter the arguments against, not just deliver a vehement oration more suitable for a party manifesto! The student who has no such opinion will need to establish by argument depending on the question set. It is excellent practice for would-be lawyers to develop arguments for or against a proposition, disguising the fact that they are indifferent to it.

Question 1

Explain how the following voting systems work and consider their respective advantages and disadvantages as methods of electing a national Parliament:

(a) First-Past-The-Post

(b) Party List

(c) Additional Member System.

Commentary

This is a pretty straightforward question. For a start, your answer must accurately describe the systems, highlighting the differences between them. A good answer would then, as required, go on to evaluate the strengths and weaknesses of each system, of itself and relative to other systems. Your argument of all sides will be all the more cogent for being substantiated by examples of what each system could produce. Whilst the UK now uses a variety of electoral systems including the three stipulated, comparative analysis from other countries may also be made. In fact, the question is not limited to the UK (or to the General Election) but unless you have particular knowledge of other countries' use of these systems, it seems sensible to major upon the UK, the focus of your study. Having decided and planned your approach, state clearly, in the introductory paragraph how you intend to interpret the question. Inevitably, a matter of particular importance is what system should be used for the General Election to the national legislature, the House of Commons, which in turn produces the national government. It is this theme that the suggested answer provided here concentrates upon, accordingly also recognising the underlying issue what reform may be appropriate.

Your conclusion, as well as drawing strands together, might point to priorities for reform and the likelihood of any such reform, or spell out which system appears best overall and why, perhaps because your chosen system best achieves what you consider to be the most important principle. For instance, one might argue that First-Past-the-Post is best as it is most likely to secure strong, stable government or you might prefer the Party List system as the best way of securing representation for all groups in society. The choice is yours as there are few 'right' answers in public law.

Answer plan

- Under First-Past-the-Post (FPtP) a minority vote can elect a government
- FPtP often secures a government with a House of Commons majority
- Party List secures proportional representation
- Under Party List there are no constituency MPs
- The Additional Member System (AMS) combines features of Party List and First-Past-the-Post
- AMS and Party List may secure better representation for minority parties
- AMS and Party List may lead to coalition government.

Suggested answer

Any liberal democracy will have a system of elections which recognises universal suffrage, the right of all adult men and women to vote in a choice of who is to govern them. Relative to its 'thousand year' history, a fully established franchise without restriction by sex, race, class or wealth is a recent development in the UK. Apart from possibly lowering the minimum age from 18 to 16 years, the focus of debate and reform has become how the various systems in use, in particular the FPtP system for the UK national, General Election, works, especially in terms of increasing voter engagement and better reflecting the wishes of the electorate. This in turn requires consideration of the type of legislature and government that each of the three different systems would likely produce. For example, how far an individual vote actually counts and the extent of representation of, for instance, minority groupings, may differ depending upon the electoral process used. Similarly, one system may be much more likely to produce a government with a House of Commons majority, and thus a government that can act, govern, as opposed to one that is emasculated and cannot.

FPtP, the 'majoritarian' system, is the system used for elections to the House of Commons. The UK is divided up into 646 separate constituencies, each with a roughly equal electorate of around 70,000 voters. Each elector in each constituency has one vote, which he casts by writing an 'X' next to the name of his chosen candidate on the ballot paper.

The winner is the candidate who receives more votes than any other single candidate. The candidate does not need an absolute majority over all the other candidates combined, just one more than the runner up. Accordingly, the winning candidate may very well be elected on a minority of the total constituency vote, that is with more electors having voted for candidates other than the successful one. Those other votes, the majority in fact, are discarded, 'wasted'. Therein lies a significant problem with this electoral system. Although the winning candidate represents all constituents including those who did not vote for him or at all, those who voted for a different candidate—perhaps a significant majority of voters in the constituency—have no direct representation of their voting preference. Nationally, this equates to millions of voters.

It is very difficult for smaller or new parties to achieve many seats under FPtP as even though they may poll a significant share of the vote in a given constituency, they may well not gain enough votes to win the seat. Thus, nationally too they may do creditably in terms of votes but relatively very poorly on seats. The experience of the Green Party illustrates this. Similarly, the so-called 'third party', the Liberal Democrats, tends to be squeezed under the system by the Conservatives and Labour. Whilst it gains lots of votes in many constituencies, this does not translate into a commensurate number of MPs returned to Westminster, and certainly not nearly enough to form a government. In many constituencies, the Liberals will come a good second or close third but of course those votes do not then count either for that constituency or nationally.

Often a general election result can seem a distortion of the true wishes of the electorate. In 2001, for example, the Labour Party won 42% of the vote nationwide, but secured 412 MPs, 63% of the total. In 2005 Labour obtained only 35.2% of the vote, but still won 355 seats, 55% of the total, while the Conservative Party, only slightly behind with 32.4% of the vote, won only 198 seats. This also shows that a party can win a constituency, and nationally, with less than half of the national votes. The party with most votes nationwide may lose the election, as happened to the Labour Party in 1951 and the Conservatives in February 1974.

FPtP also often sees very little change from election to election. It is characterised by 'safe seats' that rarely change hands, staying with the established party of that constituency election-on-election. Only about 20 or so seats change party most elections and one of the two main parties, Labour and Conservative, has always formed the government since 1945.

A principal argument of those who support FPtP is that it very usually results in a clear majority for one party, thus enabling strong, stable government able to implement the policies it promised to the electorate in its manifesto. Another advantage is that the counting of the votes is straightforward and reasonably quick. An important asset is its simplicity, involving no complicated choices for the voter to make: a complex system carries the risk of effectively disenfranchising a voter. Another key strength of FPtP is the constituency link: the outcome is a single constituency MP with whom the local electorate can identify and to whom they can—and do—take their grievances.

Party List is a very different system. There is no specific constituency-based vote. Electors vote for the party rather than for an individual. Each party puts forward a list of named candidates, hence the name, and seats are allocated in accordance with the number of votes nationally. For example, if a party wins 40% of the vote, it gains 40% of the seats nationally, the party allocating its seats, as it chooses, to the candidates on its list. This 'proportional representation', which accurately reflects the wishes of the electors, is the main advantage of this system.

One list, for the whole country, would be unusual, except in small countries, so, usually, the country is divided into 'regions' and the parties present lists of candidates for each region. That was the system used in the UK's 1999 and 2004 elections to the European Parliament. In those elections both the Green Party and the United Kingdom Independence Party, neither of whom have any representation in the House of Commons, secured MEPs. So, Party List can help small parties.

Opponents of Party List argue that a multiplicity of small parties is a bad thing. Not only might it enable extremist groups to gain representation, but it could also mean that the government would have to be formed from a coalition of two or more parties. Some see coalition as potentially beneficial, in securing wider representation of views and in the tempering effect of parties having to compromise in order to reach policy decisions. To the contrary, critics argue that coalition governments are inherently unstable; that as the government parties have to negotiate decisions and actions, either nothing gets done or all policies are so diluted that the wishes of the electorate—or any part of it—are not put into effect, satisfying no one; and that small—perhaps extremist—parties may hold disproportionate influence (even the balance of power). Lastly, the individual constituency MP disappears, so the electors no longer choose their candidate and have no obvious person to whom they can take their grievances.

The Additional Member System seems to be a happy compromise between First-Past-the-Post and Party List and has been used successfully in Germany for many years. The idea is very simple: some MPs are elected to represent individual constituencies under FPtP and other MPs are elected under Party List and do not represent a constituency. So, the elector has two votes, one for a candidate and one for a party. This system is used for elections to the Scottish Parliament and the Welsh Assembly, and is effective in reducing the distortion caused by FPtP. In the 2007 election to the Scottish Parliament, the Conservative Party won only four constituency seats (with 334,743 votes), but won a further 13 seats (and 284,005 votes) from the Party List element of the system. On the FPtP element alone, Labour won 37 seats (648,227 votes), a majority of 16 seats over the Scottish National Party (SNP) (with 21 seats, 648,374 votes); but taking into account the proportional element ('List' seats), the final tally had the SNP on 47 seats (1,297,628 votes) and Labour on 46 seats (1,243,789 votes) in total, the SNP forming a minority government, with support from the Scottish Green Party upon certain matters. The 2003 Scottish election gave Labour the strongest showing but without an overall majority; coalition government with the Scottish Liberal Democrats resulted. That no system is perfect is also illustrated here. There are perceived pros and cons of coalition government (see also p. 50–60 above). It is interesting to note also that, controversially perhaps, the SNP was not included in the 2003 Scottish government. Coalition being the 'choice' of the strongest party that did not do quite well enough not to need other parties, Labour was not going to embrace the SNP—its main rival in Scotland—if it could avoid it. The SNP have now done likewise. This distorts representation.

Also, the two different types of MP, some with constituencies and some without, may also, one day, cause disputes about relative workloads.

Different electoral systems are used in the many UK elections to different forums. However, it is the election to the most important national 'power house', the House of Commons, which doggedly and contentiously remains by FPtP. The issue of electoral reform gained ground as an issue in the 1997 General Election campaign. Since then, however, apart from sticking to its manifesto pledge to review the matter, the Labour government has done nothing. The 1998 Jenkins Commission recommended change to AMS (a refined version of it with Alternative Vote for the constituency elections). Will politicians of whatever political hue, with a vested interest in attaining and keeping power ('Buggin's turn'), ever risk giving it up? Perhaps not by choice but just possibly where it believes that it is going to lose and it seeks to prevent its main opposition from gaining power.

Question 2

What changes have been made in recent years to modernise the procedures and operation of the House of Commons? Have these reforms made the House of Commons more effective? Are there other changes that you consider desirable?

Commentary

The main element in your answer to this question will be a description of the changes made since the 1997 election in accordance with the recommendations of the Modernisation Committee. But where a question uses a vague expression like 'in recent years' you may reasonably justify bringing in material from a longer period. What will make a good answer will be your assessment of the effectiveness of the House of Commons in the performance of its principal tasks, legislating and scrutinising the Executive. Recommendations from the Modernisation Committee are the best source for suggestions for further reform; you are not expected to 're-invent the wheel' but if you have ideas of your own, then do bring them in too, all the better if grounded upon specifically identified and illustrated defects and giving analysis of strength and weaknesses alike.

Answer plan

- MPs' working conditions and sitting times
- Publishing legislation in draft
- Programme motions
- Carrying over legislation between sessions
- Prime Minister's Question Time
- Public petition
- Some reference to proposals for the new Draft Constitution.

Suggested answer

The UK is known for its traditions and pageantry and ceremony. To many, the way in which the House of Commons does its business is a prime example, steeped in history from its building to its procedures and language, as if relics of a past age—voting by herding through an 'Aye' or 'No' lobby (instead of pressing a button), to addressing each other as the 'Honourable' or 'Right Honourable' Member, to the entitlement to take snuff upon entering the Chamber. The structure seems even to be class-ridden, the Lords and the Commons. This is, of course, a product of continuity in development over a long period of time, although some might say 'without the development'. The influence of history lies perhaps in the atmosphere of the place, originally to all intents a gentleman's club where nothing changes and how it has always been done is the rule. Does this incline the House of Commons to be backward-looking and 'conservative'? It is perhaps symbolic that when the Houses of Parliament had to be rebuilt in the nineteenth century, the architectural style chosen was medieval. In recent years, however, there have seen some significant changes to the way the House of Commons operates. These have been intended to improve working conditions for MPs as well as enabling it to perform its principal functions, legislation and scrutiny of the executive, more effectively and efficiently. Much of the impetus for changes to the legislative process has come from governments, which are always trying to get substantial amounts of (its) legislation through Parliament as smoothly as possible. Governments are, however, likely to be less enthusiastic about measures to improve scrutiny of the Executive. Some long-standing criticisms of parliamentary procedures, such as the ineffective scrutiny of delegated legislation, remain to be addressed.

The first aspect that will be examined relates to the working conditions of MPs. Until relatively recently, the work of MPs was seriously hampered by a shortage of office accommodation. Many had to share offices, some had no office space at all. Now, with the opening in 2000 of Portcullis House, all MPs have an office usually with a room for a secretary and research assistant nearby; and further improvement work is in progress. This is of particular value in dealing with the substantial volume of correspondence (including email) from constituents that MPs now receive. MPs are paid a substantial allowance, towards their office costs. This payment and how some have utilised it has caused great controversy recently, with calls for a flat salary only. However, the fact remains that as matters stand appropriate assistance remains necessary for MPs if they are to perform their functions effectively.

The change that has probably had the greatest impact on MPs working conditions concerns the sitting hours of the House of Commons. Traditionally, Commons proceedings began at 2.30 p.m., except on Fridays, when sittings began at 9.30 a.m. and ended by 3 p.m. to allow MPs to travel back to their constituencies for the weekend. Debates on legislation would not normally begin until 5 p.m., normally continuing until 10 p.m. and sometimes well into the night. These hours were designed for the convenience of those MPs who had another occupation. Until well into the twentieth century, it was common for an MP to carry on a business or practise a profession, such as law, being in effect only a part-time MP. This became less common as politics developed into a full-time occupation which could thus no longer be combined with another job. A constituency demanded the exclusive attention of its MP and the amount of constituency business increased.

In any case, meetings of select and standing committees were normally scheduled for mornings, and more MPs were involved in these.

As well as being outdated, these sitting hours seriously disrupted the private lives of MPs; it was impossible to enjoy a normal family life if one frequently had to be at the House of Commons until 10 p.m. or later. Particular difficulty was caused to women with young children, and it was widely believed that these hours contributed to the reluctance of women to stand for Parliament. For particular reasons the 1997 election saw the first significant increase in the number of women elected, albeit only to 120, and this increased the pressure for a change in the sitting hours. From 1999, Thursday sittings were brought forward to the morning and afternoon only, with Commons business ending at 6 p.m. From January 2003 further reform meant that Commons' business started at 11.30 a.m. on Tuesdays and Wednesdays, ending at 7 p.m. MPs' opinions on this reform varied; those with homes and families in easy reach found them preferable, but others objected to spending isolated and unproductive evenings in rented accommodation. Some considered that the vitality of debate in the Chamber was diminished, by lesser overall attendance and a lack of 'atmosphere' that settling in for an open-ended evening debate engendered. In 2005 therefore, as a compromise, Tuesday sitting hours reverted to 2.30 p.m. to 10.30 p.m. There are political implications arising from the new hours. A government with only a small majority could be put under pressure by late night voting, and could be defeated if it let its MPs go home for the evening, pre-supposing that it is easier for the whips to keep enough MPs in Parliament to defeat the Opposition during the daytime.

There have also been adjustments to the arrangement of the yearly sessions, again partly to help MPs with family commitments. For example, there are now half-term breaks in February and May, to coincide with school holidays. The House has a long summer recess, from late July until early October (after the party conference season), with the accompanying impression that MPs have excessively long holidays. It is intended that this break be curtailed (with an extra break over the party conference season). This seems a more sensible arrangement and should produce a more rational spread of parliamentary business across the year.

Turning to the legislative process, there has long been criticism of the way in which the House of Commons examines legislation, or fails to do so. Even important laws may be rushed through without adequate scrutiny. The Anti-Terrorism, Crime and Security Act 2001 for example had only 16 hours scrutiny in the House of Commons and was not amended at all in that time. It is true that the House of Lords, as is often the case, subjected that Act to much more thorough scrutiny and forced the government to accept significant amendments, but it should be for the elected House to take the lead in questioning legislation of such significance.

There have, however, been some welcome developments in the legislative process. It is now the practice of the government to publish proposed legislation in draft form well in advance of its formal introduction to Parliament, allowing earlier consideration and comment by expert and other interested parties and the public at large, then being subjected to the new procedural stage of pre-legislative parliamentary scrutiny by committee, for example a Joint Committee specifically formed to examine a specific Bill. At the time of writing this text there were nine draft Bills before Parliament for the 2007–08 session. It is generally agreed that this early scrutiny is desirable and its use should be extended.

The timetable for passing legislation is always contentious. One issue that successive governments have refused to address is the effective stranglehold that government has upon what legislation is considered and in turn passed. The vast bulk of Bills are government Bills, and government of course wishes to get its way, specifically in getting its mandated legislative programme through. Opposition parties argue that it is to the good of the effectiveness of Parliament, in checking government generally, that it has more of a say over its own business, critically what gets debated and examined, when, and for how long.

Governments also object to delays that they attribute to Opposition obstruction. The Opposition and backbenchers generally do not wish their examination of Bills curtailed. The former practice was that discussion of Bills could only be curtailed by an Allocation of Time Order, a 'guillotine'. This Order could be made only after a Bill had suffered delay in Committee, and would itself need a substantial and often acrimonious debate. Since 2000, Programme Motions are generally used. These give the Standing Committee considering a Bill a date by which it should complete its deliberations, but additionally enables it to allocate the time available for each of the various clauses of the Bill. The use of these motions has led to a more rational and less contentious timetabling of legislative scrutiny, and it seems likely that they will replace the 'guillotine' completely.

One of the main reasons for the pressure on the parliamentary timetable is the rule that Public Bills must complete their passage through both Houses within one session. Any Bill not so passed falls and must start again from scratch next session. The Modernisation Committee recommended in 1998 that it should be possible for Bills to be carried over from one session to the next. This would encourage governments to allow more thorough scrutiny and also spread the work of legislation more evenly across the session. This proposal was accepted, in spite of misgivings that it might make life too easy for the government of the day. So far it has been used in respect of complex technical legislation and has generally been regarded as a useful innovation.

There have been other changes to parliamentary procedures. Soon after the 1997 election, Prime Minister's Question Time was moved from the traditional 3 p.m. 15-minute Tuesday and Thursday afternoon slots, to 30 minutes every Wednesday (from noon—12.30 p.m.). The intention was to allow for more extended and sober questioning, rather than the short and noisy performance of the past, but there is little noticeable difference. Whilst the trade-off of frequency for depth may be acceptable, a detraction of the single weekly session is that it lessens the range immediately, and thus the element of surprise in the matters of the moment upon which the Prime Minster may be tested by cross-questioning. A further innovation has been the introduction of a parallel chamber for simultaneous debates, using a room in Westminster Hall. This enables backbenchers to raise more issues and provides the opportunity to debate select committee reports. This has again generally been well-received as a valuable innovation.

Although many of the changes discussed, and the removal of other arcane, if harmless rules (like having to wear a hat to raise a point of order during a division!) have been largely welcomed, there remain many areas where further reform could be achieved. Many outside Parliament consider that the slow process of voting by walking through the division lobbies should be replaced by instant electronic voting. However MPs, who value the voting process as an opportunity to buttonhole a government minister, have rejected this. Some commentators suggest that the government's reforming zeal has diminished as they see the advantage in being protected from effective scrutiny by out-of-date procedures. The inherent conservatism of an institution that has existed for centuries is likely to leave many parliamentary procedures unaltered.

Question 3

At a recent general election, 10 seats in the House of Commons were unexpectedly won by the Save the National Health Service Party (SNHS). These 'first-time' MPs seek your advice as to the means available to them to try to influence government policy, especially on health issues.
   Advise them.

 ## Commentary

This question touches on a wide range of issues relating to the powers of backbench MPs. Your answer should span more than just the legislative processes and the work of select committees.

The issue, health, is of no particular significance in terms of your answer and no specialised knowledge of it is required.

As well as a good knowledge of the House of Commons' activities, an awareness of political realities will enhance the answer.

Note that although the question is not expressly confined to what the MPs can do in Parliament, this is the intended thrust (and there is likely to be little they can do outside Parliament given the absence of specific facts in the question suggesting, for example, a public campaign). Whilst the question is about the Commons, it does not preclude passing reference to the possibility of encouraging the House of Lords to assist.

Answer plan

- Scrutiny of primary and secondary legislation
- Private Member's Bill
- Raising constituents' issues, asking PQs
- Select committees
- Lobbying.

Suggested answer

The most important factor in determining the extent to which the new MPs may influence the government will be the size of the government's majority. A government with a substantial majority, as long as its own supporters remain loyal, need not worry about the attitude of Opposition parties. At the other extreme, a minority government will be dependent on the votes of other parties, which may therefore be able to exact a high price in policy terms, even to the extent of insisting upon places in a coalition government. However, even where a government has a comfortable working majority, parliamentary procedures offer Opposition and backbench MPs a variety of opportunities for the exercise of influence, and a skilful use of such procedures will maximise their effect. Although government business generally has priority, the new SNHS MPs will find opportunities to make their presence felt in Parliament.

The largest single item in the House of Commons' timetable is the consideration of government legislation. The government is bound to introduce Bills on health matters. The SNHS MPs may seek to speak in the Second Reading debate, but the Party's greatest opportunity for influence will be achieved by getting one or two of its MPs on to the Standing Committees that subject Bills to detailed scrutiny. They may then propose amendments, though these will only succeed if they attract the support of some government MPs on the committee in question; the government, provided that it has an overall majority in the House of Commons, will have a majority on each standing committee. Any amendments agreed to in committee can be reversed by the House of Commons Chamber at the Report Stage, but it may be that the government will accept reasoned amendments in order to avoid delay in passing the legislation.

Other forms of legislation may provide opportunities for intervention. If an Health Authority was to promote a Private Bill, that would give opportunities for backbench MPs to call for debates on the floor of the House, as well as participating in the quasi-judicial committee stages.

There are various methods by which an MP may propose legislation, but most of these provide no real likelihood of success. The best way to try to have a Private Member's Bill debated and even enacted is for the MPs to enter the annual ballot to promote a Bill on one of the Fridays reserved for that purpose. Competition is very great; most backbenchers enter the ballot, whether or not they have a Bill ready to propose. If one of the SNHS MPs were to be successful in gaining a high place in the ballot, that would give an excellent opportunity to change the law. One important limitation must, however, be noted. Any Bill requiring public expenditure, or the imposition of a tax, cannot be passed unless a Money Resolution is agreed, usually after the Second Reading. Only a government minister can move such a resolution, in which case there would be no real likelihood of the SNHS procuring an increase in spending against the wishes of the government. In any case, all successful Private Members Bills need at least the benevolent neutrality of government and preferably its tacit support. A modest measure, not involving public expenditure, would seem the most promising option for the SNHS MPs.

Some matters of health policy will also be dealt with by secondary legislation, but the opportunities for MPs to scrutinise this are not great. Although the most important Statutory Instruments may require the approval of the House of Commons, most do not and will become law unless a Negative Resolution is proposed and passed. The Joint Committee on Statutory Instruments examines all instruments laid before Parliament and has the power to draw matters of concern to the attention of the House, though not in respect of the substantive content of the instrument.

Apart from legislation, much of the House of Commons time is spent on various forms of debate. Although most debate is at the government's initiative, there are a certain number of Opposition days, when it can choose the subject for debate. Most of these are used by the largest Opposition party, but, by agreement, the SNHS may be allocated a half day to debate a subject of their choice. There have always been daily adjournment debates, with MPs' right to choose the topic being allocated by ballot. The opportunity for these debates has been greatly increased with the recent introduction of the parallel chamber in Westminster Hall. On Tuesdays and Wednesdays, ten slots are available for backbench MPs to debate issues, again chosen by ballot.

One of the most obvious ways for the SNHS MPs to raise health matters is by asking parliamentary questions. To obtain maximum publicity, questions should be set for oral answer, often in an oblique form in the hope of surprising the minister with an embarrassing supplementary question. MPs are, however, subject to restrictions on the number of questions they may table, because of the likelihood of the system becoming clogged and, question time being strictly limited, only some 10 to 20 questions may be dealt with on any given day. Any questions not reached are instead answered in writing, as are all questions where a written answer is requested. This procedure, while not attracting such immediate publicity as Question Time, is extremely useful as a means of obtaining information about the government's actions and policies. Application under the Freedom of Information Act 2000 also holds potential.

In recent years, the departmentally related select committees have provided MPs with enhanced opportunities for scrutiny of the Executive; the SNHS MPs will hope, having made known their interest and any expertise in the field, to obtain a place on the Health Committee. Competition for places is intense and, while places are formally allocated by the Committee of Selection, in practice the whips of each party have a considerable influence over allocation as between the parties. The government will have a majority on each committee, and the official Opposition party will take the bulk of the remaining places. Determined lobbying by the SNHS MPs might, however, secure them perhaps a single place. Select committees do generally try to operate in a non-partisan way as far as possible, and are more likely to influence government if they do so operate. The opportunities for questioning witnesses in public, and obtaining information from government and other sources tend to make select committees an effective forum. Of particular importance in the health field would be the power of the Health Select Committee to summon and question witnesses including ministers from the Health Department but also departmental civil servants who are more actively involved in implementation of policy and, often most useful, the day-to-day care healthcare providers such as key figures in Health Authorities and Hospital Trusts.

Given their specific interest, the SNHS MPs are likely themselves to be lob-bied on health issues by the various interested parties from the National Health Service (NHS) and private sector alike, for example pharmaceutical companies. Such lobbying is regulated. The 1995 Nolan Committee Report into Standards in Public Life led to the imposition of new restrictions including prohibition of paid advocacy of any cause. Unpaid advocacy and the general making and facilitating of contacts—indeed the whole 'networking' process—are going to be one of the most important tools of the SNHS MPs in the ultimate goal of influencing those with power, government ministers.

In conclusion, there is a range of possible means available to the new SNHS MPs. It may be that events, whether a newsworthy healthcare 'public cause' or a political happening such as a hung Parliament. Otherwise, it is up to them to use make effective use of the tools described, with political skill and acumen. Their efforts may be frustrated by the dominance of the major parties unless perhaps they win allies within those parties. They should at least be successful in obtaining information, which they would not have had but for their electoral success.

Question 4

What role do departmental select committees play in the scrutiny of the Executive. How effective are they?

Commentary

This is a straightforward question.

The first task is to recognise that *departmental* select committees are confined to the House of Commons.

An answer will first require an account of the committees, their structure, membership and operation. However, a good assessment question will always demand more than mere descriptive narrative. Here, the 'value added' component is the second part of the question, which challenges you to provide critical analysis and evaluation of the effectiveness of such committees since they came into being in 1979. Issues such as government influence on the choice of members, co-operation from witnesses and government reaction to reports will all be relevant. As ever, key will be your cogent, corroborated argument of all sides to the pertinent issues.

Answer plan

- Membership
- Power to summon witnesses and see records
- Non-confrontational style
- Assessing influence.

Suggested answer

As suggested by the Question, the purpose of select committees is to scrutinise the Executive, examining expenditure, administration and policy. They do this by probing investigation, including examining documentary evidence and close questioning of witnesses, work of a nature that cannot be performed adequately in the Commons chamber. Witnesses include civil servants and key personnel of Executive Agencies and other bodies ranging from energy utilities to police forces, all of whom are in any event barred from the Commons chamber pursuant to the Separation of Powers. The end product of a committee's work on a given matter is its Report, including any recommendations for change.

The present system of departmental select committees was established in 1979, when it was agreed that there should be one select committee to examine the work of each Ministry and its associated agencies, boards and 'quangos'. Originally, there were 12 such committees, now there are 19. This increase is due to changes in the structure of government and an acceptance that every department should have a committee to examine it. It is therefore now the case that select committees cover the whole range of government activities.

Membership of select committees is in practice confined to backbench MPs. Each committee has between 11 and 16 members. Membership is proportionate to party strength, for example the current Health Select Committee is 11 strong and comprises six government backbenchers, three Conservative, one Liberal Democrat and one

Independent. It is accepted practice that the Opposition can hold the Chair of some committees. Places are allocated by a Committee of Selection, which, it was hoped, would be independent of the party whips. In practice, however, each party puts forward its list of nominees, leaving the committees nothing to do. There have been various proposals for change in the procedure. The Liaison Committee (below) recommended that there be no role for the whips. It has also been proposed that the Committee of Selection be replaced by a more independent Committee of Nomination. Nothing came of either idea. It is clear that the parties wish to retain control of nominations. That control, however, is not absolute. The membership of each select committee has to be approved by a vote of the House of Commons. Usually this is a formality, but in 2001 the House rejected the proposed membership of two committees because the governing party had failed to renominate two popular and effective MPs as 'Chairs' of those committees. This demonstration of backbench power, in the face of a blatant attempt by government to exert manipulative pressure, resulted in the reinstatement of the two MPs. Whilst it was directly all about a government with a strong Commons majority not taking its own backbenchers for granted, it also showed the regard MPs have for the role of these select committees. The government has not tried such 'strong arm' tactics since, at least not overtly.

A seat on a select committee is a highly sought-after position. For newer MPs, it offers a means of making an impact; for more senior MPs, especially those who know that they will not be offered ministerial office, it offers an alternative career structure. MPs, once appointed, serve on the committee for the whole Parliament unless they choose to resign or are appointed to frontbench posts. MPs may have some relevant expertise to bring to a particular committee; for example the current membership of the Health Select Committee includes doctors (of medicine) including Dr Richard Taylor, elected as an Independent MP in 1997 on the single issue of a planned hospital closure. Of course, over time, committee membership itself will give a level of knowledge in the particular field.

Select committees have the power to send for persons, papers and records. Any individual, other than a member of either House of Parliament, may be formally summoned to appear, though in practice committees need do no more than issue an invitation, which will invariably be accepted. Many witnesses will indeed welcome the opportunity to give evidence before such a highly-regarded body. Others may be less co-operative; in 1992 the brothers Kevin and Ian Maxwell declined to answer questions from the Social Security Committee about their late father's fraudulent use of pension funds, because they were facing criminal proceedings. The committees themselves have no coercive powers. All they can do is to refer the matter to the House of Commons, which has the power to punish those found to be in contempt, but is unlikely to be willing to do so except in an extreme case. In 1985 Arthur Scargill (leader, National Union of Mineworkers) was called to the Bar of the House of Commons following his refusal to give evidence to the Energy Select Committee. No attempt was made to punish the Maxwells in this way.

Members of either House, including in particular government ministers, can only be invited, not summoned to appear. The government promised in 1979 that ministers would appear when invited, and very largely this has happened ever since. The House of Commons has the power to compel one of its members to attend a committee, but this power is unlikely in practice to be used against a government minister whilst the government retains its overall majority. It is in any case always possible that the minister who willingly attends the committee meeting may be less than helpful in actually answering the questions.

An interesting issue arises in relation to the appearance of civil servants before select committees. Civil servants are responsible to the government of the day (their departmental minister), which in turn is accountable to Parliament. The select committee system, however, can bypass the departmental minister by calling the civil servants themselves to give evidence, creating an awkward, three-sided relationship between minister, official and committee. Governments have successively issued guidance for officials appearing before committees that, though exhorting officials to be as helpful as possible, reiterates that civil servants remain subject to the instructions of ministers in giving evidence. The guidance suggests that, where issues of the conduct or misconduct of officials are concerned, the official should suggest to the committee that the minister should give evidence instead. Some serious disputes have arisen where ministers have refused to permit particular officials to attend, instead appearing themselves or sending the departmental Permanent Secretary to give evidence. The Defence select committee had difficulty investigating the 'Westland affair' because the relevant officials were not allowed to attend. Ultimately there could be a clash if the given committee compels attendance of officials and the minister instructs those officials either not to attend or not to answer any questions put. This might put the committee in an 'impossible' position but the inevitable high-profile (and now 24-hour) media attention to such behaviour concerning such a controversial matter as 'Westland' might just pressure government to reconsider its stance.

The guidance to officials also identifies various classes of material on which no information should be given to the committee without the minister's approval; these include advice given to ministers, confidential personal information, sensitive economic information and matters under international negotiation. While it is acceptable to assert that some matters are too sensitive to be discussed openly in committee, this list appears to cast a wide net, embracing some matters of legitimate concern to an investigating committee and that might be capable of open disclosure and consideration without prejudice to national (rather than government) interests. There is no mechanism for pre-determination: the government's decision is the last word.

Even more complex issues arise in relation to Executive agencies that, while remaining part of government departments, are supposed to operate with a degree of autonomy. Although the creation of these agencies was not intended to alter the arrangements for accountability, their existence has limited the scope for scrutiny through parliamentary questions and has increased the need for other methods of scrutiny to be developed. The government has accepted that, for matters concerning the day-to-day operation of an agency, the head of the agency is the appropriate witness to give evidence to a select committee, though reserving the minister's right to control the answers given.

The most striking feature of these committees is the ability of MPs from different parties to work together, symbolised by the fact that when hearing witnesses they sit together round a table, unlike the confrontational arrangement of the chamber of the House of Commons. Whilst the examination of witnesses may become somewhat adversarial on occasion, the committee itself operates 'as one' so far as possible and tries in reaching its findings to reach a consensus and to issue a unanimous report. Sometimes party divisions prevent this, but not so often as to diminish the effectiveness of the committees. Each committee can choose what topics to examine within its own remit; it will usually conduct one or two major investigations each session, as well as responding quickly to matters of immediate concern, such as banking crisis. The government has no direct control over the choice of topics and, while it may try to exert an influence behind the scenes, this has not prevented committees from choosing subjects that have gravely embarrassed the government of the day, such as that into the 'Westland affair' (1986) and concerning the Iraq war (2003).

Select committees have enhanced the powers of the backbench MP to scrutinise government actions. Just how much impact these committees have had in practice is, however, more difficult to assess. Whilst some of their reports have been followed by statutory reform, other influences have contributed to the pressure upon government to act. Government invariably makes a formal response to select committee reports, whereby it is at least forced to consider and justify its attitude to the issue in question. It is very difficult for a government to dismiss a unanimous select committee report out-of-hand; there is always the risk that the subject will arise again to embarrass the government.

It was never likely that the introduction of the reformed select committees would transform the House of Commons into as powerful a legislative chamber as the US Senate, before the committees of which even the most powerful may tremble. The Commons select committees have, however, succeeded in providing backbenchers with a source of detailed information and in encouraging the development of expertise within Parliament. Committee reports have provided insights into the inner workings of government and the televising of committee hearings shows the people that the House of Commons does not amount simply to the bear-garden of the full Chamber in 'events' like Prime Minister's Question Time, but does far more.

The select committees are now an established part of the parliamentary system. Their impact can perhaps best be assessed by trying to imagine the furore that would be caused, both inside and outside Parliament, by any attempt to abolish them.

Question 5

Consider the following situations in the light of the rules on parliamentary privilege.

(a) Giles, a backbench MP, said during a debate in the House of Commons that the directors of the three largest UK fertiliser companies met together regularly to fix prices, in breach of both UK and EU law. The Minister of Agriculture asked Giles to send him further details of the accusation and also suggested that Giles inform the European Commission. Giles wrote to both the minister and the Commission from his parliamentary office. The managing director of one of the companies is threatening to sue Giles for defamation.

(b) A private member's Bill to ban the use of chimpanzees in medical research is to be debated next week in the House of Commons. Dr Foster MP is the parliamentary consultant to the British Medical Research Society (BMRS); she is paid £5,000 a year for her services and she has declared this in the register of Members' interests. She has been told by the Society that they will end her consultancy immediately unless she votes against the Bill. Animal rights activists have warned Dr Foster that they will picket her home and her office unless she votes for the Bill.

(c) During a debate in the House of Commons on the decline in moral standards. Pecksniff MP accused Deadlock MP of fathering an illegitimate child. This accusation was false, and Deadlock was so annoyed that he punched Pecksniff in the voting lobby. The following day, the *Daily Broadsheet* published a report of the debate, including a mention of Pecksniff accusation. The *Daily Tabloid* published a front page article, under the headline 'Deadlock in Love Child Scandal', not mentioning the rest of the debate.

 Commentary

When dealing with questions on parliamentary privilege, it is important to remember that there are two arenas, the court and Parliament, and the perspective of each might not be the same. You must consider the perspective of each forum.

Answer plan

- Freedom of speech, absolute within Parliament, qualified outside
- Controls over consultancy
- Reporting parliamentary proceedings
- Procedure for dealing with breach of privilege.

Suggested answer

(a) This problem is concerned with the fundamental privilege of Parliament, freedom of speech. This is protected by Article 9 of the Bill of Rights 1689, which states:

> That the freedom of speech and debates in Parliament ought not to be impeached or questioned in any place out of Parliament.

As a consequence, the courts have accepted that words spoken in the course of parliamentary proceedings are absolutely privileged. No action for defamation can be brought in respect of such words, nor can they even be cited in court to support an action for defamation arising from words spoken outside Parliament, as in *Church of Scientology v Johnson-Smith* [1972] 1 QB 522. Giles can therefore face no legal action over what he said in the debate.

As for the letter written by Giles to the minister, the position here is less clear. If Giles had given the details orally in the course of the debate, this would be protected as a proceeding in Parliament. Does the writing of a letter count as a proceeding in Parliament? In 1957, the MP G. R. Strauss had written a letter to the minister outlining complaints from a constituent about a public utility. The utility (an Electricity Board) considered the letter defamatory and threatened legal action, which the MP suggested might be a breach of privilege. The Committee of Privileges adjudged the MP's letter a proceeding in Parliament that should have the protection of absolute privilege. The House of Commons disagreed and voted to dismiss the complaint of breach of privilege. Although suggestions have been made by various select committees that the position should be clarified by a formal extension of privilege to correspondence between MPs and ministers, no such ruling has been made.

Correspondence (including emails) is increasingly used by MPs as the best way of raising issues with a minister, parliamentary questions being reserved as the second line of attack. It may accordingly be argued that the absolute privilege should be extended. Indeed, MPs are now encouraged to deal with the new Executive agencies directly by letter rather than by asking a question of the minister in the House of Commons. An MP's correspondence on official matters will, however, have the protection of qualified privilege and it can be argued that this is sufficient. Why should an MP be immune if maliciously passing false information to a government minister or official? The call for absolute privilege, on the other hand, is that even the unfounded threat of legal action might operate to deter MPs from performing their proper function without fear or favour; arguably, anything that reduces the effectiveness of MPs is undesirable.

As far as the letter to the European Commission is concerned, it would be difficult to argue that this attracts absolute privilege as a proceeding in Parliament: EU institutions are completely separate from UK institutions. Giles would certainly be able to claim qualified privilege, however, so that he will be protected if he has acted without malice.

(b) Provided that Dr Foster has made a full declaration of her agreement with the BMRS, she will not be in breach of any rules by voting on the Bill to ban the use of chimpanzees, whether for or against. Her problem is that two different groups are attempting to force her to vote in particular ways. It is a clear breach of privilege for any outsider to attempt, by bribery or threats, to influence an MP, and any such attempt would be subject to punishment as contempt of Parliament, as well as possibly amounting to a criminal offence. It is, however, not clear how this rule relates to the practice of parliamentary consultancy. This issue was raised in 1947. W. J. Brown, an MP, was appointed by a trade union to further its interests in Parliament, but when political disagreements arose between them, the union threatened to withdraw from the contract, causing Brown financial loss. The Committee of Privileges was concerned mainly with the propriety of the original contract and, having decided that it was proper, found no breach of privilege in the contract being terminated. They also confirmed that any agreement that purported to bind an MP to behave, vote or speak in a particular way would be improper. In some later instances, the threat by a trade union to withdraw sponsorship from an MP has been classed as a breach of privilege. On each occasion the union withdrew the threat as soon as the issue of privilege was raised, and no punitive action was taken.

It therefore seems probable that any express threat from the BMRS, or any subsequent decision to withdraw sponsorship with immediate effect, would be regarded as a breach of privilege, though there would be nothing wrong with a decision to terminate the contract in due course in accordance with its terms. The Society might be satisfied to reflect that in any case, an MP may still support the causes for which he has accepted a consultancy. Pursuant to the 1994 Nolan Committee Report, Dr Foster would not be able to speak during the debate.

Any physical action taken by the protesters may be a breach of the criminal law; an offence under the Public Order Act 1986, assault or criminal damage. Dr Foster's best course of action, if subjected to harassment, may well be to involve the police. It will also be a contempt of Parliament to molest or threaten an MP. In the case of the *Sunday Graphic* (1956), a newspaper was held to be in contempt when it published an MP's telephone number and incited its readers to ring him up to complain about his actions in Parliament. The House of Commons has the power to order an outsider to appear at the bar of the House to be reprimanded, but this power is rarely used. It is probable that, as happens if people demonstrate in the public gallery, any protesters will be handed to the police to be dealt with.

(c) Because Pecksniff's statement was made during a debate, he is protected by the absolute privilege conferred by the Bill of Rights. Deadlock cannot bring any legal action against Pecksniff for defamation, even if Pecksniff knew that the accusation was false. Only if Pecksniff were to repeat the statement outside Parliament could Deadlock sue him. Deadlock might however argue that Pecksniff is abusing his parliamentary immunity, and may thus refer the matter to the Speaker as a possible breach of privilege; MPs have been reprimanded in such circumstances.

As far as the assault by Deadlock on Pecksniff is concerned, there are various possible consequences. Deadlock has apparently committed a criminal offence. Although MPs were once entitled to freedom from arrest, this no longer applies to criminal proceedings. Deadlock may therefore be arrested, charged and prosecuted just as any other person. It is, however, possible for the House of Commons to exercise its right to regulate its own proceedings. It has from time to time had to deal with disorderly conduct by MPs. It may suspend the MP from the House for a time; the MP is not paid during that time and cannot take part in any business of the House. The ultimate parliamentary sanction available against an MP is expulsion from the House. This has only ever been used in extreme circumstances, such as upon conviction for a grave criminal offence, or following gross contempt of the House. It is unlikely that Deadlock's behaviour would be regarded as justifying such an extreme sanction, though he would certainly be expected to apologise as was Ron Brown MP when in 1988, during an 'overheated' debate, he exhibited disrespect for the House by damaging the mace, the symbol of the authority of the House.

So far as newspapers are concerned, pursuant to the Parliamentary Papers Act 1840 absolute privilege only extends to material (such as Hansard) published by or under the authority of either House. A newspaper has qualified privilege for any fair and accurate report of parliamentary proceedings made without malice, as in *Wason v Walter* (1868) LR 4 QB 73. The report does not have to be verbatim to be protected. In *Cook v Alexander* [1974] QB 279, it was held that a parliamentary sketch, provided it was honest and fair comment, could attract qualified privilege. It therefore appears that the *Daily Broadsheet* may be able to claim qualified privilege for its report. The *Daily Tabloid*, however, appears not to be reporting parliamentary proceedings at all, let alone in a fair and accurate way. It will therefore be susceptible to an action in defamation and cannot plead any privilege as a defence.

Question 6

If it is to fulfil the functions of a second legislative chamber, the House of Lords needs substantial further reform.
  Discuss.

Commentary

Questions about reform of the House of Lords have become particularly topical with the removal of most of the hereditary peers under the **House of Lords Act 1999** and the publication of the report of the Royal Commission chaired by Lord Wakeham. To answer this question adequately, it is necessary to identify first the principal functions of a second legislative chamber. This will establish the criteria against which the need for further reform can be judged. By definition, there is much primary source material upon this issue. **The key papers to use include 'Wakeham' ('A House for the Future', Royal Commission on the Reform of the House of Lords (January 2000, Cm 4534)) and the Ministry of Justice White Paper (*The Governance of Britain, An Elected Second Chamber: further reform of the House of Lords* (July 2008, Cm 7438)).** This does not preclude embracing other ideas, including your own, radical or otherwise. Avoid lapsing into too much narrative: a long trawl of the history of Lords' reform will not distinguish your answer. Whilst you may wish to refer to reform of what the second chamber does or should do, and this may involve different, increased or reduced powers, the nub of the Question is reform of its composition and how that is decided upon; the premise of the question is that the second chamber, however reformed structurally, will perform, the 'typical' functions of a second chamber. Given the perspective of 'what a typical second legislative Chamber does', some comparative reference and analysis is expected. However, the focus of your answer should be the House of Lords and its relationship with the Commons.

Note that the Question is clearly confined to the *legislative* House of Lords.

Answer plan

- Representation
- Selection or election
- Checking the power of the House of Commons
- Scrutiny of legislation
- Scrutiny of the Executive
- Relationship with the Commons.

Suggested answer

In most liberal democracies, the legislature comprises two chambers. The respective powers of the two chambers will vary according to the constitutional structure of the State in question. In the UK, the House of Lords and House of Commons have developed over the centuries, and, as with much of the UK constitution, their relationship is set by statute and convention.

It is an essential element in any democratic state that the legislature should consist of representatives of the people. In a bi-cameral legislature, one of the main functions of a second chamber is to represent the people in a form different from that of the first chamber. Often the chambers differ in geographic representation. For example, in a federal state such as Germany or the United States, the first chamber is representative of the nation as a whole whereas the second chamber specifically represents the separate constituent parts of the federation, in Germany the 16 Länder and in the United States the 50 States (and 1 District). The US Senate consists of two senators from each State regardless of size. Even in non-federal states, such as France, it is common for the second chamber to consist of representatives of geographical areas.

The principal weakness of the House of Lords is that it lacks legitimacy; this lies at the root of its lack of 'teeth', having become merely a revising and delaying chamber, albeit arguably very good at what it does. It is not a democratically representative assembly. All members are there by dint of birth or by appointment, none by direct election by the people. Therefore, it is essential to change the basis of membership of the Lords to give it the legitimacy and acceptability it needs to be able to perform effectively its functions as a second chamber. The key 'rule' that has prevailed throughout Wakeham, the White Papers of 2001 and 2007 and the related cross-party discussions has been that, however the Lords is reformed, the primacy of the Commons must be maintained.

The House of Lords Act 1999 removed all but 92 of the hereditary peers, and this remainder will very probably also be removed when the reform of the Upper House is 'completed'. The life peers now form the bulk of members of the House of Lords. Whilst most of these sit and vote on party political lines, with only the minority of 'cross-benchers' being independent, the Lords is less party political in character than the Commons. Other interests are represented in the Lords; for example the 26 Bishops of the Church of England will represent the stance of the established Church. Of course, every peer – as every MP in the Commons – may exceptionally speak and vote according to individual conscience, most obviously where a 'free vote' is allowed by the parties, for instance upon matters of moral concern such as abortion or embryology research.

Wakeham favoured a wholly or largely appointed second chamber, primarily to avoid rivalry through similarity with the Commons. Following Wakeham and the 2001 White Paper, the Commons voted overwhelmingly for a wholly or largely (80%) elected second chamber whereas the Lords themselves similarly convincingly voted for a wholly or largely appointed House. The government has come round to the view of the Commons and the 2007 White Paper makes clear that it is the will of the Commons that should prevail upon reform, a message in itself to the Lords at least as currently constructed.

The government stance is that the basis of the primacy of the Commons is not the Lords' democratic deficit but the Parliament Acts 1911–1949 ('the Parliament Acts') and related conventions. Nonetheless, an elected House of Lords might challenge or even compete with the Commons. As the Secretary of State for Justice Jack Straw put it in a statement to the House of Commons, July 2008:

> we have to ensure that the mandate of this House [of Commons], and of the government it sustains, continues to hold sway.

The 2007 White Paper makes various proposals to differentiate the two Houses, some derived from Wakeham. As well as First-Past-the-Post, it moots different voting systems—Alternative Vote system, the Single Transferable Vote or (two variations of) the List system; distinct membership via larger constituencies; and a different, non-renewable term (12–15 years); a significantly smaller House (450, 400 or less); and staggered election in tranches of a third so that at no time would the complete Lords' membership be more recent than that of the Commons.

It may be that if the Lords becomes a 'hybrid House', with an appointed minority, then as well as there being a marginal democratic deficit as against the Commons, this could retain some of the wealth and diversity of experience and expertise of life peers in particular, in fields such as medicine and science, perceived as a significant asset of the Lords, rather than mirroring the Commons in attracting 'career politicians' only.

Another principal role of a second chamber is to act as a check on the first, acting as a safeguard against the concentration of too much power in the hands of one body. The powers of a second chamber vary in different constitutions from a mere power of delay to a complete veto. Under the Parliament Acts, the Lords may delay for one year legislation introduced in and passed by the House of Commons. It is significant that the 'Upper House' retains the power to reject any Bill to extend the life of the House of Commons, thus making the Lords a safeguard against any attempt to subvert democracy by postponing elections. In R (Jackson) v Attorney-General [2005] UKHL 56, the judicial House of Lords indicated that it would not accept any attempt to use the Parliament Acts to remove that safeguard, either directly or indirectly. It is likely that any further reform of the House of Lords will, as the Wakeham Commission recommended, restate and clarify relations between the two Houses.

For other legislation, the House of Lords retains some power to act as a check on the House of Commons, because it is still necessary for a Bill to be passed in identical form by each House if it is to become law in a single session.

The unrepresentative nature of the Lords as currently composed means that it is very usually reluctant to reject legislation approved by the House of Commons. However, it has done so and when this has happened in the last year of a Parliament, Bills have accordingly fallen. If the second chamber were to be wholly elected, it might justifiably expect greater powers, although a power of veto seems unlikely and might produce legislative 'gridlock'. This government has ruled out reducing the powers of a reformed second chamber.

A further task performed by a second chamber is to share the onerous work of scrutinising legislation, thus reducing the work burden of the Commons. Modern governments require the enactment of large amounts of increasingly complex legislation. In the UK, some 50 to 70 Acts are passed each year. It is an essential element in the democratic process that all legislation should be scrutinised by the Legislature and that governments should have to justify their proposals in both substance and detail. It is common practice for some legislation, particularly non-controversial measures, to start its passage in the House of Lords where detailed scrutiny can be given, thus saving time in the over-pressed House of Commons.

The House of Lords has been considered to play a very useful role in the scrutiny of legislation. Whereas in the House of Commons the intensity of the party struggle detracts from the technical scrutiny of legislation, members of the House of Lords may be able to take a more detached view, thereby ensuring that legislation, whatever its substantive merits, is well drafted. Were the House of Lords to become a fully elected chamber, it is very possible that its performance of this function would be impaired, as party political strictures would likely be more stringently applied and the quality of relative independence of the upper House may be sacrificed.

A fourth purpose that can be served by a second chamber is to assist in the scrutiny of the Executive. Whether a government is fully accountable to both chambers will vary from state to state and its arrangements for the separation of powers. It is nonetheless usual for both chambers to play a part in questioning the government and investigating its activities. In the UK, there is fusion of powers between Executive and Legislature. Government is ultimately accountable to the Commons alone through the convention of ministerial responsibility, but some ministers sit in the Lords. So, most government departments will be represented there and members of the House of Lords can ask oral and written questions of them. The House of Lords also uses its power to set up select committees to scrutinise aspects of government behaviour, though there are no departmental select committees like those in the Commons. Were the House of Lords to be wholly elected, its members would likely shed their caution and expect a greater role in the scrutiny of the Executive.

It is as yet unclear if the changed upper chamber would be granted greater or new powers. In the absence of a legally enforceable written constitution and strong separation of powers, and with a government commanding a majority in the House of Commons being thus able to control the legislative programme with arguably little effective restraint, the case for an effective second chamber in the workings of the UK constitution is compelling. The challenge in giving the upper chamber democratic legitimacy is in finding a workable, effective balance between its enhanced role and the maintenance of the primacy of the Commons.

Question 7

How effective has the Parliamentary Commissioner been in providing redress for citizens aggrieved by acts of maladministration?

Commentary

This is a fairly straightforward question. The answer requires a description of the jurisdiction, powers and practices of the Parliamentary Commissioner (the Commissioner). To produce a good answer, the student needs to cite some examples of the Commissioner's work, and to make explicit the criteria against which effectiveness is being judged. Any comparisons with Ombudsmen from other countries will enhance the answer.

One clarification. The proper, full title is 'Parliamentary and Health Service Ombudsman'. Our concern is with the parliamentary aspect only, although there is brief reference to the other sphere of work in the Suggested Answer.

Answer plan

- Power over central government
- Exclusions
- Relationship with judicial review
- The MP filter
- Maladministration defined.

Suggested answer

The office, originally entitled Parliamentary Commissioner for Administration, or Ombudsman, was introduced into the UK in 1967, because of concern that existing methods of redress were inadequate. Following the example of Scandinavian states, it was hoped that an Ombudsman would provide a simple and understandable means by which citizens' complaints could be dealt with. Since 1967, the idea of redress through Ombudsmen has spread widely through both the public and private sectors in the UK, but some disappointment has been expressed that the Commissioner, the most senior Ombudsman with the most important area of jurisdiction, has not been more effective.

The Commissioner's powers of investigation cover most government departments and very many non-departmental government bodies. It appears to be accepted practice that as such bodies are created they are brought within the Commissioner's jurisdiction, though there may inevitably be some time lag. There are, however, various matters specifically excluded from the Commissioner's remit by sch. 3, Parliamentary Commissioner Act 1967 (the Act). Some of the exclusions can be justified on the grounds that alternative methods of redress are available. Other exclusions are open to criticism, particularly the exclusion of contractual and other commercial transactions entered into by the government. Governments use contracts as an instrument of policy and their maladministration could easily cause injustice. In recent years there has been an increase in the contracting out to the private and voluntary sectors of services traditionally performed by the government itself, and it is clearly undesirable if this process is excluded from investigation. Personnel matters in both the military and Civil Services are also excluded from the Commissioner's jurisdiction, in spite of the fact that sensitive issues may arise. The introduction of a formal appeal machinery for the dismissal of civil servants has alleviated this problem, but in many other countries, complaints from civil servants form an important part of the Ombudsman's work.

A further limitation on the Commissioner's powers is found in s. 5(2) of the Act, which forbids investigation of matters that the aggrieved person could have taken to a tribunal, or brought before the ordinary courts, unless the Commissioner considers that it was not reasonable for the person to have used that forum. It seems acceptable that, where a specific statutory recourse has been provided, such as the tribunals dealing with taxation or social security, the individual should be expected to use it. There is more difficulty where the remedy is not specific, and those who drafted the 1967 Act cannot have anticipated the huge growth of judicial review. The Commissioner seems to take the view that it is generally reasonable for a person to use her services rather than seek judicial review, given the cost and uncertainty of that method of redress. It is important to note that the Commissioner's services are free to the complainant, whether the complaint is upheld or not. There is inevitably some overlap between the roles of courts and Commissioner. For example, the Commissioner criticised the heavy-handed treatment by HM Customs and Excise of travellers carrying too many cigarettes; in *R (Hoverspeed) v Customs & Excise Commissioners* [2002] EWCA Civ 1804, [2003] 2 All ER 553, the courts found that the treatment constituted a breach of EU law on the free movement of goods and persons. If legal action is started after the Commissioner has received a complaint, she may drop her investigation, as happened with complaints about the discriminatory treatment of widowers by the Inland Revenue.

The aspect of the Commissioner's powers that has always caused most controversy is the fact that, unlike virtually every other Ombudsman in the world, she cannot accept complaints directly from the public. Instead, they must be referred to her by an MP. This system was imposed partly because of 'floodgates' fears, and partly to help preserve the traditional method of redress through Parliament. It has, however, acted as a severe limitation upon the availability of the Commissioner as a method of redress. The number of complaints referred by MPs has rarely exceeded 2,500 in any year, and many of these are rejected as outside the Commissioner's jurisdiction. The Commissioner does try to ensure that all MPs are aware of her services and understand her powers, but this does not seem to be effective. In any case, MPs prefer to deal with constituents' complaints themselves, perhaps in part to gain credit, and thus votes at the next election.

The lack of direct access creates a 'circular problem'. There is little point in the Commissioner embarking upon any large-scale publicity campaign when any matters referred directly to her would have to be sent back, and complainants advised instead to contact their MP. Few people have heard of the Commissioner and fewer still would suggest to their MP that the Commissioner might be used. Research indicates that the MP will rarely make the suggestion of reference to the Commissioner if the constituent does not raise it. The Commissioner therefore remains under-used. Many critics have argued for the abolition of the MP filter, and a recent Cabinet Office paper supported this view. There is the further issue that, if the number of complaints increased substantially, the Commissioner's staff would have to be expanded, with a consequent increase in public expenditure, always unpopular with governments. When direct access to the Commission for Local Administration was introduced, the number of complaints shot up from 3,000 to 12,000 a year, and the same would almost certainly happen with the Commissioner.

The Commissioner's function is defined in s. 5(1) of the Act as being to investigate complaints of 'injustice in consequence of maladministration'. The term 'maladministration' was deliberately not defined in the Act, though Richard Crossman gave some examples during the passage of the Bill: 'bias, neglect, inattention, delay, incompetence, ineptitude, perversity, turpitude, arbitrariness and so on'. The Act did, however, make it clear that the Commissioner was not to reconsider the merits of discretionary decisions taken without maladministration (s. 12(3)); she was not providing a means of appeal against decisions that people did not like. The Commissioner may only investigate the matter that is complained about. In R (Cavanagh) v Health Service Commissioner [2006] 3 All ER 543, a parent complained that medical treatment of his daughter had ceased.

This did not entitle the Commissioner to investigate whether the treatment was suitable in the first place.

There were initial concerns that the first Commissioner was taking too narrow a view of maladministration. He was encouraged by the select committee to extend his definition to include both bad decisions, that is decisions appearing at first glance to be unreasonably perverse, and bad rules, that is rules that produced excessively harsh results in practice. Most cases concern defects in the way decisions are made and unfair treatment of individuals. Common examples are delay, giving incorrect or misleading advice, failing to inform people of their rights and unfairness as between individuals.

The process of investigation is generally seen as painstaking and thorough. The Commissioner has power to demand all government papers, with the exception of Cabinet papers (although a recent stance of the Information Commissioner may impact here), which may be withheld by the Cabinet Secretary with the Prime Minister's approval. The Commissioner has all of the powers of a court to summon witnesses and take their evidence, on oath if necessary, and can order the production of documents. She is not bound by the Official Secrets Acts, Crown privilege or by public interest immunity. It is therefore possible for the Commissioner to go deeply into the decision-making processes of the government and uncover what lies behind the public façade. It would be quite impossible for an individual MP to do this. A striking example is the Commissioner's investigation in 1989 into the 'Barlow Clowes affair', where the Department of Trade and Industry had failed to exercise its regulatory powers properly. This complex investigation resulted in the production of a 120,000-word report detailing a history of maladministration lasting 13 years.

The only problem with the thoroughness of the Commissioner's investigations is that it makes them slow, averaging over one year, though this is partly explained by the fact that only complex cases get through the MP filter, MPs managing the straightforward cases themselves. A former Commissioner has pointed out that the mere fact of a reference may induce a government department (knowing it has not behaved properly) to offer immediate redress, thereby avoiding an adverse finding. Only the debatable cases will need full investigation.

The Commissioner has the power to make recommendations, but has no power to force the government to follow them. However, as a general rule, the government will comply with the recommendations even if reluctant. In the Barlow Clowes case, the government disputed the Commissioner's finding of maladministration but nonetheless accepted the obligation to compensate the investors, at a cost of £150 million, by far the largest sum ever paid out upon a Commissioner's recommendation. By contrast, the Commissioner succeeded in obtaining compensation for only a few of those the property of whom had been blighted by delays in choosing and building the Channel Tunnel rail link. In general, it is politically very difficult for a government to reject what is seen, by Parliament and the country, as an independent, impartial and thorough assessment of the complaint. This was reinforced in *R (Bradley) v Secretary of State for Work and Pensions* [2008] 3 All ER 1116, where the Commissioner stated that there had been maladministration in the rules governing pension schemes and recommended pensioners be reimbursed from public funds. The Secretary of State rejected the finding of maladministration, but the court quashed the decision as irrational. The court could not order the government to pay compensation, but if the government has to accept that there was maladministration, it is more difficult for it to refuse to pay. Government will also be mindful of media attention and the public mood.

If difficulties do arise in persuading the government to accept the Commissioner's recommendations, the matter may be taken up by the Public Administration select committee, which monitors the Commissioner's activities and government response to them. The existence of this committee increases the effectiveness of the Commissioner by ensuring that any failure to follow the recommendations is followed up. The minister or Permanent Secretary of the department in question is likely to be asked to appear before the committee to explain and justify the failure and the committee will not hesitate to issue an adverse report. In some countries, Ombudsmen do have the power to enforce their decisions, but such a power is rarely used.

In evaluating the overall effectiveness of the Commissioner, the first point to make is that the Commissioners have succeeded, over the last 40 years, in obtaining redress for many hundreds of people who would probably otherwise have gained no redress. Those matters that are investigated are dealt with thoroughly and impartially and it is never suggested that the Commissioner has failed to get to the bottom of the problem and find out the truth. Dissatisfaction is concentrated on the issue of access; the limits on the Commissioner's jurisdiction and the MP filter have been the subject of sustained and cogent criticism, though reform still seems unlikely. It is perhaps unfair to criticise the Commissioner, not for the cases with which she deals, but for those that never reach her because of the systemic obstructions.

The hopes of those who initially advocated the introduction of a UK Ombudsman may not have been entirely fulfilled. That said, the role has grown, with the establishment of 'regional' Commissioners, reflecting devolution, and the 'Westminster' Commissioner in particular has become one essential part of the machinery for redressing the grievances of individual citizens. Even the growth of judicial review during the last 40 years has not removed the need in the UK, as in many other countries, for a citizen's defender in this form.

Further reading

Bradley, A. and Ewing, K. *Constitutional and Administrative Law*, 14th edn (Longman, 2007), chs 9–11; ch 29D.

Barnett, H. *Constitutional and Administrative Law,* 7th edn (Routledge-Cavendish, 2008), ch 27.

Loveland, I. *Constitutional Law*, 3rd edn (Butterworths, 2003), chs 5–8.

Parliamentary Sovereignty

Introduction

Parliamentary sovereignty (or supremacy) is the most important and controversial aspect of the UK constitution, and a very common assessment question. Although it is possible for a question to be set that concentrates on the traditional doctrine, and an example of such a question is given here, a common slant is the effect of membership of the European Union on parliamentary supremacy. Two examples are given, in the form of an essay and a problem question. The principal difficulty that students experience in answering such questions lies in distinguishing between the approach of European Union (EU) law, as laid down by the European Court of Justice, and that of English law, as shown by the English courts. Only precedents from the English courts should be cited as authority for what English law actually is. Whether this complies with European Union law is a separate issue, and may not always be relevant, depending on the terms of the question asked.

It is a truism that to understand the standing and operation of parliamentary sovereignty today requires full cognisance of its historical development, that is, how it came to be over time.

Question 1

What is meant by the term parliamentary supremacy? What are its implications in matters other than those raised by the UK's membership of the European Union?

Commentary

This question requires the student to demonstrate a general understanding of the theoretical basis of parliamentary supremacy and its effects. Because it specifically excludes the problems arising from membership of the EU, which are dealt with in a subsequent question, the student can concentrate on some of the other issues that have attracted attention, such as the ability of Parliament to impose special procedures for the passage of later legislation. In many Examination or coursework questions, this type of question will include discussion of the EU; the student should assume that the EU is meant to be discussed if it is not, as here, expressly excluded.

Answer plan

- Parliament may make or unmake any law on any subject
- An Act of Parliament will be obeyed by the courts
- Parliament can repeal, amend or simply ignore any current legislation
- An inconsistent later Act will impliedly repeal an earlier Act to the extent of the inconsistency
- But this may not apply to 'constitutional statutes'.

Suggested answer

In most states, the validity of any law can be traced back to a written constitution, which forms the basis of the organisation of the State. In the UK, however, once the origin of a legal rule is traced back to an Act of Parliament, there is no further document by which the validity of that Act can be determined. Instead, the lawyer is forced simply to assert the proposition that an Act of Parliament is law, because Parliament has the power to enact laws. Why Parliament has that power is an interesting historical and political question, but the lawyer is generally happy to accept the existence of Parliament's power as very much established and thus unquestioned and unquestionable.

The historical origins of parliamentary supremacy lie in the gradual development of the accepted practice that changes to the law required not merely the personal decision of the Monarch but also the 'advice and consent' of the representatives of Lords and Commons, formally assembled in the two Houses of Parliament. This understanding was challenged in the seventeenth century, but was confirmed once and for all by the Bill of Rights 1689, Art 1:

> That the pretended power of suspending of laws, or the execution of laws by regal authority without consent of Parliament is illegal.

From this point, the creation of new law has been a power possessed by Parliament alone. What was not clear, however, was whether there were any limits upon that power. During the seventeenth century there were suggestions that any Act of Parliament that was unreasonable, repugnant or impossible would be declared invalid by the courts. These suggestions were heavily influenced by the philosophy of natural law, by which human law is judged against the standards set by an ideal, God-given law. With the decline of this philosophy and the growth of positivism, the expression of such sentiments waned and, as Parliament was not in any case interested in enacting unreasonable legislation, the courts were content to accept the validity of any Act passed by traditional parliamentary procedure. Parliament was thus established and treated as the supreme lawmaker, and parliamentary sovereignty a common law rule.

The most celebrated statement of parliamentary supremacy is that of Dicey:

> that Parliament has the right to make or unmake any law whatever; and further that no person or body is recognised by the law of England as having a right to override or set aside the legislation of Parliament.

It received judicial confirmation in *Madzimbamuto v Lardner-Burke* [1969] 1 AC 645, where Lord Reid said:

> It is often said that it would be unconstitutional for the UK Parliament to do certain things, meaning that the moral, political and other reasons against doing them are so strong that most people would regard it as highly improper if Parliament did these things. But that does not mean that it is beyond the power of Parliament to do such things. If Parliament chose to do any of them, the courts could not hold the Act of Parliament invalid.

It is clear that Parliament can do, and has done, many things that in other countries might be regarded as unconstitutional. It may break international law (*Mortensen v Peters* (1906) 8F(J) 93), legislate retrospectively (War Damage Act 1965), provide for detention without trial (Terrorism Act 2006).

It is virtually impossible to imagine any circumstances (other than a breach of EU law) where the UK courts would refuse to accept the validity of an Act of Parliament properly passed and 'enrolled'. Further, the courts will not involve themselves in questions relating to the way in which the legislation was passed. In *British Railways Board v Pickin* [1974] AC 765, the Respondent alleged that a private Act of Parliament had been passed only after Parliament had been misled by the Appellant. The court upheld the validity of the Act, stating that it would be for Parliament itself to investigate any defects in the procedure.

An interesting exception, where the court was prepared to consider parliamentary legislative procedure in relation to the courts interpretive role, is *R (Jackson) v Attorney-General* [2005] UKHL 56, where it was argued that the Parliament Act 1949 was invalid as an Act because, in amending the Parliament Act 1911 procedure, it was itself passed under the 1911 Act procedure. The court, though it accepted that the 1949 Act was an Act of Parliament and not delegated legislation, nevertheless held that the interpretation of the 1911 Act, and hence the validity of the 1949 Act, was a justiciable issue. The court distinguished between its role in interpretation of the law as passed by Parliament, and issues relating to the parliamentary process, a matter for Parliament.

There remains one disputed area. Can Parliament bind its successors? The orthodox view is that it cannot. The Parliament that is supreme is the current

Parliament, so it has the power to amend or repeal the legislation of any previous Parliament. Normally such repeal is expressed in the later Act. But if, through inadvertence or caution, Parliament simply enacts something inconsistent with an earlier Act, the courts will treat this as an implied repeal of the earlier Act by the later. In *Ellen St Estates Ltd v Minister of Health* [1934] 1 KB 590, the Court of Appeal rejected an attempt to argue that the Housing Act 1925 should be read subject to inconsistent provisions in the Acquisition of Land Act 1919. The 1925 Act impliedly repealed those provisions.

What is the origin of this rule that Parliament cannot bind its successors? If it is regarded as a rule of common law, then logic would suggest that, like all other rules of common law, it would be subject to alteration by Act of Parliament. However, Wade argued in his 1955 article, 'The Basis of Legal Sovereignty', if the rule is regarded as the rule of recognition, on which the whole basis of constitutional legality rests, it is not like other common law rules, and nothing short of a legal revolution could change it. Any attempt by an Act of Parliament to change the basis on which Acts of Parliament are treated as law is doomed to failure. But, in various contexts, the issue of Parliament's ability to bind its successors has arisen and given rise to legal and academic debate.

The first concerns grants of independence to former colonies, which are given legal effect by an Act of Parliament stating that Parliament will no longer legislate for the country in question. Could such an Act be repealed? Legal theory suggests that it could, but, as was pointed out in *British Coal Corporation v R* [1935] AC 500, that has no relation to realities. The independent State would simply take no notice of any attempt to revoke its independence without its consent. There would likely also be considerable political fall-out in terms of international criticism, condemnation and diplomatic pressure. It appears that the UK courts would consider themselves bound to obey the express terms of the UK statute but such legislation is most unlikely even to be tabled.

There have been some differences of opinion between Scottish and English lawyers over the status of the Acts of Union 1707, various provisions of which are deemed to be unalterable. It is argued that as the Acts were the work of the then separate English and Scottish Parliaments, they could not be repealed by the UK Parliament that replaced them and that owes its very existence to those Acts. In fact some of the 'unalterable' provisions have been altered, without successful legal challenge in Scotland or England. It is conceivable that any attempt to alter such fundamental matters as the status of Scots law or the nature of the Church of Scotland would be rejected, at least by the Scottish courts. Again, however, such change is highly unlikely given the political unacceptability of such a measure.

The question that has given rise to most debate is whether Parliament could prescribe special procedures for the passing of future legislation that might then bind a future Parliament (or the same Parliament), that is that Parliament would have to use the special procedure even if only to pass an Act to get rid of it. There is nothing to prevent Parliament creating special procedures; for example, the Northern Ireland Act 1998, s. 1 requires the holding of an approving referendum before any legislation changing the constitutional status of Northern Ireland can be passed. However, this so-called constitutional guarantee derives its validity from the 1998 Act, which could itself be repealed without a referendum. Would it be possible to prevent this by stating in an Act that the Act itself could not be repealed without a referendum? This would in any event not prevent Parliament simply ignoring the 'mandatory' prerequisite of the referendum: it might be extremely controversial politically but it would be the law, the *Act* having been properly passed (by Commons, Lords and Assent).

There is a school of thought that Parliament may be bound by such special provision regulating the 'manner and form' of future legislation, providing partial entrenchment by the likes of a referendum or special majorities in each House for amendment or repeal. However, the only authority for this contention is Commonwealth cases such as *Attorney-General for New South Wales v Trethowan* [1932] AC 526, *Harris v Minister of the Interior* 1952 (2) SA 428, and *Bribery Commissioner v Ranasinghe* [1965] AC 172. Significantly, in all of these cases, the requirements as to the manner and form of future legislation were contained in the original statutes emanating from the 'mother of Parliaments', the Westminster Parliament, by which independence was granted. Accordingly, these 'entrenching' provisions could not be changed by the different legislatures in question. The problem in applying these precedents to the UK Parliament is that it would have to limit itself, rather than being subjected to external constitutional constraints. Whilst successive Parliaments could choose to abide by the limit, none has to: in other words, the real 'problem' is the circular argument that the sovereignty of the Westminster Parliament vests in its membership for the time being, and whilst MPs, peers and monarchs come and go, sovereignty continues. It can be said that some manner and form changes have bound Parliament, such as His Majesty's Declaration of Abdication Act 1936.

In *Thoburn v Sunderland City Council* [2002] EWHC 195 Admin, [2002] 4 All ER 156, Laws LJ confirmed the orthodox view that Parliament 'cannot stipulate as to the manner and form of any subsequent legislation' and could therefore repeal any previous legislation. However, he went on to suggest that the courts had begun to recognise a special category of constitutional statutes, those concerning fundamental constitutional rights or otherwise affecting the social contract between citizen and state. These statutes, he said, could not be impliedly repealed. If Parliament wished to repeal them, it would have to use express, unambiguous words. Otherwise the courts would assume that Parliament intended the constitutional rights to be protected, even against later statutes. Which statutes are 'constitutional' in this sense? Laws LJ suggested some examples: the Bill of Rights 1689, the Acts of Union 1707 and the Human Rights Act 1998.

This interesting suggestion would provide a means by which the courts could retain the traditional theory of parliamentary supremacy while offering some protection to individual rights. It would retain the right of Parliament to deal with war, terrorism or other emergencies unhindered by the courts, while ensuring that any such legislation would have to be politically acceptable. It remains to be seen whether this new interpretation of parliamentary supremacy is adopted. The greatest test is always in such situations of exigency, when government implores Parliament and people that a given measure is 'vital' and would be for use only 'exceptionally', as has been raised post '9/11', not always successfully, in the attempts to extend detention without charge of suspected terrorists.

Question 2

What impact has UK membership of the European Communities had on the doctrine of parliamentary sovereignty?

 ## Commentary

The issues raised by this question are likely to be central to any constitutional law course. Students must be careful to discuss this question in the light of case law, not the often ill-informed pronouncements of politicians. There have now been enough cases to enable definite answers to be given to most issues, but the exact boundaries to the courts' obedience to EU rather than UK laws remain uncertain and therefore debatable. The student will need to explain the general doctrine of parliamentary supremacy, but there is no need to go into detail about the other complex issues that would arise in a more general question.

 ## Answer plan

- By EU law, EU law has supremacy over the national law of member states
- By UK law, the law passed by Parliament has supremacy
- These principles are contradictory, but may be reconciled as follows:
  - Any UK law passed before 1972 can be impliedly repealed by the **ECA 1972**
  - Any UK law passed after 1972 will, if possible, be interpreted by UK domestic courts so as to comply with EU law
  - The *Factortame* cases ruled that UK laws passed after 1972 and being inconsistent with EU law will not be enforced by the UK courts
  - The **ECA 1972** can be expressly repealed (or amended), but not impliedly repealed or amended.

Suggested answer

When the UK joined what is now the EU, concerns were expressed in many domestic quarters about the constitutional implications for the UK. In particular, how could EU membership be reconciled with the conventional doctrine of parliamentary supremacy? In states with a written constitution, it was generally possible to spell out the implications of EU membership by an appropriate constitutional amendment. However, the UK constitution being unwritten, no such process was available. All that the UK could do was to pass the European Communities Act 1972 (ECA 1972), by the same procedure as for all other statutes and with, prima facie, the same legal force as all other statutes, leaving many unanswered questions.

According to Dicey, 'no person is recognised by the law of England as having a right to over-ride or set aside the legislation of Parliament'. This doctrine forms the very basis of the UK constitution with the effect that the current Parliament can pass any legislation it wishes, including legislation to amend or repeal, expressly or impliedly, prior legislation of that or an earlier Parliament. Although there has been considerable academic debate about possible exceptions to this power, and possible methods of entrenching legislation, the orthodox view accepted no limits on Parliament's authority.

Before the UK joined the EU, the European Court of Justice had established, in *Costa v ENEL*, Case 6/64, [1964] CMLR 425, that EU law prevailed over incompatible member state law. The doctrine of direct effect obliged national courts to give effect to rights arising under EU law, regardless of any national law to the contrary. No doubt, in an ideal world, no national law inconsistent with the state's EU obligations would ever be enacted. In the real world, however, it was all too likely that a state would enact such legislation, whether by inadvertence, or perhaps in the hope that the inconsistency would not be noticed or challenged. A particular problem faced by the UK legislators was to find some way to instruct the courts to give effect to EU law in preference to Acts of Parliament whenever passed.

It was straightforward to provide, in s. 2(1) of the European Communities Act 1972, that all rights arising under the EU Treaties were to be given effect in preference to pre-existing UK law. The orthodox doctrines of express and implied repeal authorised that. However, the real problem concerned legislation passed after 1972 which was inconsistent with EU law. This was dealt with in s. 2(4) of the ECA 1972 which provides that legislation passed, or to be passed in the future, should be construed and have effect subject to the rule laid down in s. 2(1), that is, that effect must be given to EU rights. This was reinforced by s. 3(1), which instructed the courts to decide any issues of EU law 'in accordance with the principles laid down by, and any relevant decisions of, the European Court of Justice'. This would include the principle of the supremacy of EU law laid down in *Costa v ENEL* (1964).

The ECA 1972 therefore appeared to provide the courts with an instruction that they should obey EU law, but left unresolved the question of what would happen if different instructions were provided—to the UK courts—in a later Act of Parliament. What if an Act passed after 1972 'simply' contained provisions inconsistent with Community law? By the conventional methods of interpretation, where provisions in an earlier Act are inconsistent with a later Act, the earlier Act is impliedly repealed to the extent of the inconsistency: *Ellen St Estates Ltd v Minister of Health* [1934] 1 KB 590. It could therefore be argued that any Act passed after 1972 could impliedly repeal the ECA 1972, so that the phrase 'legislation passed or to be passed' would be read with the proviso 'except this new Act'. This would leave the UK in breach of its obligations under the EU treaties. How could the courts avoid this?

The solution, for many cases, was found in the long-standing rule of statutory interpretation that, where legislation is passed to implement the UK's international obligations, any ambiguity should be construed so as to comply with those obligations rather than conflict with them. This rule, taken with the express wording of s. 2(4) of the ECA 1972, has been treated by the domestic courts as a clear instruction to interpret any UK legislation passed to implement EU law in such a way as to ensure that there is no discrepancy between them. In *Garland v British Rail Engineering* [1983] 2 AC 751, the court preferred the interpretation of the Sex Discrimination Act 1975 which was consistent with Article 119 (now 141) EU Treaty, to the interpretation that created conflict between them. The courts have been willing to use purposive methods of interpretation rather than traditional literal methods to ensure compliance with EU law. In *Pickstone v Freemans plc* [1989] AC 66, and *Lister v Forth Dry Dock* [1990] 1 AC 546, the courts went far beyond literal interpretation, even implying extra words into a regulation in order to ensure compliance with EU law. This approach has proved to deal satisfactorily with all cases where UK legislation is passed in order to incorporate EU directives and treaty provisions into UK law.

A different problem was posed by the decision of the European Court of Justice in *Marleasing*, C-106/89, [1992] 1 CMLR 305 that all national legislation, whenever passed, should be interpreted in the light of EU law in order to give effect to rights even if they did not have direct effect. The UK courts had earlier refused, in *Duke v GEC Reliance Ltd* [1988] AC 618, to interpret UK statutes passed in 1970 and 1975 in the light of a 1976 directive, on the grounds that that could not possibly have been Parliament's intention; the rules stated in the statutes were unambiguously in conflict with the directive. But in *Webb v EMO Air Cargo (No. 2)* [1995] 4 All ER 577, the House of Lords without debate interpreted an ambiguous 1975 Act to give effect to a 1976 directive, just as the European Court of Justice decision required. There remains considerable uncertainty in both UK and EU law as to just how far a national court is supposed to go in effectively rewriting existing national laws under the guise of interpretation, but the UK courts seem willing to follow the instruction given by the ECA 1972.

The above cases, being treated as issues of statutory interpretation and the reconciling of apparently contradictory rules, managed to avoid the fundamental problem of a direct clash between EU law and a statute passed after 1972. The issue finally arose in an unavoidable form in the *Factortame* cases, C-213/89, [1990] 3 CMLR 375 and C-221/89, [1991] 3 CMLR 589. These concerned an apparent clash between the EU laws forbidding discrimination on grounds of nationality and the Merchant Shipping Act 1988, which imposed discriminatory rules concerning fishing boats. When *Factortame* challenged the application of the 1988 Act, it sought an interim injunction suspending the Act pending a reference to the European Court of Justice. UK law would not permit such a suspension as it would clearly breach the Diceyean formulation of parliamentary supremacy, but the European Court of Justice held that EU law could require it. The House of Lords was therefore faced with the ultimate choice, or dilemma: to obey the 1988 Act, as the newest statement of Parliament's intentions, or to obey the 1972 Act and enforce EU law. The House of Lords decided to obey the ECA 1972 and awarded the injunction. In effect, the ECA 1972 was held not to be subject to the doctrine of implied repeal. All legislation passed after 1972 thus contains an implicit proviso: 'unless EU law provides otherwise'. The ECA 1972 Act was treated by the courts as having an exceptional status, but perhaps not a unique one. In *Thoburn v Sunderland City Council* [2002] EWHC 195 Admin, [2002] 4 All ER 156, Laws LJ suggested that other 'constitutional' statutes might share this protection against implied repeal.

The ECA 1972 Act can of course be expressly amended or repealed pursuant to parliamentary sovereignty, and if that happened then EU law would lose its primary effect within the UK in the eyes of the UK courts. Parliament would be specifically, expressly directing the UK the courts, and its supremacy would be restored to its Diceyean form by the change.

It is interesting to consider the effect of an express parliamentary enactment, short of a complete repeal of the ECA 1972, stating that some particular provision of the Act was to prevail over any EU law to the contrary and expressly instructing the domestic courts, the ECA 1972 notwithstanding, to follow the given statutory provision instead of the conflicting EU law. What would the domestic courts do? Would they follow the ECA and the EU law, or the later statute? In *Macarthys Ltd v Smith* [1981] QB 180 Lord Denning suggested that in such a case, unlikely though it was, the UK courts would have to obey the new statute as the expression of the current will of Parliament. Whilst the matter would no doubt reach the ECJ, ultimate resolution of what would be a constitutional crisis would be in the political arena, not just domestic but also involving EU bodies and member states. Whilst the ECJ is generally recognised as having provided innovative 'fixes' throughout the legal and political development of the EU and its relations with its member states, the UK courts are confined purely to interpretation and application of 'the law'. Nonetheless, here they would be between a 'rock and a hard place', which law to apply, which to breach and with which sovereign law-making entity to clash? Perhaps rather than try to differentiate between ranks, the domestic courts would be bound to obey the last order, the unambiguous, express instruction of the Westminster Parliament. This would then leave it to the respective politicians to resolve matters somehow. The 'offending' Act would almost inevitably have been a government measure (to have been passed) and so the key question would be begged, just who does or should govern the UK and have the last word in the setting of its laws.

In conclusion, it can be argued that the UK Parliament, through its power expressly to amend or repeal the ECA 1972 or to legislate expressly contrary to it, does retain its ultimate supremacy in spite of the fact that in its daily operation it is now restrained (or constrained) by EU law. The domestic courts have in effect taken Parliament at its word as expressed in 1972, and will continue to do so until expressly instructed to the contrary. Any other decision would have led to the courts provoking clashes with EU law. Parliament (essentially the elected House of Commons) chose in 1972 to give up exercise of its domestic sovereignty over some (albeit arguably an unexpectedly wide and growing realm of) matters, unless and until it chooses to take it back. As with devolution, it may be ever more difficult—politically—for Parliament to reclaim what it relinquished but it seems legitimate that the ultimate decision as to whether EU law should continue to have force in the UK should rest with the UK Parliament.

Question 3

In January 2003 the EU Commission issued Directive 1/2003 which provided, inter alia, that:

In the event of property of a European Union citizen being compulsorily acquired into public ownership that citizen shall be entitled to prompt, adequate and effective compensation from the nationalising government.

In 2008, due to the world financial crisis, the government of the UK wishes to obtain powers to take banks, which are struggling financially, into public ownership. The Nationalisation of Banks Bill 2008 is placed before Parliament. This Bill passes through all its stages in the House of Commons and is at its Third Reading in the House of Lords. It contains a controversial clause that stipulates that:

No compensation shall be payable to any shareholders in any bank, taken into public ownership.

In the Commons debate on the Bill, the Minister for Europe explained that this clause was to prevent anyone making excess profits from the collapse of a bank.

Joan is a major shareholder in Farrows Bank, which is named in the Nationalisation of Banks Bill 2008 as one of the banks that is to be nationalised. She wishes to challenge the legality of this Bill.

Advise Joan.

Commentary

The major constitutional question raised by the UK's membership of the European Union (EU) is the effect that EU law may have on the traditional doctrine of parliamentary sovereignty. This question is asked in essay form in Question 2, but it can equally well be asked in problem question form, as illustrated here. The most common mistake that students make in answering such questions is to think that there is an easy, straightforward answer and just give that answer. The European Court of Justice (ECJ) has said that EU law is supreme over national law; the House of Lords has accepted this. Often, a student explains *R v Secretary of State for Transport ex parte Factortame Ltd* [1991] 1 AC 603 and leaves it at that. *Factortame* is a vitally important case and cannot be omitted, but there is much more to the supremacy issue than that. Examiners would expect an explanation of traditional ideas about parliamentary supremacy and the case law that preceded *Factortame*. A really good answer would also consider the cases after *Factortame*. An answer to an essay question will be discursive whereas a problem question will demand application of the material law.

The type of EU law specified in this problem is a Directive. This is the most awkward type of EU law for the courts of an EU member state to deal with, because, first, the court has to decide whether the directive is even enforceable in the national law of that state. This is called the doctrine of 'direct effect'. If the directive lacks direct effect, no issue of whether the EU law or national law has supremacy even arises, because the directive is not enforceable in that state. How direct effect works for directives is explained in the Suggested Answer below.

Watch out however if other types of EU law arise in a problem. They work in a different way from directives. If it is a Regulation, then it is directly applicable and there is no need to go into the problems of whether or not it has direct effect. Similarly, Treaty Articles do not cause many problems as the ones that grant individual rights have direct effect (*Van Gend en Loos v Nederlandse* [1963] CMLR 105). Unlike with directives, this is not limited to vertical direct effect (see the Suggested Answer below).

As discussed in the Introduction to this book (Chapter 1), the key with problem questions is to analyse them very closely, use the information supplied to the full, not skip over anything in your planning or writing, and of course to apply the law to the facts. A line-by-line approach may suit unless, for example, you are 'advising', in which case it may be appropriate to group facts or issues for each 'client' being advised. If you adopt the approach of 'doing the law' first and then applying it to the facts, be careful: there is an uncanny knack then to miss out some points at the application stage.

With a complex problem scenario, as here, it is probably best to pick out the main issues and tackle them one by one. These are identified in the bullet points. It may be best to start with the issues, with which you are most confident. This creates a favourable impression with the person marking the piece of work and enables you to gain in self-belief before tackling the more difficult areas.

Whatever the form and style of the question asked, never lose sight of the key issue in questions of this type: how have the UK courts adapted to the supremacy of EU law?

Answer plan

- The traditional principles of parliamentary sovereignty: an Act of Parliament cannot be overridden
- The **European Communities Act 1972 (ECA 1972)**: EU law becomes part of the law of the UK
- *Costa v ENEL*: the ECJ holds that EU law has supremacy over national law
- The three conditions for the direct effect of a Directive
- *Marleasing*: interpret national law in accordance with EU law
- *Factortame*: UK courts accept the supremacy of EU law
- Governments must compensate for breach of EU law
- References to the ECJ
- **ECA 1972** can be expressly repealed.

Suggested answer

A good starting point for the traditional theories of parliamentary sovereignty are the writings of A.V. Dicey:

> The principle of parliamentary sovereignty means neither more nor less than this: namely, that Parliament thus defined has, under the English constitution, the right to make or unmake any law whatever; and, further, that no person or body is recognised by the law of England as having a right to override or set aside the legislation of Parliament.
>
> A.V. Dicey *Introduction to the Study of the Law of the Constitution*, 10th edn (1885 edn: Macmillan, 1959), p. 39

According to this theory Parliament can always change its mind, so no Act of Parliament can be protected from being amended or repealed by a later Act of Parliament. Parliament may repeal an Act either by explicitly referring to the previous Act, which is known as express repeal or, if two Acts conflict, the latter is taken to be the law — implied repeal. Even if an Act was worded so as to prevent repeal, that wording would be ineffective: *Ellen Street Estates Ltd v Minister of Health* [1934] 1 KB 590. So, according to Dicey's view, there is nothing to prevent the Nationalisation of Banks Bill 2008 repealing any previous legislation. Similarly an Act of Parliament always overrides any other form of law, and this would include foreign legislation: *Mortensen v Peters* (1906) 8F (J) 93. No person or body can set aside legislation made by Parliament.

So, traditionally, the courts have always rejected any attempt to challenge an Act of Parliament. This was confirmed by the House of Lords in *Pickin v BRB* [1974] AC 765. Once a Bill has been passed by both the House of Commons and the House of Lords and has received Royal Assent, it cannot be questioned. Joan might well argue that she does not wish to challenge an Act, but stop a Bill from becoming an Act. *Pickin* offers her no greater chance of success with this. The Lords stated that they did not have the power to investigate what went on in parliamentary proceedings. Other cases, though on delegated legislation, support the idea that the courts will not make any rulings on parliamentary proceedings: *R v Secretary of State for the Environment ex parte Notts CC* [1986] AC 240. Indeed Article 9 of the Bill of Rights 1689 states that '. . . proceedings in Parliament ought not to be. . . questioned in any court. . . '

According to traditional views, then, Joan has no case at all, but membership of the EU has changed this, although, at first, this was not clear. Section 2(1) ECA 1972 stated that all EU law was part of the law of the UK. Section 3(1) stated that the UK courts now had to abide by the decisions of the ECJ. The Act did not clearly state what would happen if EU law conflicted with a UK Act of Parliament. Under the traditional theory of implied repeal, EU law would take priority over any Act of Parliament enacted before the ECA 1972: see *Ellen Street Estates* above. Section 2(4) of the ECA 1972 has attracted attention, although its exact meaning is obscure. It states that:

> . . . any enactment passed or to be passed. . . shall be construed and have effect subject to the foregoing provisions of this section. . .

This could mean that EU law has supremacy over Acts of Parliament passed after 1972, or it could just mean that such Acts should be interpreted ('construed') so as to try to avoid any conflict with EU Law. Both interpretations seem to have found favour with the UK courts (below).

It is clear that some time before the UK joined the EU, that organisation's own court, the ECJ, had decided that the law of the EU had sovereignty over incompatible national laws:

> The EEC Treaty created its own legal order which is directly applicable to member States and to their nationals, as a result of the partial transfer of sovereignty from member States to the community. Consequently a subsequent unilateral law which is incompatible with the aim of the Community cannot prevail.
> (*Costa v ENEL* [1964] ECR 585 at 593)

The Nationalisation of Banks Bill 2008 would seem to be 'subsequent unilateral law which is incompatible' with the 2003 Directive, in that it denies any compensation.

First, however, it must be decided whether the directive is actually applicable, that is can it be enforced in UK law? The UK is obliged, under Article 249 of the EU Treaty, to give legal effect in its own national legal system to a directive, but appears not to have passed any legislation to do this. The ECJ has ruled that, in certain circumstances, a directive can have direct effect and be enforceable in the courts of a member state, despite the lack of national legislation.

The ECJ decided this in two UK cases, *Van Duyn v Home Office* [1975] Ch 358 and *Marshall v Southampton and SW Hants AHA* [1986] QB 402, and this has been accepted by the UK courts.

The directive must meet three conditions to have direct effect. The date for the implementation of the directive must have passed, which is the case here. Secondly, the wording of the directive must be clear, precise and unconditional, so that there is something that a court may enforce. Directive 1/2003 grants a clear right to compensation, which Joan should be able to enforce. The third condition is the 'vertical direct effect' condition, in that the directive can only be enforced against a public body, 'an emanation of the state'. Joan is going to be denied compensation by an Act of Parliament. She cannot sue the sovereign body, Parliament, so she would have to sue the government minister responsible for the legislation, qualifying as an 'emanation of the state': *R v Secretary of State for Transport ex parte Factortame* [1991] 1 AC 603. Farrows Bank would also be a possible Defendant, if it becomes nationalised and therefore a 'public body': *Foster v British Gas* [1991] 1 AC 306.

The problem is that Directive 1/2003 seems to be in direct contradiction to the 'no compensation' clause proposed in the Bill. The ECJ held in *Costa v ENEL* that EU law has supremacy, but in *Pickin v BRB*, the House of Lords insisted upon the supremacy of Acts of Parliament. The ECJ suggested a solution to this difficulty in *Marleasing SA v La Commercial Internacional de Alimentacion SA* [1990] ECR I-4135, in that the national court is obliged to interpret its own national law 'as far as possible, in the light of the wording and the purpose of the directive'.

The House of Lords accepted this obligation in *Webb v EMO Air Cargo (UK) Ltd* [1995] 1 WLR 1454, but it seems impossible to reconcile a directive that requires compensation to be paid and an Act of Parliament stipulating that it should not.

There appears a clear conflict between the UK Act and the directly effective EU directive. Lord Denning was one of the earliest judges to say, in *Macarthys Ltd v Smith* [1981] QB 180, that the UK courts should accord supremacy to EU law in such a case of conflict. His fellow Court of Appeal judges were not willing to go that far and endorse such a radical break with the traditional theories. It was not until *R v Secretary of State for Transport ex parte Factortame* [1991] 1 AC 603 that the House of Lords was willing to accept that EU law now had supremacy. Significantly, the House of Lords did not consider this in any great detail, as they would not wish to be seen to be questioning traditional theories too openly. Lord Bridge merely said, at p. 659, that:

> Under the terms of the Act of 1972, it has always been clear that it was the duty of a United Kingdom court, when delivering final judgment, to override any rule of national law found to be in conflict with any directly enforceable rule of Community law.

This is what s. 2(4) ECA 1972 required.

Joan could therefore follow the precedent of *Factortame*, but the exact remedy that the court could grant her is more problematic. In the light of the traditional theories of parliamentary supremacy, it is unthinkable that the UK courts would order Parliament not to legislate or order that an Act of Parliament is of no legal force. In *Factortame* itself, the House of Lords merely issued an interim injunction against the government minister responsible for that piece of legislation, telling him not to enforce the offending Act of Parliament. Joan would probably be obliged to wait for the Bill to become an Act. She could then ask the courts to follow *Factortame* and issue an injunction forbidding the enforcement of the Act and the confiscation of her shares, without compensation. The court might even prefer to issue a lesser remedy, a Declaration, as in *R v Employment Secretary ex parte Equal Opportunities Commission* [1995] 1 AC 1.

The ECJ has also provided another remedy for claimants in Joan's position. If a government or public body breaches EU law and causes loss to the claimant, particularly if the government is acting intentionally and persistently, it must compensate the claimant. The directive here confers a right to compensation upon Joan and this would seem to be a serious breach of EU law: *R v Secretary of State for Transport ex parte Factortame Ltd (No. 4)* [1996] 2 WLR 506. Joan could sue the relevant government minister, for compensation.

If Joan brings legal proceedings they have to commence in a UK court and the final order or ruling must come from a UK court, as indicated in *Factortame* and in *Equal Opportunities Commission*. It is very likely though that, at some stage of the proceedings, the UK court would seek a ruling, on the meaning of EU law, from the ECJ under the Article 234 procedure. This occurred, for example, in *R v Secretary of State for Transport ex parte Factortame (No. 1)* [1990] 2 AC 85. The UK court then applies the ruling of the ECJ.

There is one final possibility that is not favourable to Joan's case. Lord Denning observed in *Macarthys Ltd v Smith* [1981] QB 180 that EU law only had supremacy in the UK because an Act of Parliament says so. Parliament could always change its mind about the ECA 1972 Act and repeal or amend it. Denning went on to say that the words of the repealing Act would have to be clear or 'express'. This is confirmed by *Thoburn v Sunderland City Council* [2002] 1 CMLR 50, which held that the ECA 1972 Act was a 'constitutional statute', which could not be impliedly repealed. Only express repeal could remove EU law and replace it with a UK statute. The wording of the Nationalisation of Banks Bill 2008 seems clearly to contradict EU law, but the court might consider that it would need to consult the record of parliamentary proceedings, as happened in *Pickstone v Freemans plc* [1989] AC 66, in order to ascertain whether Parliament intended to contradict or implement EU law.

If an Act of Parliament clearly did intend to remove this EU Directive, then the UK courts would be bound to follow the intention of Parliament. The ECJ would assert the supremacy of EU law, so there would be a clash between the two courts. As seen in the *Factortame* litigation, it would probably be the UK that had to back down and remove the offending part of the Act of Parliament. Otherwise, political ramifications would likely ensue. though this goes beyond what is pertinent to Joan's situation.

Further reading

Bradley, A. and Ewing, K. *Constitutional and Administrative Law*, 14th edn (Longman, 2006), chs 4 and 8.

Bradley, A. 'The Sovereignty of Parliament,' in J. Jowell and D. Oliver (eds) *The Changing Constitution*, 5th edn (OUP, 2004).

Craig, P. 'Britain in the EU', in J. Jowell and D. Oliver (op cit.)

Munro, C. *Studies in Constitutional Law*, 2nd edn (Butterworths, 1999), chs 5 and 6.

Oliver, D. *Constitutional Reform in the UK* (OUP, 2003) ch 4.

7

The Rule of Law; the Separation of Powers

Introduction

Any constitutional and administrative law module will devote time to the Rule of Law and the Separation of Powers, whether considered under Constitutional Sources, Fundamental Principles or otherwise. Here, we consider the conceptual nature and practical application of each in the context of the check they provide upon government and Parliament in particular, having first examined the 'engine' of the UK constitution, parliamentary sovereignty.

Question 1

In so far as Dicey's general statement of the rule of law may be taken to involve the existence in the English constitution of certain principles almost amounting to fundamental laws, his doctrine is logically inconsistent with the legislative supremacy of Parliament.
    (O. Hood Phillips *Constitutional and Administrative Law* (1987))

Discuss.

Commentary

Students often dislike answering questions on the rule of law because the topic seems too vague. Lots of different ideas and theories are identified as the rule of law, which is what causes the confusion. The student must be familiar with at least some of these theories, be able to criticise them and compare them. A good starting point is Dicey's version of the rule of law. It should be referred to in any question on the rule of law even if, unlike in our question, it is not specifically raised in the question set. Students should also be able to discuss at least one other theory of the rule of law.

Here, the particular slant of the question is how the rule of law sits with the power of the Westminster Parliament.

 Answer plan

- The law must authorise all government action
- Equality before the law
- The common law protects individual liberty
- The supremacy of Parliament
- The Judiciary and the Executive
- The **Human Rights Act 1998**.

Suggested answer

The idea of the rule of law was not invented by Dicey, but he popularised it in the late nineteenth century. His book, *Introduction to the Study of the Law of the Constitution* (1885) can be seen as a strong defence of the English constitution when compared with the constitutions of other countries, particularly those with written constitutions. De Smith states:

> His ideas . . . were very influential for two generations; today they no longer warrant detailed analysis.
> (*Constitutional and Administrative Law* (1998))

It is true that Dicey's ideas went out of fashion for a time, but they have now come back into favour, particularly with senior members of the Judiciary. Indeed they are now specifically mentioned in sections of the Constitutional Reform Act 2005. So, once again, these ideas demand detailed analysis.

It is often said that the UK has an 'unwritten constitution', meaning that it is not codified and much of it has no formal legal status. Dicey argued that not only did this not matter, but in fact it was a positive advantage. In the UK there was a long tradition of respect for individual liberty and democracy. This tradition was upheld in the country's constitutional arrangements. For short, it could be called the rule of law. Dicey (referring to the 'English' constitution) summarised it under three main principles.

His first principle concerned the rule of law and discretionary powers. No person could be punished or interfered with by the authorities unless the law authorised it. Put another way, all government actions must be authorised by the law. This contrasted the situation in England with a country where there were no rules. In the latter, the government could do as it pleased and there would be no legal controls over its activities. Examples would be imprisonment when someone had broken no law, or the lack of any trial before punishment.

Dicey also considered that governments should not possess wide discretionary powers. These ideas were classically illustrated in *Entick v Carrington* (1765) 19 St Tr 1030 where the courts declared that the Secretary of State could not order the search of Entick's house, because there was no law authorising such searches. The court would not accept arguments of 'state necessity' or that there was one law for government activities and another for ordinary people.

Dicey's second principle has the resounding title of 'equality before the law', namely that the government and its officials should not have any special exemptions or protections from the law. He did not like the French *Droit Administratif* system where government activities were dealt with by separate administrative courts. These he considered to be too partial to the government, and inferior to ordinary courts of law.

The final principle concerns individual rights. The English constitution respects personal liberty. There is no need for a Bill of Rights because civil liberties are respected anyway. The courts protect them in their decisions by developing the common law in a way that respects individual liberty. Parliament legislates on particular problems. In contrast, Bills of Rights are documents that promise all sorts of rights. These promises are so general and capable of so many meanings that they are meaningless. Also, the Bill of Rights might not be respected by the government and might be unenforceable.

Dicey's theory is open to many objections, some applicable when he wrote, some pertaining to the workings of different constitutions now. Some might say that these ideas are so vague and wide ranging that they have no real meaning. De Smith argues that: 'The concept is one of open texture; it lends itself to an extremely wide range of interpretations ' and that: ' ... everyone who tries to redefine it begins with the assumption that it is a good thing, like justice or courage'.

Some might say that Dicey's theory is so obvious that it is not worth stating it. Of course the government must obey the law and the courts enforce it in a modern constitutional system. R. F. V. Heuston ('The Rule of Law' from *Essays in Constitutional Law* (1964)) claims that Dicey misunderstood French administrative courts. They are not biased in favour of the government and they do at least as well, if not better, in controlling the government as the 'English' courts. Separate 'public law' or 'constitutional' courts are the normal arrangement in continental Europe. E. Barendt ([1985] Public Law 596) argues that Dicey also misunderstood the nature of written constitutions. Although in 1885 Bills of Rights might just have been pious declarations that no one could enforce, nowadays most countries that have them possess sophisticated enforcement mechanisms.

Of course there is a rule of law in the United Kingdom and arguably the Diceyean model still holds credibility at least in its fundamentals. However, the main criticism is that it fails to deal with the supremacy of Parliament. In passing legislation

Parliament must comply with the procedural strictures of the rule of law. Beyond this, at least theoretically the sovereignty (or supremacy) of the UK Parliament means that it may pass whatever laws it wishes. If Parliament legislates in a way that is contrary to the value-laden principles of the rule of law, it is still the law and there is nothing that the courts can do about it. For example statutes can effectively annul inconvenient court decisions, as with the War Damage Act 1965 which reversed, with retrospective effect, *Burmah Oil v Lord Advocate* [1965] AC 75, where the House of Lords had ordered the government to pay compensation to Burmah Oil for the wartime destruction of its oil installations. Statutes also grant government officials some immunity from legal action, for instance the Crown Proceedings Act 1947. Some Acts of Parliament grant the government wide and uncontrolled discretionary powers, such as the Deregulation and Contracting Out Act 1994. Dicey claimed that Parliament would restrain the government. Perhaps that was true in 1885, but nowadays the government of the day controls Parliament through its majority and can nearly always get its own way.

A key element of Dicey's rule of law was that the government must possess clearly defined legal powers to authorise its actions. Under the UK's unwritten constitution it is in fact difficult to be precise about the legal powers that government possesses. Prerogative powers still exist and it can be difficult to identify those powers accurately. For instance in *R v Home Secretary ex parte Northumbria Police Authority* [1988] 1 All ER 556 the court accepted the existence of a prerogative power, to maintain peace in the realm, which had not previously been identified. Again much of the constitution is convention, not law, for example, the powers of the Prime Minister. As they are not law, the courts cannot control these powers. Indeed there must be some doubts about whether the courts are always keen to ensure that the government keeps within its legal powers. In *Malone v Metropolitan Police Commissioner* [1979] Ch 344, Malone's telephone had been tapped by the police. He claimed that there was no law that authorised telephone tapping. These facts have strong similarities to the classic rule of law case, *Entick v Carrington* (1765). However, in *Malone* the judge came to the opposite conclusion: no law forbade telephone tapping by the police, therefore it must be legal.

Despite these criticisms, the rule of law still has its defenders. T. R. S. Allan ([1985] Cambridge Law Journal 111) stressed that Parliament still has a controlling effect on the government, particularly as the Commons is elected by the people. The government does not always get its way in Parliament and although Parliament can be persuaded to change the law in a way favourable to the government, until that has happened the government must obey the existing law. Judges will ensure that they do. Judges can also minimise the effects of 'unjust' laws by using techniques of statutory interpretation.

Perhaps Dicey never intended his rule of law as an accurate description of the 'English' constitution. Perhaps he was just trying to say that this is the way it should be, not the way it actually was. These were the ideals that government, administrators and judges should endeavour to uphold.

Since the 1990s, the rule of law has attracted the attention of many senior judges. In *M v Home Office* [1994] 1 AC 377 the House of Lords confirmed the rule of law in its basic meaning. The government must obey the law. It had no immunity from court orders and government ministers were liable for contempt.

More significantly, the courts began showing a keen interest in the rule of law in its wider sense. In *Bennett v Horseferry Road Magistrates* [1993] 3 All ER 138, the defendant had been illegally abducted from South Africa to stand trial in England. Despite the fact that no English laws had been broken, the House of Lords threw the case out on the grounds that it would be an abuse of fair procedure to try Bennett. The courts would not 'turn a blind eye, to the authorities' involvement in law-breaking.

Although Dicey disagreed with the idea of a Bill of Rights, the Human Rights Act 1998 (HRA 1998) has increased interest in, and, perhaps, the standing of the rule of law. Many of the Convention rights now domestically enforceable under HRA 1998 embody values similar to those espoused in the rule of law. For example, detention without trial was disapproved of by Dicey and potentially breaches Convention Articles 5 (liberty of the person) and 6 (fair trial) for starters. It was considered by the House of Lords in *A v Secretary of State for the Home Department* [2005] 2 AC 68. This involved the detention, without trial of foreign nationals who were suspected of terrorism. The House held that this was contrary to human rights on the narrow ground that this was unjustifiable racial discrimination: UK nationals were just as likely to be suspected of terrorism. Lord Bingham (at p. 113) quoted Professor Lauterpacht: 'The claim to equality before the law is in a substantial sense the most fundamental of the rights of man.'

Equality before the law was of course one of the main elements of Dicey's theory. In the follow-up case, *A v Home Secretary (No. 2)* [2006] 1 All ER 575 the House of Lords rejected the use of evidence obtained by torture, not just because it was forbidden by various international Human Rights Conventions, but because it was contrary to the common law traditions of this country. That is just the sort of argument that Dicey would have used.

Despite the views of the senior judiciary, the greatest problem with the rule of law, as defined by Dicey, is that it gives no protection if Parliament legislates in an unfair or unjust way. HRA 1998 has arguably enhanced the protection of freedoms of the individual, providing positive, enforceable rights and a significantly broadened interpretative remit to the courts (s. 3 in particular). However, the Act has no effect upon parliamentary supremacy.

An intrinsic aspect of parliamentary sovereignty is that there can be no judicial review of Acts of Parliament. If Parliament wishes to pass 'unconscionable' legislation, it may. Perhaps the best protection against this happening is however the political responsibility of those who govern and legislate, essentially MPs, as their very jobs lie ultimately in the hands of those who may be affected by such draconian laws, the electorate.

Question 2

Explain what is meant by the 'Separation of Powers'. To what extent is it an important element in the constitutional arrangements of the UK?

Commentary

Questions on the separation of powers are somewhat easier to approach than questions on other constitutional theories like the rule of law. At least the separation of powers has a clearly defined meaning.

Our example is a pretty typical question on this subject. To answer, the candidate must be able to explain the theory of the separation of powers, ideally illustrated by reference to an example of a constitution based on those principles, such as that of the United States or France. Then it is necessary to show how the UK's constitution does not conform to the theory. The difficulty in questions on separation is in what the question asks you to do next. There being both separation and fusion in the UK constitution, the focus of the given question might be upon either or both elements. The same basic material can be deployed to answer either type of question.

The second part of this question really directs us to consider both 'sides' of this equation, requiring then an evaluation of how significant a part separation plays in how the UK constitution works as a whole.

One point of clarification. You need always to define your terms: in our suggested answer 'the Executive' refers to central government except where otherwise stated.

Answer plan

- The Executive proposes the laws
- The Legislative makes the laws
- The Executive administers and implements the laws
- The Judiciary interprets, applies and enforces laws
- The fusion of the legislative and executive functions in the UK
- The independence of the Judiciary in the UK.

Suggested answer

The separation of powers is an ancient and very simple idea: governance of the State should not be concentrated in the hands of one person or body, otherwise tyranny results. Ancient Greeks, such as Aristotle in his *Politics*, first propounded a version of this theory, but the most famous version is that put forward by

Montesquieu in *The Spirit of the Laws* (1748) (A. Cohler, B. Miller and H. Stone (eds), Cambridge, 1989). Montesquieu argued that there were three functions of government. The Legislative, or Lawmaking function, which is the enactment of rules for the society. The Executive, or Law-Applying function, which covers actions taken to maintain or implement the law, defend the State, conduct external affairs and administer internal policies. Finally came the Judicial, or Law-Enforcing function, which is the determining of civil disputes and the punishing of criminals by deciding issues of fact and applying the law. His view was that: 'There would be an end to everything, if the same man, or the same body ... were to exercise those three powers ....'

This can be interpreted in several ways, but the most likely is that he meant that the three functions should be carried out by separate organs of state and that each organ should only carry out its own function. For instance, the Legislature should not judge, nor should the Executive make laws. The Legislative, Executive and Judicial branches should have equal status so each could control the excessive use of power by another branch.

These theories were adopted and developed by James Madison and incorporated into the Constitution of the United States in 1787, which still remains a classic example of an attempt to implement the separation of powers. Article I declares that: 'All legislative power herein granted shall be vested in a Congress of the United States', Article II that 'The executive power shall be invested in a President of the United States' and Article III that 'The judicial power of the United States shall be invested in one Supreme Court and inferior courts as the Congress may from time to time ordain and establish.'

The President is not a member of Congress and elections for the President and for Congress are separate. There is also an elaborate system of checks and balances between the three branches of governance of the United States. For example, under Article I, Section 7, the President may, in effect, veto legislation passed by the Congress, if at least one-third of either House of Congress agrees with him. The Supreme Court has the power to declare the acts of both the President or Congress unconstitutional and illegal, but this power is not found in the written constitution, but rather case law: *Marbury v Madison* (1803) 1 Cranch 137.

The constitution of the UK is nothing like this, in that there is no written constitutional document and no formal separation of powers. Historically, the King and his *Curia Regis* were all three branches of government. Even today, formally, the Queen still appoints all government ministers and all the members of the Judiciary from the County Court upwards, she summons Parliament and Assents to all Parliamentary Bills before they become law. The Executive is part of the Legislature, in that ministers must be members of one of the Houses of Parliament, and even the senior judges are members of the Legislature as they sit currently in the House of Lords as 'Law Lords'.

This has lead many constitutional commentators to dismiss the relevance of the theory of the separation of powers to the UK constitution. Instead they have concentrated on the 'checks and balances' such as ministerial accountability to Parliament. More recently, some writers, such as Munro (*Studies in Constitutional Law* 2nd edn (Butterworths, 1999)), have tried to reinterpret these 'checks and balances' as a UK version of the separation of powers. Many senior judges have echoed this (below).

It is argued that although all members of the government are also members of the Legislature, these two groups are not identical. There are just over a hundred government ministers, but they are greatly outnumbered by 'ordinary' members of the Legislature amongst the 646 MPs and 741 or so Lords. The Executive does not have complete control over the Legislature, as even MPs of the governing party do not always do as they are told. The Legislature can also hold the Executive to account by means of debate, oral and written questions and the system of select committees.

The personnel of the Legislature and the Judiciary are also largely separate, for under sch. 1 of the House of Commons Disqualification Act 1975, judges cannot be members of the House of Commons. The Lords of Appeal in Ordinary (Law Lords) sit in the Legislature as members of the House of Lords, but by convention, they do not usually participate in the legislative work of the House.

The office of Lord Chancellor, once a classical illustration of fusion of power, has now been reformed by the Constitutional Reform Act 2005 (CRA) so as to enhance judicial independence and separation of powers between the Judiciary and Legislature. The Lord Chancellor is still a Cabinet minister but no longer a judge, head of the Judiciary or 'Speaker' of the legislative House of Lords. The office of Attorney-General has recently attracted much, similar criticism in terms of lack of separation of powers and it may be that this post will be reformed in like fashion. Once fully implemented the 2005 Act will also remove the Law Lords from the House of Lords, housing them as 'Justices' of a new, separate 'Supreme Court of the United Kingdom'. Judges are now selected by a Judicial Appointments Commission. The Lord Chancellor will only be able to appoint judges recommended by this Commission, although he does not have to accept their first choice. This lessens executive control of the Judiciary.

The Legislature cannot tell the Judiciary how to decide a case and, in order to protect judicial independence, it is extremely hard for the Legislature to dismiss a judge from office. Under s. 133 CRA, judges of the High Court and above hold office during good behaviour, but may be removed, on an address by both Houses of Parliament. Thus a judge cannot be removed because a politician does not like her decision in a given case.

The courts accept the supremacy of Parliament but assert an entitlement to interpret laws made by Parliament. As Lord Diplock put it in *Duport Steel v Sirs* [1980] 1 All ER 529 at 541:

> it cannot be too strongly emphasised that the British constitution, though largely unwritten, is firmly based on the separation of powers: Parliament makes the laws, the judiciary interprets them.

The courts will decide against government ministers if they exceed their legal powers, as seen in *M v Home Office* [1992] QB 270 where the House of Lords held the Home Secretary in contempt of court for disobeying a court order. The modern Judiciary has asserted the separation of powers as can be seen in *R v Secretary of State for the Home Department ex parte Fire Brigades Unions* [1995] 2 AC 513, where the Law Lords refused to allow the Executive to ignore the legislative will of Parliament. As Lord Mustill put it:

> It is a feature of the peculiarly British conception of the separation of powers that Parliament, the executive and the courts have each their distinct and largely exclusive domain. Parliament has a largely unchallengeable right to make whatever laws it thinks right. The executive carries on the administration of the country in accordance with the powers conferred on it by law. The courts interpret the laws and see that they are obeyed.
> (*Fire Brigades Unions*, at 567).

Despite these arguments that there is a form of the separation of powers operating in the UK constitution, it has to be reiterated that this is not a formal separation as suggested by Montesquieu or as found in the United States. Since the Human Rights Act 1998 came into force in 2000, this has caused problems. Article 6 of the Convention provides the right to a fair trial including a hearing 'by an independent and impartial tribunal established by law'.

This led the House of Lords to rule in *R (Anderson) v Secretary of State for the Home Department* [2002] 4 All ER 1089, that the Home Secretary should not play a part in setting the minimum custodial tariff to be served by a murderer, as the Home Secretary was a member of the Executive, not the Judiciary, and the minimum tariff was an aspect of sentencing. As Lord Steyn put it (at 1106):

> Article 6(1) requires effective separation between the courts and the executive, and further requires that what can, in shorthand, be called judicial functions may only be discharged by the courts ...

s. 3 CRA contains the first statutory guarantee of judicial independence. The Lord Chancellor and other ministers of the Crown 'must uphold the continued independence of the Judiciary' and 'must not seek to influence particular judicial decisions through any special access to the Judiciary'. So it can be seen that the UK is becoming more concerned about the lack of a formal separation of powers in its constitution and is trying to do more to ensure the independence of the Judiciary. A full separation of powers looks unlikely, however, as this would require the Legislature to be separate from the Executive, which would mean a totally different way of electing a government, selecting a Prime Minister and holding government to account. Such radical change does not seem imminent or pressing.

Further reading

Bradley, A. and Ewing, K. *Constitutional and Administrative Law*, 14th edn (Longman, 2007), chs 5, 6.

Barnett, H. *Constitutional and Administrative Law* 7th edn (Routledge-Cavendish, 2008), chs 3 and 4.

Loveland, I. *Constitutional Law, Administrative Law, and Human Rights*, 4th edn (OUP, 2006), ch 3.

Turpin, C. and Tomkins, A. *British Government and The Constitution*, 6th edn (Cambridge, 2007), ch 2.

The Human Rights Act 1998

Introduction

Although the Labour government that won the 1997 General Election had promised, in its election manifesto, to enact the European Convention on Human Rights into British law, the speed with which this was done took many by surprise. The Human Rights Act 1998 adopted an existing human rights treaty, the European Convention on Human Rights and gave it force in UK law from 2 October 2000. In a sense this was nothing new, since the European Convention on Human Rights had existed since 1951. It was issued by the Council of Europe, *not the European Union*, which is a common mistake made not just by students, but by the media and even some judges as well! The UK was a founder member of the Council that was established, in 1949, to promote democracy, human rights and the rule of law in a Europe devastated by war. Britain played a leading role in drafting the Convention, but it was not then thought necessary to give it legal force in British law as it was considered that the rights protected in the Convention were already respected in this country.

Despite this, it was always possible to enforce the Convention on an international level. Any of the 47 member states could bring a complaint of breach of human rights against any of the other members, alleging that that the State had not respected the rights laid down in the Convention. This procedure is rarely used, but the Convention also allows individual 'victims' the right to bring a complaint against the State that they claim has infringed their human rights. Nowadays these complaints go directly to the European Court of Human Rights, which is an international court staffed by judges from the 47 member states, sitting in Strasbourg. (Note that this is not to be confused with the quite separate European Court of Justice, which is the court of the European Union and sits in Luxembourg.) The European Court of Human Rights will rule upon whether there has been any infringement of human rights and may order the offending State to award compensation to the victim. member states, including the UK, have a very good record for obeying these judgments, which often mean that domestic law has to be changed. Over the years the European Court of Human Rights has decided thousands of cases, which means that there is a lot of guidance upon what the Convention actually means in practice.

All that the Human Rights Act 1998 does is provide that the 'Convention rights' can be enforced in British courts. British legislation must be interpreted in a way that is consistent with the rights granted under the Convention. All public authorities must also act in a way that is compatible with the Convention. As 'public authorities' includes courts, this means that case law must be interpreted to 'take into account' the cases decided by the European Court of Human Rights.

Since Gordon Brown became Prime Minister he has tried to initiate a debate upon whether the UK should go further and draw up a 'British Bill of Rights and Duties'. This would help to show what it means to be British and the core values that British people share. It seems from the document in which these ideas are raised, *The Governance of Britain* (Cm 7170) that these rights and duties would be in addition to the rights already protected under the Human Rights Act 1998. The other major political parties support the idea of a UK Bill of Rights, but it is unclear what would go into it, what form it might take and, crucially, how it would be enforced.

So what would an examiner expect you to know about all this? At the very least you would need to know what the Human Rights Act actually says. It would also be helpful to know the procedure to make a complaint to the European Court of Human Rights, which has been mentioned above. Even after the Human Rights Act came into force this procedure still exists and someone dissatisfied with the British courts might choose to go there. Even more important, it is essential to have some idea of which rights are actually protected in the 'Articles' of the Convention and some idea of the major cases that tell us what those rights actually mean. A more difficult question is the discussion essay on what difference the Act and/or the Convention has made to the protection of rights in this country. Of course there is no definite answer to this but armed with some *factual* knowledge about the Act, Convention and case law any student should be able to at least offer some sort of answer.

Question 1

The response to terrorism has been at a considerable cost to traditional liberties formally protected by the European Convention on Human Rights and the Human Rights Act ...
    (Bradley and Ewing *Constitutional and Administrative Law*, p. 627)

Discuss.

Commentary

This is a discussion question on human rights, which draws attention to a recently controversial area, a common tactic amongst lecturers. When threatened with problems like terrorism, most governments consider it necessary to alter the normal legal rules on how suspected criminals are treated. This can bring the courts into conflict with the government or executive. Judges may not agree with the legal changes and may feel that they unnecessarily threaten human rights or the liberties of the individual.

The question seems straightforward, but the words 'formally protected' may cause some concern. All that they mean is that liberties were traditionally respected by the UK courts, but now they are listed as rights in the **Human Rights Act 1998**. That is the 'formal' part.

There has been a lot of legislation on terrorism. In a relatively short essay for coursework or in an examination, it would be difficult to cover it all. Even if you could it would make for a boring read. Students should not just repeat information but should try to criticise and analyse. It would pay to be selective and just to look at the legislation that you consider most significant. I have taken this a stage further and decided to look at the most important cases. I would hope that this would make for a more interesting read. It is also much easier to remember a few cases than to try to recall hundreds of pages of statute.

Answer plan

- Statutory definition of terrorism
- The right to life
- Torture and inhuman or degrading treatment or punishment
- Detention without trial
- The right to a fair trial
- Reasonable suspicion
- The right to legal assistance
- Public emergency and derogation from the Convention.

Suggested answer

Some people might think that terrorism is a problem that has only affected the United Kingdom since the attack on the Twin Towers in New York on 11 September 2001, but in fact it is not a new problem. If we only consider recent history, there has been a terrorist problem in Northern Ireland since the late 1960s.

Terrorism is defined in s. 1 of the Terrorism Act 2000 as threatening serious violence against a person, serious damage against property, endangering a person's life, creating a serious risk to the health and safety of the public or seriously interfering with an electronic system. These threats must be designed to influence the government or to intimidate the public. Crucially the threat must be made for the purpose of advancing a political, religious, racial or ideological cause. Threats involving using a noxious substance were added in the Anti-terrorism, Crime and Security Act 2001 and the Terrorism Act 2006 added threats against 'an international governmental organisation' in s. 34. This is a very wide definition, but even so governments have found it hard to convict terrorists using the normal processes of the criminal law. So a succession of special measures has been introduced, which have sometimes brought the government into conflict with the courts.

Article 2 of the European Convention of Human Rights guarantees the right to life and this has come up in the courts, when alleged terrorists have been shot by the security services. In the notorious 'Death on the Rock' case, *McGann, Farrell and Savage v UK* (1995) 21 EHRR 97, three members of the Provisional IRA were shot dead by plainclothes members of the SAS. The victims were given a command to stop and appeared to reach for remote-control devices in order to detonate a car bomb. They were shot dead before they could do this. Although the soldiers had been told that there was a bomb on Gibraltar, this was not the case and the deceased were not carrying remote-control devices. The European Court of Human Rights concluded that the soldiers honestly believed that the victims were carrying detonators and that it was necessary to kill them. However, the majority of judges concluded that the UK authorities were to blame. They could have arrested the three earlier, when they entered Gibraltar, they wrongly believed that a remotely controlled bomb would be used and maybe the victims could have been wounded rather than killed. In the words of the Convention, the killing was not 'absolutely necessary'.

Jordan v UK (2001) 11 BHRC 1 also involved IRA men shot dead by the SAS and Royal Ulster Constabulary. Again there was a breach of Article 2, because there was not an independent and effective investigation into the circumstances of their deaths.

Article 3 outlaws 'torture and inhuman or degrading treatment or punishment'. In *Ireland v UK* (1978) 2 EHRR 25 suspected terrorists in Northern Ireland were imprisoned and subjected to harsh interrogation techniques such as beatings, wall-standing, hooding, noise, sleep-deprivation, and deprivation of food and drink. These were not isolated incidents, but were a systematic practice authorised at a high level of the British government. The European Court concluded that the use of these techniques had led to physical and mental suffering, but were not severe enough to amount to torture. They were, however, inhuman and degrading and the UK was in breach of the Convention. The Court is keen to prevent torture as it is one of the most basic human rights, to which no exceptions are permitted. In *Chahal v UK* (1997) 23 EHRR 413, Chahal was an Indian citizen, living in the UK, who advocated a Sikh homeland, Khalistan. The British Home Secretary wanted to deport Chahal to India, as a suspected terrorist and threat to national security. This was forbidden by the Court, because there was a real risk that he would be tortured if he was returned to India. There was evidence that the Punjab police had previously used such measures against Sikh militants.

The UK House of Lords considered the history of the use of torture, both within Britain and worldwide in *A v Secretary of State for the Home Department (No. 2)* [2006] 1 All ER 575. They concluded that evidence obtained by torture in other countries was inadmissible in UK legal proceedings. This was the common law rule long before there were Human Rights Conventions. Lord Bingham said at p. 586:

> In rejecting the use of torture, whether applied to potential defendants or potential witnesses, the common law was moved by the cruelty of the practice as applied to those not convicted of crime, by the inherent unreliability of confessions or evidence so procured and by the belief that it degraded all those who lent themselves to the practice.

Because it is difficult to prove involvement in terrorism the authorities have often resorted to prolonged detention of suspected terrorists, who have not been convicted of any offence. This can be a form of preventive detention or it can be a way of providing extra time to question suspects. In 1971 hundreds of suspected terrorists in Northern Ireland were indefinitely detained, a practice known as internment. This was questioned in *Ireland v UK* (above), but because of a derogation (see later) the Court accepted the practice. Under the Prevention of Terrorism (Temporary Provisions) Act 1984, it was possible for the police to detain arrested persons suspected of terrorism for up to a week for questioning. In *Brogan v UK* (1988) 11 EHRR 117, the European Court of Human Rights condemned the treatment of Brogan. In their view, this length of detention had to be authorised by a judicial authority. In the recent Terrorism Act 2006, the government sought the power for the police to detain suspected terrorists that had been arrested, for up to 90 days. The Houses of Parliament refused to accept this and the maximum period was extended to 28 days, but crucially this has to be authorised by a High Court judge.

The government had another problem with suspected terrorists of foreign nationality. The Home Secretary has power to deport foreign nationals, who she considers to be a threat to national security, but under *Cheblak*, above, she cannot do so if they are likely to be tortured or ill-treated on their return to their home country. It might also be difficult to prosecute these alleged offenders in the normal way because of a lack of evidence that could be used in court. The solution adopted in s. 23 of the Anti-terrorism, Crime and Security Act 2001, was to give the Home Secretary power to detain suspected international terrorists, indefinitely and without trial. The nine detainees challenged their detention in the House of Lords' case *A v Secretary of State for the Home Department (No. 1)* [2005] 2 AC 68 and succeeded on the very narrow grounds that it was discriminatory to detain foreign nationals, but not UK nationals. Both could be a terrorist threat. After this case the government had to think again and came up with 'control orders' in the Prevention of Terrorism Act 2005, which apply to both UK and foreign terrorist suspects. These are a form of 'house arrest' where the suspect is not put in any form of custody, but allowed to remain in their own home, with severe restrictions upon where they are allowed to go and who they are allowed to contact. The courts have expressed some concern about control orders, in particular that the procedure to make them infringes Article 6, the right to a fair trial. In *Secretary of State for the Home Department v MB* [2008] 1 All ER 657 and *Secretary of State for the Home Department v AF (No. 2)* [2008] 2 All ER 67, the House of Lords condemned control orders, on the grounds that the person being subjected to the order was not allowed to see the evidence against them, because to reveal that evidence would itself be a threat to national security. In *Secretary of State for the Home Department v JJ* [2008] 1 All ER 613, another control order was quashed on the grounds that it contravened Article 5, the right to liberty. JJ was confined to his home, away from family and friends, for 16 hours a day, and heavily restricted on who he could contact.

Much of the anti-terrorism legislation also allows the police to arrest on less evidence than for 'normal' crimes. This too has led to court cases, but here the cases tend to depend on the facts rather than any wider legal principle. A police officer arrested O' Hara claiming that he had reasonable grounds for suspecting him to be concerned in an act of terrorism. The officer had been told to arrest O'Hara by a superior. This would not be enough for reasonable grounds by itself, but the briefing to the officer did contain information on which he could form a reasonable suspicion (*O'Hara v Chief Constable of the Royal Ulster Constabulary* [1997] 1 All ER 129). Article 5(1)(c) of the European Convention permits the arrest of a person 'on reasonable suspicion of having committed an offence'. The European Court of Human Rights recognised in *Fox, Campbell and Hartley v UK* (1991) 13 EHRR 157, that in terrorist crime, information often had to be kept secret to protect sources, so the standard of reasonable suspicion could be lower. Even so, suspicion had to be based on some facts and the applicants' convictions for terrorist activity seven years before were not enough. In contrast, in *Murray v UK* (1994) 19 EHRR 193 the Court accepted that there was enough evidence of terrorist activity, from other family members, to justify reasonable suspicion.

The UK House of Lords returned to this issue in *R (Gillan) v Commissioner of Police of the Metropolis* [2006] 2 WLR 537, which involved a power in the Terrorism Act 2000 to stop and search without the need for reasonable suspicion. The view of the court was that this minor infringement of a person's liberty did not breach any of the Articles of the European Convention.

After a person is arrested there is a recognised right for that person to contact a lawyer, under Article 6.3(c) of the Convention and under common law: *R v Chief Constable of South Wales ex parte Merrick* [1994] 2 All ER 560. In terrorist cases, particularly in Northern Ireland, access to a solicitor has often been delayed for up to 48 hours. The European Court of Human Rights has repeatedly condemned this in a whole series of cases such as *Murray v UK* (1996) 22 EHRR 29, *Magee v UK* (2001) 31 EHRR 822 and *Averill v UK* (2001) 31 EHRR 839. Yet the Court of Appeal upheld the use of evidence obtained from a 'safety interview', held without the defendant's lawyer, in *R v Ibrahim* [2008] 4 All ER 208.

It can be very difficult to prove that someone is a terrorist, so some terrorist offences reverse the normal burden of proof. An example is s. 11 of the Terrorism Act 2000, which makes it a criminal offence to belong or profess to belong to a proscribed (terrorist) organisation. The defendant has to prove in his defence that he belonged to the organisation, before it was proscribed and did not take part in its activities. In *Attorney-General's Reference (No. 4 of 2002)* [2005] 1 AC 264, the House of Lords thought this unfair and interpreted the section to mean that, if this defence was raised, the prosecution would need to prove involvement in terrorist activities.

A state may suspend some of the rights guaranteed under the Convention under Article 15 if there is a 'war or other public emergency threatening the life of the nation'. This is a process known as 'derogation' and in its early days, the European Court of Human Rights insisted that they would be the final judge of whether there really was a public emergency and whether the measures taken were justified: *Lawless v Ireland (No. 2)* (1961) 1 EHRR 15. The UK has frequently used derogations to counter the terrorist threat in Northern Ireland. In *Brannigan and McBride v UK* (1993) 17 EHRR 539, the Court accepted that there was evidence of a public emergency caused by terrorism emanating from Northern Ireland and that this justified up to seven days detention without trial for police questioning. In *Ireland v UK* (above) a derogation existed and could perhaps justify detention without trial, but not torture, which is protected by Article 3. Detention without trial was also the issue in *A v Home Secretary (No. 1)* and there the majority of the judges were willing to defer to the government's view on whether there actually was a public emergency. Lord Hoffmann vigorously dissented on the grounds that although lives were threatened this was not the same as 'threatening the life of the nation': 'Whether we would survive Hitler hung in the balance, but there is no doubt that we shall survive Al-Qa'ida.' [2005] 3 All ER 169 at 220.

Both the European Court and the UK courts have recognised that terrorism is a serious problem and have been willing to allow some suspension of normal rights in order to combat it. The UK courts have seemed more willing to allow this, perhaps because the problems are closer to home, but the two *A v Home Secretary* cases have indicated that the domestic courts will still insist that the most basic and most important human rights should be respected.

Question 2

What effect has the Human Rights Act 1998 **had upon English law?**
  Discuss.

Commentary

Since the Act was passed there has been a torrent of court cases and a welter of academic opinion based on its provisions. A good structure for an answer is to go through the most important provisions of the Act and explain their effect. This is not very difficult to do and this is not a very long Act. A good answer though must refer to some of the case law. No student could possibly be familiar with all the cases, but textbooks and your lecturers will give you some guidance on the best examples. Another approach, but not the one taken by the example below, is to look at the effect of the Act on just one area of the law. One could look at prisoners' rights, criminal trials, privacy, family law or whatever interests you. This is still an evolving area of law, so watch out for important new cases to give your examination answer something different from other students'.

Answer plan

- A tradition of civil liberties in the past
- Legislation must be interpreted in a way that is compatible with human rights
- Courts may make a declaration of incompatibility
- Judicial deference to the legislature and executive
- It is unlawful for a public authority to act in a way that is incompatible with human rights
- The **Human Rights Act 1998** may also apply in private disputes.

Suggested answer

The Human Rights Act 1998 came into force on 2 October 2000 and made it far easier to enforce the European Convention of Human Rights in British courts. There have already been a large number of court decisions that refer to the provisions of the Act. As we will see, although there have been inconsistencies, particularly in the lower courts, a trend of cautious application by the judges has begun to appear.

Before this Act Britain had a tradition of civil liberties, popularised by the late nineteenth-century writer, A. V. Dicey. Citizens did not have rights guaranteed by the constitution, but rather they had liberties, they could do anything that the law did not forbid. Judges would prevent governments taking actions for which they did not have legal power, as in the classic case of *Entick v Carrington* (1765) 19 St Tr 1030. If any problems remained Parliament would enact legislation to deal with the matter.

Unfortunately, that is not always what happened. Sometimes judges would decide that public authorities, such as the police, could take action against a person, simply because there was no law to say that they could not, as in the telephone tapping case *Malone v Metropolitan Police Commissioner* [1979] Ch 344. This is the exact opposite of what Dicey said. Similarly, although Parliament sometimes passes Acts that add to the liberties and rights of the people, as in the Freedom of Information Act 2000, they can also legislate in a way that greatly reduces liberties and adds to the power of the police and similar agencies, as in the Regulation of Investigatory Powers Act 2000.

The United Kingdom has been a party to the European Convention of Human Rights since 1951. Even before the Human Rights Act 1998, the courts of this country could refer to the provisions of the Convention to help interpret ambiguous legislation: *R v Home Secretary ex parte Brind* [1991] 1 AC 696. The courts had also said that breaches of the European Convention would encourage them to judicially review a minister's decision and hold it to be unreasonable and therefore illegal: *R v Ministry of Defence ex parte Smith* [1995] 4 All ER 427.

The 1998 Act requires more of the courts. Section 3 states that:

> So far as it is possible to do so, primary legislation and subordinate legislation must be read and given effect in a way which is compatible with the convention rights.

The courts have held that this requires them to go much further than ordinary statutory interpretation, where the court might depart from the ordinary language of the statute to avoid absurd consequences. If necessary the judge could read words into a statute that were not there to ensure compliance with the Convention. As Lord Steyn put it in *R v A (Complainant's sexual history)* [2002] 1 AC 45:

> The techniques to be used would not only involve the reading down of express language in a statute but also the implication of provisions.

Section 43(1)(c) of the Youth Justice and Criminal Evidence Act 1999 forbids the questioning of a rape complainant about her previous sexual history. The court reinterpreted this to mean that the judge could allow such questioning, if to do otherwise would prevent a fair trial. Similarly, in *R v Offen* [2000] 1 WLR 253, the Court of Appeal looked at s. 2 of the Crime (Sentences) Act 1997, which says that a defendant should be given a life sentence if they commit two serious offences, unless there were 'exceptional circumstances'. The court took account of the European Convention and interpreted it to mean that a life sentence should only be imposed if the defendant was a serious risk to the public. So far a lot of the cases on the Human Rights Act have involved a consideration of the fairness or otherwise of criminal and, sometimes, civil trials, which is covered by Articles

5 and 6 of the Convention. If the court concludes that there is no breach of the Convention, as they often do, then the judges do not have to do any 'interpreting' under s. 3 and the existing law remains: *Poplar Housing v Donoghue* [2001] 3 WLR 183.

If there is a clear breach of a Convention Article and the courts cannot interpret the difficulty away under s. 3, the court has no power to declare the Act void. Such a power would conflict with the supremacy of Parliament. Instead, s. 4 allows the courts to make a 'declaration of incompatibility'. The court merely states that the Act of Parliament in question is 'incompatible' with human rights. Only the High Court and above can do this. Then it is up to Parliament to amend or repeal the offending Act, if Parliament chooses to do so. There is a special 'fast-track' procedure to do this under s. 10 of the Human Rights Act 1998, using delegated legislation. This was done after the declaration of incompatibility in *R (on the application of H) v London North and East Mental Health Review Tribunal* [2001] QB 1, where the court held that it was a breach of Article 5 to place the burden of proof on a restricted patient to show that he was no longer suffering from a mental disorder warranting detention. In fact, declarations of incompatibility have not been that common and it has not been unusual for a higher court to overturn the declaration of incompatibility made by a lower court, on the grounds that there is no breach of the Convention. Examples of this would be *Matthews v Ministry of Defence* [2003] 1 All ER 689, where Crown Immunity prevented a sailor suing the government and *Wilson v First County Trust (No. 2)* [2003] 4 All ER 97, where a lender was denied access to the courts. In contrast, the House of Lords made a declaration of incompatibility in *R (Anderson) v Home Secretary* [2002] 4 All ER 108, and said that the Home Secretary could not decide the minimum period that a murderer must stay in prison. This was not a fair trial under Article 6, because a trial should be conducted by a judge, not a politician. The government and Parliament decided upon satisfactory legislation to implement this judgment in the Criminal Justice Act 2003.

In fact the courts have been rather cautious in their application of the Convention. Indeed, Richard Edwards has eloquently argued that a culture of 'judicial deference' has developed, in that judges can be reluctant to interfere with laws enacted by a democratically elected Parliament: (2002) 65 MLR 859. In *R v DPP ex parte Kebilene* [2000] 2 AC 326, a case involving the Prevention of Terrorism Act 2000, the Court of Appeal issued a declaration of incompatibility. The House of Lords disagreed that there was a breach of the Convention and Lord Hope observed that:

> In some circumstances it will be appropriate for the courts to recognise that there is an area of judgment within which the judiciary will defer, on democratic grounds, to the considered opinion of the elected body or person whose act or decision is said to be incompatible with the Convention.

On some questions, the courts will also defer, not only to the legislature, but also to the executive. In *Secretary of State for the Home Department v Rehman* [2003] 1 AC 153, the House of Lords declined to interfere with the Secretary of State's decision to deport Rehman as a possible threat to national security. As Lord Hoffmann said at p. 192:

> On the other hand, the question of whether something is 'in the interests' of national security is not a question of law. It is a matter of judgment and policy. Under the constitution of the UK and most other countries, decisions as to whether something is or is not in the interests of national security are not a matter for judicial decision. They are entrusted to the executive.

Section 6 of the Human Rights Act 1998 makes it 'unlawful for a public authority to act in a way which is incompatible with a Convention right'. This combined with the succeeding ss 7 and 8, creates a new right of action and allows the 'victim' of a human rights abuse to sue and recover damages among other remedies. The courts have had some difficulty in deciding what is a public authority, as it is not defined in the Act. In *Yarl's Wood Immigration Ltd. v Bedfordshire Police* [2008] EWHC 2207, the court held that a private company, operating an immigration detention centre under a contract with the Home Office, was a public authority. In contrast, the House of Lords held that private care homes that accommodated persons paid for by the local authority were not public authorities. The *YL v Birmingham City Council* [2008] 1 AC 95 decision has been reversed by s. 145 of the Health and Social Care Act 2008.

The European Court of Human Rights can award damages, but sees its function as to make rulings on the law rather than to compensate victims. In cases like, *R (KB) v Mental Health Review Tribunal* [2003] 2 All ER 209, the UK courts have awarded torts-type damages. In *R (Greenfield) v Secretary of State for the Home Department* [2005] 2 All ER 240, the House of Lords decided that the purpose of the Human Rights Act 1998 was not to give victims better remedies at home than they could recover at Strasbourg. It was more important to ensure 'just satisfaction' and issue an order remedying the breach of rights.

A much-discussed question is whether the Human Rights Act applies to legal disputes between private individuals or just when a public authority infringes a person's human rights. Section 2 would suggest that the Act could apply to any legal dispute because it states that all courts and tribunals must 'take into account' decisions of the European Court and Commission of Human Rights, whenever a 'Convention' right arises. Also, under s. 6, the courts are themselves public authorities and bound to promote Convention rights. The courts have so far not been willing to recognise completely new rights based on the Convention in disputes between private individuals. In *Wainwright v Home Office* [2004] 2 AC 406, the House of Lords rejected a free-standing right of privacy, but the UK courts have tentatively moved towards using the Convention in private disputes to reinforce claims that already exist in English Law. In *Hello! v Douglas* [2001] 2

All ER 289, *Venables & Thompson v News Group Newspapers Ltd* [2001] 1 All ER 908 and *Campbell v MGN* [2004] 2 AC 457, Convention rights were used to reinforce claims for breach of confidence.

The public maybe has a misleading impression of the Human Rights Act 1998. Some cases generate enormous publicity, such as *R (Pretty) v DPP* [2002] 1 AC 800, on whether the right to die allowed assisted suicide and *R (Begum) v Denbigh High School* [2006] 2 All ER 487 on the right to wear a particular form of Islamic dress to school. What is lost in all the publicity is that the applicants lost in both cases and English law remained the same.

Most judges, particularly in the higher courts have taken a cautious approach. This was recognised by the House of Lords in *Bellinger v Bellinger* [2003] 2 AC 467, where their Lordships refused to recognise the marriage of a male to female transsexual to a man. They were aware that, unlike Parliament, they are not elected and may not represent the democratic wishes of the country. Besides they are not yet used to deciding so many cases dealing with complicated political, social and moral issues and prefer to leave it to the politicians in Parliament.

Question 3

What effect has the European Convention of Human Rights had upon the protection of civil liberties in English law?

Discuss.

 ## Commentary

The **Human Rights Act** was enacted in 1998, coming into force in 2000. It allowed the rights protected by the **European Convention on Human Rights** to be more easily enforced in UK courts. This country already had a long established tradition of civil liberties, referred to in the Suggested Answer to Question 2 in this chapter. In addition, the UK had been a party to the Convention since its beginning, in 1951, and the judgments of the European Court of Human Rights had already had a considerable effect upon English law. Not only had legislation been required, but the courts had adapted the common law to reflect the Convention. The Human Rights Act 1998 just makes this process easier.

The problem with writing an essay like this is that there are so many possible examples, and therefore it is difficult to know what to leave out. It is certainly unwise though to attempt an all-inclusive answer and it is better to be selective and carefully *plan* what you wish to write, concentrating on only a few themes.

Answer plan

- Petition to the European Court of Human Rights in Strasbourg
- Corporal punishment has been abolished
- Discrimination against homosexuals has been reduced
- Interference with communications is now regulated by statute
- Release from prison is now decided by the courts
- The fairness of criminal trials has been improved
- Delays in the hearing of asylum and mental health applications have been reduced.

Suggested answer

The European Convention on Human Rights came into existence in 1951, sponsored by the Council of Europe. It had been drafted with the help of British civil servants and the future Lord Chancellor, Lord Kilmuir, and it was intended to extend the same standard of protection of civil liberties that existed in Britain to other European states.

In 1966 the UK lead the way in allowing the right of individual petition, which allows aggrieved individuals to bring a complaint against the UK. There have been many successful cases which have led to many changes in English law. The person who considers themselves a 'victim' of a human rights abuse petitions the European Court of Human Rights. They have six months in which to do this and they must first have 'exhausted domestic remedies'. In other words they must have done all that they reasonably could to pursue their case in the British legal system. Before 1998, the petition would be preliminarily investigated by the Commission of Human Rights, but now this is done by the Court itself. The Court issues 'final and binding' judgments, which will explain whether there has been any infringement of the Convention Articles. Although the Court may conclude that some of a state's laws are defective it does not give instructions upon how those laws should be changed. It is up to the state affected to abide by the judgment and make any changes to its laws that are necessary. Enforcement is by international pressure, the disapproval of the Council of Europe and other Convention states. That said, offending states nearly always comply with the judgments of the Court and Britain has a particularly good record in this respect. Let us consider some of the changes in English law precipitated by the European Court of Human Rights.

Corporal punishment, particularly of children, used to be an established part of British life. *Tyrer v United Kingdom* (1978) 2 EHHR 1, held that sentencing Tyrer to be 'birched' under Manx law was unacceptable as it was 'degrading treatment' under Article 3. This punishment had once been used in mainland Britain, but continued in use only on the Isle of Man and, although the British Crown controlled

Man's foreign relations and adherence to treaties, it did not control the Isle's internal affairs. Hence Britain could not legislate directly to abolish 'birching'. Instead, a compromise was reached and such punishments were discontinued, although Manx law did not formally change until 1994.

Corporal punishment in schools also fell foul of the Convention, but this time it was Article 2 of the First Protocol, wherein the State must respect the philosophical convictions of parents when educating their children. In *Campbell and Cosans v United Kingdom* (1982) 4 EHRR 293, some parents objected to the possibility that their children might be beaten at school and this was held to be a breach of the above Article. The government was undecided upon how to react to this, as corporal punishment still seemed to enjoy public support. Could there be a system where some children could be beaten, if their parents agreed, while, if their parents objected, other children could not? Eventually, the House of Lords resolved the problem by amending the Education (No. 2) Act 1986 with a new s. 46, which had the effect of abolishing corporal punishment in state schools. Although not legally obliged to do so, most public schools have followed suit. So maybe a court decision can help to change public opinion. Lastly, *A v United Kingdom* (1999) 27 EHRR 611, throws doubt upon the extent to which parents can use physical force to discipline children. 'A' had been beaten by his stepfather with a garden cane, leaving visible bruising and, although the English courts had held that this was not actual bodily harm, the European Court of Human Rights held that this was a breach of Article 3. Legislation on this subject was planned, but it has proved difficult to define the level of force that will be permitted.

The European Court of Human Rights has also made a number of important decisions on what we might loosely term sexual conduct, because a person's right to a private life is protected under Article 8 and cannot be restricted unless it is 'necessary in a democratic society'. *Dudgeon v United Kingdom* (1981) 4 EHRR 149 exposed an anomaly in British law, because whilst homosexual acts had been legalised in 'mainland' Britain as long ago as 1967, they remained a criminal offence in Northern Ireland. The European Court held this to be a breach of Article 8, as they could see no good reason for having such a law, and legislative reform swiftly followed in Northern Ireland. More recently the same issue resurfaced in relation to homosexuals serving in the Armed Forces, where 'buggery' was still a serious criminal offence and homosexual personnel were discharged from the service. Again, in *Lustig-Prean and Becket v United Kingdom* (2000) 29 EHRR 548, the European Court of Human Rights could see no good reason for such a restriction and, in response, the law in Britain was soon changed. The Court is consistent in its line that discrimination against homosexuals is not acceptable and in *ADT v United Kingdom* (2001) 31 EHRR 33, where five men had been engaging in sexual activity, it held that the offence of 'gross indecency', which can only be committed between men, was a breach of Article 8. The different age of consent for men and women was eliminated in the Sexual Offences

(Amendment) Act 2000, reducing the discriminatory aspect of this offence. Transsexuals have frequently questioned why British law refuses to recognise a change in sex, in cases such as *Rees v United Kingdom* (1987) 9 EHRR 56 and *Sheffield and Horsham v United Kingdom* (1999) 27 EHRR 163, among others. Finally, there was a successful case in *Goodwin v UK* (2002) 35 EHRR 18 and the law has been changed in the Gender Recognition Act 2004.

Article 8 has also proved useful to those who have wished to challenge unjustified government interference with their correspondence and other communications. The police had listened in to Malone's telephone communications. The English courts held that this must be legal, as there appeared to be no law against 'telephone tapping': *Malone v Metropolitan Police Commissioner* [1979] Ch 344. Malone was more successful before the European Court of Human Rights, which held that this was a breach of his right to respect for his correspondence, because there were no laws to govern 'telephone tapping' and no 'appeal', hence no judicial control. Parliament responded by passing the Interception of Communications Act 1985, which brought in a system of warrants, appeals to a tribunal and supervision by a Commissioner. This Act did not regulate the use of other listening devices, which was exposed in *Khan v United Kingdom* (2001) 31 EHRR 1016, where the police had attached a listening device to a house. At the time there was no legal regulation of police 'bugging', and Khan was unsuccessful in having the evidence, obtained by the listening device, excluded in an English court: *R v Khan* [1996] 3 All ER 289. This practice, of placing listening devices, is now legally controlled in the Regulation of Investigatory Powers Act 2000.

Article 8 has also caused problems for Britain in a long series of 'prison cases', starting with *Golder v United Kingdom* (1975) 1 EHRR 524, which involved a prisoner's right to communicate with his solicitor and ended with a general right to correspond with the outside world in *Campbell v United Kingdom* (1993) 15 EHRR 137. These rulings led to the abandonment of the automatic censoring of prisoner's mail.

The UK courts have also made a great number of decisions on the fairness of criminal trials. In *R v A (No. 2)* [2002] 1 AC 45, the Home Secretary stated that the complete exclusion of questioning about a rape complainant's previous sexual history could sometimes lead to an unfair trial. Similarly, in *R v Offen* [2000] 1 WLR 253, it was held that jailing an offender for life, who had committed two serious offences, was only justified if the offender was a danger to the public.

Similarly, there have been many cases where judges have been critical of delays and inefficiencies in the asylum system that infringe upon the applicant's human rights, as in *EB (Kosovo) v Secretary of State for the Home Department* [2008] 4 All ER 28. Changes have also occurred in Mental Health Review Tribunals. In *R (H) v MHRT, North and East London Region* [2001] QB 1 the House of Lords did not accept that a patient had to prove that he no longer suffered from a mental disorder in order to obtain release. This reversed the burden of proof, and is unacceptable under Article 5. Delays in Mental Health Review Tribunal hearings also contravene the same Article: *R (KB) v Mental Health Review Tribunal* [2003] 2 All ER 209.

Coroners investigate causes of death. The adequacy of this system has been criticised in a number of cases: such as *R (Amin) v Secretary of State for the Home Department* [2004] 1 AC 653, which involved one young offender killing the other prisoner in his cell and *R (Al Skeini) v Secretary of State for Defence* [2006] HRLR 7, which concerned the deaths of Iraqi civilians at the hands of British troops. Article 2, the right to life was infringed, because the investigations of the deaths were unsatisfactory.

The right of the Home Secretary to decide upon the release of life prisoners has been removed by a series of judgments in the European Court of Human Rights and the UK courts. As a 'politician', he does not satisfy Article 6.1 of the European Convention on Human Rights, which requires trial 'by an independent and impartial tribunal established by law'.

The process began when the European Court of Human Rights decided that it was not acceptable for the Home Secretary to decide upon the release on parole, or recall from parole of discretionary life prisoners in *Thynne, Wilson and Gunnell v UK* (1991) 13 EHRR 666. Both the courts of the UK, in *R v Home Secretary ex parte Venables and Thompson* [1998] AC 407 and the European Court of Human Rights, in *T v UK and V v UK* (2000) 30 EHRR 121, objected to the Home Secretary setting the 'tariff' or minimum period of detention for juveniles convicted of murder.

Then in *R (Anderson) v Home Secretary* [2002] 4 All ER 1089, the House of Lords declared that the Home Secretary's role in fixing the tariff and deciding upon the release of an adult convicted of murder, was incompatible with human rights. The law has now been changed in the Criminal Justice Act 2003. Since then, the courts have questioned, but finally accepted, the involvement of the Home Secretary in the decision to release any sort of prisoner: *R (Black) v Secretary of State for Home Affairs* [2009] 2 WLR 282.

The decisions of the European Court of Human Rights have already had a major impact upon civil liberties in this country. The UK courts have just begun exploring human rights and are feeling their way towards what it is acceptable for the courts to do and what they must leave to Parliament.

Question 4

Parliament decides to strengthen the law prohibiting the hunting of wild mammals with dogs and enacts the Hunting Act 2009. The Act makes any organisation engaged in hunting an illegal organisation and membership of such an organisation a criminal offence. Members of such an organisation can be arrested and held without trial for a period of up to three months. Under the Act the Home Secretary decides whether a person detained can be released.

Anonymous informers say that Dougie, Karen and Paul are all members of the Borchester Hunt, so the three are arrested and detained at a disused army camp. The camp, which is run for the government by a private security company, lacks any heating and the food and conditions are very poor. Dougie is placed in a cell with another inmate, Boris, who is known to be violent. Boris kills Dougie.

Karen and Paul are denied access to lawyers, but friends of theirs petition the Home Secretary to release them, but he refuses.

Karen, Paul and Dougie's widow, Sharon, are wondering whether any legal action would be worthwhile.

Advise Karen, Paul and Sharon.

Commentary

This question raises various important issues of human rights, but in a problem format, rather than an essay. So you need to be familiar with what is in the **Human Rights Act 1998** and how that Act works. You also need to be acquainted with the different Articles in the **European Convention of Human Rights** and what those Articles actually say. It is also extremely useful to be able to give the extra detail that the leading cases on this area can provide. Unfortunately, there are a huge number of cases on this subject and, as can be seen by the profusion of '[2008]s' in the case references in the suggested answer, the number is increasing all the time. So a useful tactic to adopt is to look out for new cases, which often make the headlines in the ordinary media, not just legal journals, and show that you are up to date by including them in your answer. The facts of this problem are fairly unlikely, but they do raise issues on common human rights problems such as unlawful detention and fair trials, which you would probably have studied in your course. Try to spot each human rights issue as it is raised, identify the relevant Article of the **European Convention of Human Rights** and try to establish whether there has been a breach of human rights. This can be done by comparing the facts to the wording of the Article, with the help of any cases that you know of, that have been decided on that point.

Answer plan

- Article 11—freedom of assembly
- Article 5—the right to liberty and security
- Imprisonment without trial
- Article 15—derogation in time of emergency
- Article 6—the right to a fair trial
- Article 3—prohibition of torture
- Article 2—the right to life
- Public authority
- Proceedings under the **Human Rights Act 1998**
- Declaration of incompatibility.

Suggested answer

What has happened to Dougie, Karen and Paul would seem to raise some serious human rights issues. Since the Human Rights Act 1998 came into force these issues can be raised in an English court, and, if the three fail to gain satisfaction, they could still raise a complaint with the European Court of Human Rights in Strasbourg. First we need to advise them upon whether there are any human rights breaches and then upon who would be liable for those breaches and what remedies the courts might grant.

The real Hunting Act 2004 made hunting mammals with dogs a criminal offence and was challenged in the courts on a number of grounds, including that it infringed human rights, in *R (Countryside Alliance and Others) v Attorney-General and Another* [2008] 3 All ER 1. Participants in hunting claimed that it was part of their private life and to stop them doing it was a breach of Article 8, the right to a private life. The House of Lords disagreed, stating that fox hunting, for instance, was a very public activity carried out in daylight with considerable colour and noise and so could hardly be termed 'private'. Article 11 guarantees freedom of association and it was argued that this included the right to form and join 'hunts'. The court held that freedom of association was intended to protect political activity and, anyway, according to Article 11.2 it was permissible to restrict this freedom for a number of reasons, which included 'the protection of morals'. Article 8.2 also allowed the right to a private life to be restricted for the same reason. The aim of the Hunting Act 2004 was to prevent or reduce unnecessary suffering to wild animals, but there was also a moral objective: Parliament regarded causing suffering to animals for sport as unethical. The court accepted that there was a difference of opinion on whether hunting animals actually caused excessive suffering, but were willing to defer to the decision of Parliament on this sort of moral issue. So it would seem acceptable to have laws banning hunting, but any law that restricts rights must be proportionate to the aim; it must not restrict rights any more than necessary to stop hunting. In *R (Countryside Alliance and Others) v Attorney-General and Another* [2008] 3 All ER 1, it was acceptable to make hunting illegal, but to make hunting organisations illegal and to imprison their members without trial would not seem to be a proportionate response to the problem and might be a breach of Article 11.

Imprisonment without trial has always been regarded as a serious breach of civil liberties (*Liversidge v Anderson* [1942] AC 206) and is now clearly prohibited by Article 5, the right to liberty and security. *Brogan v United Kingdom* (1988) 11 EHRR 117 held that detention without trial for only four days was excessive. The detainee must be brought before a judge, who can determine the legality of the detention, but we know from our facts that Karen and Paul's only remedy is to the Home Secretary, an elected politician, and that is unacceptable. *Brogan* is a decision of the European Court of Human Rights, which, under s. 2 of the Human

Rights Act 1998, must be 'taken into account' by any UK court, when deciding upon the meaning of a 'Convention right'. Despite this wording, which would suggest that a UK court is not bound to follow an ECHR decision, the House of Lords would nearly always follow such a decision. For example, it is possible for a state to suspend some of the human rights protected by the Convention, such as Article 5, by making a 'derogation' under Article 15. This can only be done if there is a 'war or other public emergency threatening the life of the nation'. In *Lawless v Ireland (No. 3)* (1961) 1 EHRR 15, the European Court of Human Rights was prepared to accept the view of Ireland that IRA activity constituted a public emergency, even though there was not much evidence of a serious threat. The House of Lords was willing to follow this case in *A v Home Secretary (No. 1)* [2005] 2 AC 68, despite at least one judge expressing some scepticism whether there was a terrorist threat serious enough to threaten the life of the nation. Both *Lawless* and *A* involved suspensions of Article 5 and imprisonment without trial, but there is no evidence in the facts of our problem that there is any form of public emergency and no evidence that the UK government has applied for a derogation. Hunting does not threaten the life of the nation.

The trio have been arrested and Article 5.1(c) requires there to be 'reasonable suspicion' that they have committed the offence. The European Court of Human Rights accepted that information from unnamed informants could amount to reasonable suspicion in *Fox, Campbell and Hartley v UK* (1991) 13 EHRR 157, but that was a case involving terrorists and the Court did say that that could justify a lower standard of evidence upon which to reasonably base suspicion. So maybe there is not enough evidence to justify Dougie, Karen and Paul's arrests and the House of Lords has recently held in *R v Davis (Iain)* [2008] 3 WLR 125 that it is not permissible to convict anyone, solely on the evidence of anonymous witnesses. This is a breach of common law principles and Article 6; the right to a fair trial, specifically Article 6.3(d), which states that everyone charged with a criminal offence, has the right to examine witnesses.

Dougie, Karen and Paul have clearly not received a fair trial. Legal advice is an essential preparation in making a proper defence and to deny access to a lawyer is a breach of Article 6.3(d): *Golder v United Kingdom* (1975) 1 EHRR 524 and *Silver v United Kingdom* (1981) 3 EHRR 475. There is no doubt that the English courts accept that defendants, prisoners and arrested persons must be allowed to communicate with their lawyers without any interference from the authorities, as shown by the prison case *R (Daly) v Home Secretary* [2001] 2 AC 532. The House of Lords accepted that it was a basic right existing in English law, irrespective of anything in the European Convention. The three, in fact, have not received any trial at all, as we are not told that the Home Secretary has held 'a fair and public hearing' as required by Article 6. The hearing must also be held by 'independent and impartial tribunal' and a number of cases have held that a politician, who may be influenced by electoral considerations, should not act as a judge.

It was held in *R (Anderson) v Home Secretary* [2003] 1 AC 837 that the Home Secretary should not decide upon the minimum sentence or release date of life prisoners. The principle was also used in *R v Home Secretary exparte Venables and Thompson* [1998] AC 407, where the House of Lords stated that the Home Secretary should not decide upon the minimum sentence of child prisoners as, according to Article 5.4, release should be decided by a court.

The treatment of Dougie, Karen and Paul, while detained, leaves something to be desired. 'Inhuman or degrading treatment' is prohibited under Article 3 and, although what has happened to the three is not as severe as the beatings and psychological interrogation techniques in *Ireland v United Kingdom* (1978) 2 EHRR 25, sending a prisoner to the harsh conditions of 'death-row' in the United States was a breach in *Soering v United Kingdom* (1989) 11 EHRR 439. So poor prison conditions could be an infringement of human rights, as could allowing a prisoner to be murdered, because, under Article 2, the State has a duty to protect the right to life. *R (Amin) v Home Secretary* [2004] 1 AC 653 has quite similar facts to the killing of Dougie by Boris, for it concerned a young prisoner who was killed by a cell mate, whom the prison authorities knew to be both racist and violent. Article 2 required that there should be full investigation into his death, in which his family could be involved. The State is also required to do all that is reasonable to protect a person from a real and immediate risk to their life, if the State has knowledge of that risk. This duty applied when the police failed to protect a boy from the persistent threats of his eventual murderer in *Osman v United Kingdom* (1998) 29 EHRR 245 and so it could also apply to Dougie's death.

The three detainees would clearly seem to have suffered human rights infringements and so would be 'victims' of an unlawful act and able to bring a case against a 'public authority' under ss 6 and 7 of the Human Rights Act 1998. The Act does not define a public authority, but the Home Secretary clearly is, as seen by the cases against him mentioned earlier in this essay. The private security company that runs the camp might not be so straightforward, as in *YL v Birmingham City Council* [2008] 1 AC 95 it was held that a private care home that took residents placed there by the council, which paid their fees, was not a public authority. In contrast, *Yarl's Wood Immigration Ltd v Bedfordshire Police* [2008] EWHC 2207 decided that a private company, operating an immigration detention centre under a contract with the Home Office, was a public authority, albeit under different legislation. The company exercised the coercive power of the State, as does the company running the detention centre in our problem, so Karen, Dougie's widow and Paul can bring their case. They could seek a judicial review of the decision to detain and not release them and compensation for the harm that they have suffered under *R (Greenfield) v Secretary of State for the Home Department* [2005] 2 All ER 240.

According to s. 6(2) of the Human Rights Act 1998, the court cannot overturn an Act of Parliament, even if it is contrary to human rights, but has to enforce it: *Doherty v Birmingham City Council* [2008] 3 WLR 636. So the court would have to consider making a 'statement of incompatibility' under s. 4 of the Act as they did in the similar cases where the Home Secretary had the statutory power to detain without trial: *R (Anderson) v Home Secretary* [2003] 1 AC 837 and *A v Home Secretary (No. 1)* [2005] 2 AC 68. There seems little likelihood that the Hunting Act 2009 could be interpreted in a human rights friendly way, as courts are required to do by s. 3 of the Human Rights Act 1998.

So Karen, Paul and Sharon might well be granted a declaration of incompatibility by the courts, then it would be up to Parliament to amend or repeal the Hunting Act 2009. If Parliament decides not to do so, or delays excessively, there is nothing to stop the three applying to the European Court of Human Rights itself. In the light of the gross human rights abuses detailed in this answer, that Court would rule in their favour. The UK government might be ordered to pay compensation to the three and would come under pressure from the Council of Europe, to remedy these breaches of human rights.

Further reading

Barnett, H. *Constitutional and Administrative Law*, 7th edn (Cavendish, 2008), ch 18.

Bradley, A. and Ewing, K. *Constitutional and Administrative Law*, 14th edn (Longman, 2007), ch 19.

Edwards, R. 'Judicial Deference under the Human Rights Act' (2002) 65 MLR 859.

Loveland, I. *Constitutional Law, Administrative Law and Human Rights: A Critical Introduction*, 4th edn (OUP, 2006), chs 18–21.

Freedom to Protest and Police Powers

Introduction

This is sometimes known as the law of public order. There are a number of criminal offences involved so, occasionally, it is treated as part of a criminal law syllabus. It, however, concerns a very important civil liberty, that of protest against the government or other powerful bodies, so historically it has been an important constitutional law issue. How far may the citizen lawfully go to indicate their dislike of government? According to the British tradition of civil liberties, citizens may protest in any way that they want, as long as they do not break the law.

The Human Rights Act 1998 introduced Article 11, the right of peaceful assembly into UK law, but as yet, this has made little difference.

To study this subject we need to know, fairly accurately, which laws may be broken. Problem questions are common in this area. All that you need to do is to identify which laws may have been broken or offences committed. Many students find essay questions more demanding: you have to have a point of view, argue it and marshal evidence to support it. You may be asked whether you think that there is sufficient liberty to protest or whether you approve of the Criminal Justice and Public Order Act 1994 for example.

There is a lot of duplication in the laws on this area. The old common law such as breach of the peace remains. Added to this was the Public Order Act 1936. Some of that Act still remains although much of it was replaced by the Public Order Act 1986. On top of that the Criminal Justice and Public Order Act 1994 creates additional criminal offences and police powers. Anti-social behaviour orders under the Crime and Disorder Act 1998 and dispersal powers under the Anti-Social Behaviour Act 2003, could also impinge upon freedom to protest. Sections 132–138 of the Serious Organised Crime and Police Act 2005 require that anyone wishing to stage a demonstration in the vicinity of Parliament must obtain prior authorisation. This was aimed at the one-man protest of Brian Haw against government action in Iraq and was considered in *R (Haw) v Secretary of State for the Home Department* [2006] All ER (D) 94. The measure has been seen as heavy handed and oppressive and is to be repealed in the Constitutional Renewal Bill 2008.

We must now also take into consideration the Human Rights Act 1998, which introduced Article 11, the right of peaceful assembly, and Article 10, freedom of expression, into UK law. This has had an influence on how the existing UK law is interpreted. For instance in *DPP v Jones (Margaret)* [1999] 2 AC 240 it was conceded that a right to peaceful assembly on the highway might exist. The House of Lords also accepted in *R (Laporte) v Chief Constable of Gloucestershire* [2007] 2 AC 205 that the police had no power to stop persons travelling to a demonstration unless a breach of the peace was imminent. It was not enough for the police just to act 'reasonably'.

So it can be seen that it is perfectly possible for the same set of facts to give rise to liability under several different laws. The more one looks at a public order problem the more offences one can see. Under examination conditions this is not a problem, time will limit what you can identify. If it is an essay you have to be sensible about what you are going to cover. Select material to support your argument.

If you are considering a problem question only deal with the legal issues raised by the facts. For instance, if you are given a set of facts indicating fairly minor public disturbances it is unlikely that you would be expected to consider riot. A reasonably high level of violence would indicate riot.

Question 1

Twelve members of the 'No Abortion Campaign' are protesting on the pavement outside an abortion clinic on Eastby High Street. They are displaying placards with the words 'No to abortion' and speaking to each woman who enters the clinic asking her to consider whether she is 'doing the right thing'.

The owner of the abortion clinic summons the police and PC Kent arrives. She stands on the pavement observing the 'No Abortion Campaign' members, but takes no action.

Then 12 members of a group in favour of abortion, Women's Choice, arrive and start shouting at the 'No Abortion Campaign' members, insulting them with words such as 'religious fanatics go home.' Three of the members of Women's Choice throw stones, breaking the windows of the clinic.

PC Kent asks the 'No Abortion Campaign' members to leave, which they unwillingly do. They slowly walk the half a mile down the High Street to the railway station.

PC Kent, together with other police officers who have joined her, arrest the 12 members of the 'No Abortion Campaign'.

Advise the 'No Abortion Campaign' on whether they have committed any public order offences and whether the police actions are legal.

Commentary

This is a fairly standard sort of problem question on public order law. What you have to do is to identify and discuss possible offences that might have been committed and consider the police's powers to control public protest. The question asks you to confine yourself to public order law, so do not stray off into ordinary criminal law and consider things like criminal damage. Nor is it necessary to consider civil matters such as nuisance. Your answer will be quite long enough and complicated enough just confining yourself to public order law! This area of law has many overlapping provisions and some contradictory case law. A good answer will make sense of this law by applying it to the problem and trying to come to a conclusion. Reasoned conclusions show that you understand the law. There are 12 members of the No Abortion Campaign, 12 members of Women's Choice and three women throw stones. This is not just chance, as numbers of participants are important in public order law and give the student a clue as to which area of law they should be considering.

The **Human Rights Act 1998** means that the **European Convention on Human Rights** is now relevant to this area of law, in particular **Article 10**, which provides for freedom of expression and **Article 11,** which provides for freedom of assembly. This is actually helpful, because court decisions on these Articles are helping to clarify what English law on public order should be.

Answer plan

- The police have discretion
- Wilful obstruction of the highway
- Threatening, abusive or insulting words or behaviour
- Immediate unlawful violence or provocation of immediate unlawful violence
- Conduct likely to cause harassment, alarm or distress
- An assembly of two or more persons in a public place open to the air
- Riot is 12 or more persons present together using or threatening unlawful violence for a common purpose
- Violent disorder is three or more people present together using or threatening unlawful violence
- Breach of the peace is an act or threat of violence against a person or their property in their presence
- The organiser of a procession must give the police six days' notice.

Suggested answer

There are a number of public order offences that could have been committed by both the 'No Abortion Campaign' and Women's Choice and also a number of powers that PC Kent could have used to control the developing situation. According to *R v Chief Constable of Devon and Cornwall ex parte The Central Electricity*

Generating Board [1982] QB 458, the police have discretion on how they use their public order control powers. They are not obliged to arrest for crimes or to use their powers to disperse protesters. This was confirmed by the more recent *R v Chief Constable of Sussex ex parte International Trader's Ferry Ltd* [1999] 1 All ER 129. The opposite is not, however, the case, the police cannot arrest for something that is not a crime, nor prevent lawful protest.

A gathering on the pavement has been held to be obstruction of the highway in *Arrowsmith v Jenkins* [1963] 2 QB 561. It is still the offence of wilful obstruction, even if there was no intention to obstruct and even if no one was actually obstructed. The highway is for passage and repassage and purposes incidental to that movement. However, the European Court of Human Rights has ruled, in *Platform Arzte fur das Leben* (1988) 13 EHRR 204, that there is a right to hold meetings in a public place. Another case more favourable to the 'No Abortion Campaign' is *DPP v Jones (Margaret)* [1999] 2 AC 240, where the House of Lords held that a small protest on a roadside verge, near Stonehenge, was not an obstruction of the highway. Lord Irvine, the Lord Chancellor, thought that a right of peaceful assembly on the highway might exist and that the common law should develop to conform to Article 11 of the European Convention, which gives a right of peaceful assembly. The 'No Abortion Campaign's' protest is certainly peaceful and quite small in number, so it is probably not obstruction of the highway.

They also do not seem to be committing any offences under the Public Order Act 1986. They are not using 'threatening, abusive or insulting words or behaviour' nor are their signs 'threatening, abusive or insulting' and there are no threats of violence, so there is no offence under s. 4 of the Act. Even the lesser offence in s. 5, where it is enough for 'disorderly behaviour' to be likely to cause 'harassment, alarm or distress' is not committed. *DPP v Clarke, Lewis, O'Connell & O'Keefe* [1992] Crim LR 60 also involved a protest outside an abortion clinic, but the protesters had no intent to be threatening, abusive or insulting. All that the defendants did in that case was to show pictures of an aborted foetus to police officers and one passer-by. To commit an offence under s. 5 the protest needs to be more vigorous, as in *DPP v Fidler and Moran* [1992] 1 WLR 91, where there were also shouts and threats against those attending the clinic, in addition to the display of photographs and models of dead foetuses. *Percy v DPP* (2002) 166 JP 93 confirms that the 'No Abortion Campaign' are unlikely to have committed an offence. Even if behaviour is held to be insulting, this must be balanced against the right to freedom of expression under Article 10 of the European Convention of Human Rights.

Women's Choice appear to have committed criminal offences. Unlike the 'No Abortion Campaign', they are using insulting words, which seem intended or likely to cause their opponents to fear immediate personal violence: *R v Horseferry Road Magistrate ex parte Siadatan* [1991] 1 All ER 324. There is a more serious version of this offence, under s. 31 of the Crime and Disorder Act 1998, if it is racially or religiously aggravated. This means that the offender demonstrates hostility based on the victim's membership, or presumed membership, of a racial or religious group. In *R v Rogers (Philip)* [2007] 2 AC 62 the defendant referred to three Spanish women as 'bloody foreigners'. The offence is committed if hostility is shown to foreigners in general as a particular racial group does not have to be identified. So by analogy hostility to religious people in general could also be an offence.

There is also a lesser offence under s. 5 of the Public Order Act 1986. It seems likely that the 'No Abortion Campaign' would experience harassment, alarm or distress, unless the courts decide that by their frequent protesting they will have become used to insulting, threatening and abusive words or behaviour, rather like the police officers in *DPP v Orum* [1988] 3 All ER 449.

It is possible that more serious offences have been committed. Section 1 of the Public Order Act 1986 defines riot as '12 or more persons who are present together use or threaten violence for a common purpose . . . as would cause a person of reasonable firmness present at the scene to fear for his personal safety'. There are over 12 members of Women's Choice and according to s. 7 'violence' can include violence towards property, not just people and would include the throwing of missiles. It would have to be proved, though, that at least 12 of them had a common purpose to violently attack the clinic or their opponents: *R v Jefferson* [1994] 1 All ER 270. This could prove difficult, so s. 2, which makes violent disorder an offence, is more likely. This is similar to riot, but only requires three participants and does not require a common purpose. The three window breakers would have committed this offence as the 'No Abortion Campaign', the inmates of the clinic, bystanders and even the police officer would have been put in fear. Affray, under s. 3, has not been committed, as under s. 8, violence against persons is required.

Section 14 of the Public Order Act 1986 allows the senior police officer on the spot to impose conditions upon a public assembly, if he reasonably believes that it may result in serious public disorder, serious damage to property, intimidation or serious disruption to the life of the community. A public assembly used to require a minimum number of 20 persons, but this was reduced to two by the Anti-Social Behaviour Act 2003. PC Kent could give directions as to the place, number of people and duration of the assembly. This would seem to allow her to act against either 'Women's Choice' or the 'No Abortion Campaign'. In addition to these powers, she also has common law and other statutory powers to disperse assemblies.

Section 30 of the Anti-Social Behaviour Act 2003 allows the police to disperse groups of protesters according to *R (Pritpal Singh) v Chief Constable of West Midlands* [2007] 2 All ER 297. Members of the public have to have been 'intimidated, harassed, alarmed or distressed' and then a senior police officer has to give an authorisation allowing dispersal in that locality. An authorisation would only exist if there had been trouble in the area of the abortion clinic before, but the facts suggest that this is not a long-running protest, so it is unlikely that an authorisation is in force. Section 42 of the Criminal Justice and Police Act 2001 allows the police to disperse persons who are outside a dwelling and 'likely to cause harassment, alarm or distress to the persons living at the residence'. The clinic is not a 'dwelling' though.

PC Kent does, however, have a common law power to take reasonable measures to prevent a breach of the peace. The accepted definition, today, of a breach of the peace is an act or threat of violence against a person or their property in their presence, which puts someone in fear of violence: *R v Howell* [1982] 2 QB 416 and *Percy v DPP* [1995] 3 All ER 124. This power has been used to disperse meetings as in *Duncan v Jones* [1963] 1 KB 218 and to refuse to obey the reasonable instructions of a police constable is the offence of obstruction of a police officer in the execution of his duty: *Duncan v Jones* (ibid.)

On the facts it seems reasonable for PC Kent to assume that violence might break out, but has she acted against the wrong group? The old case of *Beatty v Gillbanks* (1882) 9 QBD 308 held that the Salvation Army should not be forbidden from marching through Weston-super-Mare, just because they might be violently opposed by the rival Skeleton Army. In *Platform Arzte fur das Leben* (above), the European Court of Human Rights has ruled that this is the correct approach and that, in certain circumstances, the State has a duty to protect peaceful protesters from those who would oppose them with violence. In *Redmond-Bate v DPP* (1999) 163 JP 789, the defendants were women preaching from the steps of Wakefield Cathedral but, as the listening crowd were becoming hostile, the police stopped the women. Sedley LJ said that the police were wrong to do this and that 'the common law should seek compatibility with the values of the European Convention on Human Rights'. 'The question for the police officer was whether there was a real threat of violence and if so, from whom it was coming.' So PC Kent should really have taken action against the troublemakers, Women's Choice.

Processions and marches are well regulated by law and under s. 11 of the Public Order Act 1986—the organisers must give the police six days' written notice 'unless it is not reasonably practicable to give any advance notice of the procession' or 'the procession is one commonly or customarily held in the police area'. There is no definition of a procession in the Act and even a mass cycle ride held as a protest in London was held to be a procession, but as it was customarily held, once every month, there was no requirement to notify under the Act: *R (Kay) v Commissioner of Police of the Metropolis* [2008] 1 WLR 2723. So possibly walking back to the station could be a procession, if they were still continuing their protest and it certainly could not be said to be 'customary'. It is surely arguable here that it is not reasonable to expect the 'No Abortion Campaign' to notify the police in advance as their march has, in effect, been caused by the police. Section 12 allows a senior police officer to give directions to the organisers if he 'reasonably believes that' the procession 'may result in serious public disorder, serious damage to property or serious disruption to the life of the community' or the purpose of the march is intimidation. As these directions have to be in writing, they are hardly practical in this situation. The law, in the *Public Order Act 1986*, makes a clear distinction between assemblies and processions, for instance there has never been a minimum number for processions and assemblies do not have to be notified to the police in advance. The facts of this problem illustrate, that there may not be a clear-cut distinction between assemblies and processions, as was shown in *DPP v Jones* [2002] EWHC 110, where the police illegally imposed assembly conditions on what was in fact a procession.

In conclusion, PC Kent took legal action against the wrong people, the 'No Abortion Campaign' group, who were merely exercising their peaceful right of protest. She should have taken action against the violent and threatening Women's Choice.

Question 2

Margaret and her friends oppose the use of British and US troops in Iraq. They travel from London to protest outside RAF Blackham, an airfield where both British and US aircraft are based.

She and 10 of her friends set up an encampment on the roadside just outside the main gates of RAF Blackham. This attracts a lot of attention from passing motorists, many of whom slow down, causing a delay to other traffic.

Two of the group, Janet and Steve, climb over the perimeter wall into Blackham and enter a hanger, where they damage an aircraft by hitting it with hammers. Janet also burns the US flag, the 'Stars and Stripes', which distresses the US service personnel standing nearby.

The police arrive, arrest Janet and Steve and the nine others, dismantle their camp and take them all back to London, which takes six hours.

All the protesters say that they have not broken the law. They claim that they have a legal right to protest and that they were trying to prevent the aircraft being used in Iraq, which would be an illegal use of force in international law.

Advise them on the law relating to their case.

 Commentary

This problem is designed to mirror the modern kind of protest, where a small group has very strong views about government policy and wishes to take action to publicise their views. You may think their actions silly or you may think them justified, depending on your own political views, but leave those aside and try to analyse what the legal decision would be on facts like these. Freedom to protest is a right guaranteed under the **European Convention on Human Rights** and under common law, so that needs to be stated in any answer. Often the inspiration for a problem is an important new case, so it is always worthwhile for the student to take note of new cases, particularly if their lecturers seem interested in them. Here, those cases are *R v Jones* [2007] 1 AC 136, where the House of Lords dealt with a defence that had become increasingly common: we had to break the law in order to prevent an even worse breach of the law and *R (Laporte) v Chief Constable of Gloucestershire* [2007] 2 AC 105, which dealt with breach of the peace. Unsurprisingly, the court rejected the idea that citizens could take the law into their own hands. The other part of the problem concerns the ancient legal concept of breach of the peace. There are hundreds of cases on this subject, but you are being pointed towards modern developments. It always pays to keep up to date.

Answer plan

- **Article 11** Right to protest
- Unless it causes disorder or crime
- **Criminal Justice and Public Order Act 1994**—caravans and raves
- Wilful obstruction of the highway
- Public nuisance
- A public assembly of two or more persons in a public place open to the air
- Aggravated trespass—intimidate, disrupt or obstruct a lawful activity
- Lawful activity does not include preventing breaches of international law
- Insulting behaviour causing harassment, alarm or distress
- Reasonable action to prevent a breach of the peace.

Suggested answer

Article 11 of the European Convention on Human Rights guarantees that 'Everyone has the right to freedom of peaceful assembly and to freedom of association with others . . . ' Freedom of expression is also guaranteed by Article 10. Both these 'Convention rights' must be taken into account by courts and tribunals of the UK under s. 2 of the Human Rights Act 1998. Under s. 3, UK legislation 'must be read and be given effect in a way that is compatible with Convention rights'. Irrespective of this, English common law has long recognised that people are allowed to protest and to hold public meetings, as illustrated by the case of *Beatty v Gillbanks* (1882) 9 QBD 308. The Salvation Army should have been allowed to march in Weston-super-Mare, even though they knew that they would be violently opposed by the Skeleton Army. The Salvation Army was acting lawfully and it was not their fault if this caused another organisation to act unlawfully.

Protest can become unlawful though. This is recognised both by English common law and by the European Convention. Article 11(2) states that the right to freedom of assembly can be restricted 'for the prevention of disorder and crime' . . . 'or for the protection of the rights and freedoms of others'. Let us examine whether Margaret's protest has become unlawful or not.

The encampment by the roadside may be trespass, but that is usually only a civil matter that does not involve the police. The Criminal Justice and Public Order Act 1994 criminalises certain forms of trespass. Under s. 60 there is a power to remove trespassers, but this was aimed at travellers who are trespassing and requires there to be at least one caravan and one vehicle present. None of this seems to be the case here. Under s. 63 of the same Act, there is a police power to disperse raves and seize equipment. This is definitely not a rave as that requires at least 20 persons to be present and requires amplified music to be played during the night. Even if it was a rave, the police have no power to seize camping equipment, so dismantling their camp seems to be illegal.

Obstruction of the highway is an offence under s. 137, Highways Act 1980 and can be used by the police to disperse peaceful, non-violent protest. The offence is committed 'if a person without lawful authority or excuse in any way wilfully obstructs the free passage along a highway'. Pavements and grass verges are part of the highway and a person can even be off the highway and yet cause an obstruction on it, as shown by *Nagy v Weston* [1965] 1 All ER 78, where a hot dog van in a lay-by caused the obstruction on the highway. *Arrowsmith v Jenkins* [1963] 2 QB 561 involved a public meeting in the road, which was held to be an obstruction. It was no defence that there was no intent to cause an obstruction, nor that the road was only blocked for five minutes. *DPP v Jones* [1999] 2 AC 240 moderates this strict approach. This consisted of a peaceful, non-obstructive assembly of 21 people, including Margaret Jones, on the verge of the A344 road at Stonehenge. Lord Chancellor Irvine said, at p. 257, that:

> the public highway is a public place which the public may enjoy for any reasonable purpose, provided the activity in question does not amount to a public or private nuisance and does not obstruct the highway by unreasonably impeding the primary right of the public to pass and repass: within these qualifications there is a public right of peaceful assembly on the highway.

The Lord Chancellor thought this was the case irrespective of the right guaranteed under Article 11 of the ECHR, as the Human Rights Act was not yet in force at the date of this case.

Margaret and her friends would have a stronger argument that they have the right to protest now that the Act is in force, as they are only causing minor inconvenience to motorists.

Lord Irvine referred to public nuisance, which is a more serious charge than obstruction of the highway. The House of Lords stated in *R v Rimmington,*

R v Goldstein [2006] 1 AC 459, that this offence should now be rarely used, when there was a statutory equivalent available, which might give the defendant the benefit of statutory defences. So the prosecution should use obstruction of the highway, to which, as we have seen, Margaret may have a defence.

The Public Order Act 1986 gives the police powers to control a public assembly, which is defined in s. 16 as 'an assembly of 20 or more persons in a public place which is wholly or partly open to the air'. The minimum number was reduced to two by s. 57 of the Anti-Social Behaviour Act 2003, so Margaret's gathering would meet the definition. Also, under s. 16, a 'public place' includes a highway. By s. 14 a senior police officer may impose conditions on a public assembly such as the place it is held, its maximum duration or the maximum number of persons. Ignoring police directions is a criminal offence. It is important to note that the police may only impose conditions if they reasonably believe the assembly may result in serious public disorder, serious disruption to the life of the community, intimidation to others or serious damage to property. The 'attack' on the aircraft could be damage or intimidation, so this probably gives the police power to act under this section. However, the 1986 Act gives the police no power to ban or forbid a public assembly of this kind. This can only be done if the protest is moving and therefore becomes a 'procession' or if it is a 'trespassory assembly' under the Criminal Justice and Public Order Act 1994. A trespassory assembly has to cause serious disruption to the life of the community or damage to some sort of historical monument. Neither seems to be the case here.

The actions of Janet and Steve in entering the air base and damaging an airplane could be aggravated trespass under ss. 68 and 69 of the Criminal Justice and Public Order Act 1994. They have trespassed on land. Even entering the aircraft hanger is included, because although the offence originally only covered land in the open air, this was changed by the Anti-Social Behaviour Act 2003 to include all land. They have obstructed or disrupted 'lawful activity': the activities of the military. These issues were discussed, by the House of Lords, in *R v Jones* [2006] 2 WLR 772. Jones (the same Jones as in *DPP v Jones* above) and others had entered RAF Fairford and carried out or planned to carry out various acts of damage to military property. They argued that they could not have committed aggravated trespass, because the military were not engaged in 'lawful activity'. The war against Iraq was the crime of aggression and the military were preparing for it. Their Lordships accepted that, ever since the Nuremberg Military Tribunal at the end of the Second World War, 'aggressive war' was a recognised crime in international law. However, it had never been made a crime in the domestic law of the UK, as only an Act of Parliament could do this. Anyway, this crime could only be committed by the leaders of a state, not by low-ranking service personnel. The decision to go to war and to conduct foreign policy was part of the prerogative power of the Crown, with which the courts would not interfere. The defendants were also guilty of criminal damage under s. 1(1) of the Criminal Damage

Act 1971. This offence is not committed if the defendants have a 'lawful excuse', so they tried to argue the same defence as with aggravated trespass. They claimed that they were using reasonable force to prevent the crime of aggressive war from being committed. This too was rejected by the House of Lords for the same reasons. So it does seem likely that Janet and Steve have no defence to the charges of aggravated trespass and criminal damage.

Janet destroyed the 'Stars and Stripes', but it is not a crime to destroy a flag, even the flag of the United Kingdom. In *Percy v DPP* (2002) 166 JP 93, Ms Percy performed a similar action at RAF Feltwell, by writing 'Stop Star Wars' across the US flag and standing on the flag. Five US service personnel gave evidence that this caused them distress, so Percy was charged under s. 5 of the Public Order Act 1986. The offence is that she used insulting words and behaviour likely to cause harassment, alarm or distress. On appeal, the court held that her right to freedom of expression, under Article 10 of the European Convention, outweighed any distress she might have caused. Janet could use a similar argument.

The police could use the ancient common law power to control a breach of the peace, to justify their dispersal of the demonstration. In another case involving Ms Percy, *Percy v DPP* [1995] 1 WLR 1382, breach of the peace had to involve violence or a threat of violence. This could include provoking others to violence, or as the court put it where violence from some third party was a natural consequence of her action. In that case Percy had repeatedly trespassed on a military base, but she had not committed a breach of the peace as highly trained military personnel were unlikely to respond to an unarmed trespasser with violence. So applying this case, it does not look like Janet has committed a breach of the peace.

According to older cases such as *Moss v McLachlan* [1985] IRLR 76, if a police officer honestly and reasonably considers that there is a real risk of a breach of the peace in close proximity both in place and time, then the officer may take reasonable measures to prevent the breach of the peace. This permitted a police road block in *Moss*. In *R (Laporte) v Chief Constable of Gloucestershire Constabulary* [2007] 2 AC 105, the police prevented three coachloads of demonstrators from joining an anti-Iraq war demonstration outside RAF Fairford in Gloucestershire. They were stopped at some distance from RAF Fairford and then conducted non-stop back to London. The House of Lords did not think that the police could reasonably apprehend that a breach of the peace was imminent. The protesters were nowhere near the protest site and there were plenty of police at Fairford to deal with any breach of the peace. The police action was excessive and indiscriminate as only a few of the coach passengers were known troublemakers. This can be contrasted with the later House of Lords case, *Austin v Metropolitan Police Commissioner* [2008] 1 All ER 564, where there was a large May Day demonstration in London. The police confined around 3,000 people in Oxford Circus for seven hours, without toilet facilities or food and drink. Not all the persons detained were protestors. It was held that a breach of the peace was imminent and that these were extreme and exceptional circumstances. Violence had occurred at previous May Day demonstrations and there was no other way to contain any possible disturbance.

So, in conclusion, the police are probably justified in moving Janet and Steve away. They have committed the crimes of aggravated trespass and criminal damage and breach of the peace does include violence against property, not just people: *R v Howell* [1982] QB 416. Janet and Steve are inside the perimeter fence and can be easily separated from Margaret and the other protesters, which was not the case in *Austin v Metropolitan Police Commissioner* [2008] 1 All ER 564. Following *R (Laporte) v Chief Constable of Gloucestershire Constabulary* [2007] 2 AC 105, Margaret and the other demonstrators should be allowed to continue their peaceful protest. The European Court of Human Rights would agree that as long as a protest is peaceful the law should not forbid it: *Steel v UK* (1999) 28 HHRR 603.

Question 3

Article 11 of the European Convention on Human Rights **refers to the right to freedom of peaceful assembly, subject to the imposition of lawful restraints on the exercise of that right. Consider whether citizens of the UK enjoy the right to peacefully assemble or whether the lawful restraints mean that such right exists only so far as the police in the exercise of their discretion allow it.**

Discuss.

 # Commentary

For a number of reasons, this looks to be a fairly intimidating essay question! For a start it seems to cover what to many students would seem to be two quite separate topics, the **European Convention on Human Rights** and public order law. However, since the **Human Rights Act 1998** came into force, on 2 October 2000, such questions will be seen as increasingly relevant. Whether the existing law measures up to these new standards could be asked of several areas of constitutional law. Fortunately, there is plenty of material with which to answer this question. A critical account of the existing public order law would just about get by. Ask yourself the question, how much freedom to protest have we really got when all the various offences and police control powers are taken into account? There are also some cases, involving the UK, which the European Court of Human Rights has already decided. The issue of police discretion seems tricky, but has been dealt with in cases as old and as well-known as *Beatty v Gillbanks* **(1882) 9 QBD 308.** Structure and argument are everything in an essay like this. Do not just write down every case that you can remember and list all the offences in the **Public Order Act 1986**, but select the cases and offences that you want to discuss. Only use those that advance your argument, i.e., do they reveal a respect for peaceful protest or are they unnecessarily restrictive?

Answer plan

- **Article 11 of the European Convention of Human Rights** declares that everyone has the right to freedom of peaceful assembly
- Protest must be peaceful
- Processions may be prohibited if there is a threat of violence
- Violence or the threat of violence is an essential constituent of breach of the peace
- Restrictions on the right to protest must be clearly prescribed by law
- Peaceful protest may allow obstruction of the highway
- The State has a duty to protect peaceful protest.

Suggested answer

Some have suggested that English law unduly hinders peaceful protest. Take, for example, the views of Lord Bingham in *R (Laporte) v Chief Constable of Gloucestershire Constabulary* [2007] 2 AC 105 at 126–7: 'The approach of the English common law to freedom of expression and assembly was hesitant and negative, permitting that which was not prohibited. Lord Hewart CJ reflected the then current orthodoxy when he observed in *Duncan v Jones* [1936] 1 KB 218 at 222 that "English law does not recognise any special right of public meeting for political or other purposes"'.

The 1998 Act, giving effect to Articles 10 and 11 of the Convention, represented what Sedley LJ in *Redmond-Bate v DPP* (1999) 7 BHRC 375 at 380 aptly called a 'constitutional shift'. Article 11.1 of the European Convention on Human Rights states that: 'Everyone has the right to freedom of peaceful assembly . . . '. Article 11.2 allows this right to be restricted, but the restrictions must be 'prescribed by law' and must meet one at least of the legitimate aims listed there such as, 'national security', 'public safety', 'the prevention of disorder or crime' or 'the protection of the rights and freedoms of others'. The restriction on the right to protest must also be justified as 'necessary in a democratic society'. In other words it must be genuinely designed to protect, for example, 'public safety', but must go no further than is necessary to achieve that purpose. This is known as 'proportionality'. Article 10.1 states that 'Everyone has the right to freedom of expression. . . ' and there are similar restrictions on this right in Article 10.2. This essay aims to explore whether Sedley LJ is right, and whether English law does now guarantee a right of peaceful protest in accordance with the European Convention.

It is clear that any protest must be peaceful, as the European Commission held in *Christians against Racism and Fascism v United Kingdom* (1980) 21 DR 138 at 148: 'Disruption incidental to the holding of the assembly will not render it "unpeaceful", whereas a meeting planned with the object of causing disturbances will not be protected by Article 11.' Therefore there seems to be nothing objectionable to the offences in the Public Order Act 1986, for an essential element of riot, violent disorder and affray is that violence or threats of violence is used, so, by definition, they are not 'peaceful' actions. Even the 'threatening, abusive or insulting words or behaviour' in s. 4 must carry with them a threat of violence or at least provoke violence. Section 5, which merely requires the 'threatening, abusive or insulting words' etc. to be likely to cause 'harassment, alarm or distress' seems more suspect, as violence is not a constituent of the offence. In *Chorherr v Austria* (1993) 17 EHRR 358, however, the European Court of Human Rights held that a protest that caused annoyance or agitation was not protected by Article 11. Hence, s. 5 of the Public Order Act 1986 might well be acceptable.

Some have argued that it is an undue interference with public protest to prohibit processions, under what is now s. 13 of the Public Order Act 1986. This has, however, been considered acceptable under the European Convention, if there is a likelihood of violence in the area: *Christians against Racism and Fascism v United Kingdom* (1980) and *Rai v United Kingdom* (1995) 82 ADR 134. Turning aside from the statutory provisions of the Public Order Act 1986, the ancient common law power to control a breach of the peace has often caused concern amongst civil libertarians. According to Lord Denning in *R v Chief Constable of Devon and Cornwall ex parte CEGB* [1981] 3 All ER 383: 'There was a breach of the peace whenever a person who was lawfully carrying out his work was unlawfully and physically prevented by another from doing it'. Other cases have preferred a tighter definition, which involve threats of harm or violence. This was expressed in *R v Howell (Erroll)* [1982] 2 QB 416 as 'an act done or threatened to be done which actually harms a person, or in his presence his property, or is likely to cause such harm or which puts someone in fear of such harm being done'. This was further explained in *Percy v DPP* [1995] 3 All ER 124, that to be conduct that was a breach of the peace, it had to involve violence, a threat of violence or carry a real risk that it would provoke violence in others.

The use of breach of the peace has been questioned three times in the European Court of Human Rights. Each time the Court has been satisfied that the restriction that breach of the peace makes upon the right to protest is 'prescribed by law'. In other words it is sufficiently well-defined for someone to be able to understand what it is they are forbidden to do. The Court has, however, preferred the definition in *Howell* and *Percy*, which stresses the need for violence to make the conduct unlawful, for 'peaceful assembly' is a right. On the facts though, the court has disapproved of the use of breach of the peace in some circumstances. In *Steel v United Kingdom* (1999) 28 EHRR 603, Ms Steel walked in front of a grouse shoot and Ms Lush stood in front of a JCB digger in order to hinder the building of the M11. This was an acceptable restriction upon their rights to protest as Ms Steel might have been accidentally shot and Ms Lush might have provoked violence, so their protests were not peaceful. Ms Needham, Mr Polden and Mr Cole were conducting an entirely peaceful protest, outside a sale of 'fighter helicopters', when they were arrested. This was unacceptable under Article 11, Article 10, which guarantees freedom of expression and Article 5.1, which guarantees that no one will be deprived of their liberty unless they break the law. The three had not broken English law as they had not threatened or provoked any violence and so there was no breach of the peace.

In *McLeod v United Kingdom* (1999) 27 EHRR 493, the police had been present when Mr McLeod entered and removed items from his ex-wife's house, because they claimed that they feared a breach of the peace. The Court held that this was unjustified, as there was in fact little or no risk of disorder or crime occurring, as Mrs McLeod was not there at the time. This was a breach of Article 8, Mrs McLeod's right to respect for her home.

Finally, in *Hashman and Harrup v United Kingdom* (2000) 30 EHRR 241, hunt saboteurs were bound over to keep the peace. The words used by the English magistrates were to be of 'good behaviour'. The European Court of Human Rights found this to be unacceptable, because it did not tell the protesters what it was they were forbidden to do. It was particularly difficult for them to know, because they had not been convicted of or charged with any offence. Restrictions on the right to protest must be 'prescribed by law' and this lacked any clear definition.

So, in summary, the European Court has not found breach of the peace unacceptable, as properly defined, but has just required it to be used properly, to restrict violent protest only. The English courts have also been moving tentatively towards accepting a right of peaceful protest on the public highway. Completely peaceful assemblies, protests and demonstrations have often fallen foul of s. 137 of the Highway Act 1980, because it is a criminal offence to obstruct the highway. Cases such as *Arrowsmith v Jenkins* [1963] 2 QB 562, have held that the only lawful use of the highway is for passage and repassage, so a public meeting in the street was an obstruction. Other cases, such as *Hirst v Chief Constable of West Yorkshire* (1987) 85 Cr App R 143, have taken a slightly more lenient line, that very minor protests, which cause no real obstruction, can be tolerated. Some judges have been willing to go further and find that a right of peaceful assembly on the highway might exist. The Lord Chancellor, Lord Irvine, gave tentative support for such an idea in *DPP v Jones* [1999] 2 All ER 257 and felt that, if necessary, the common law should develop in order to conform to Article 11. Lord Hutton was confident that such a common law right already existed and cited Lord Denning's spirited dissent in *Hubbard v Pitt* [1976] 1 QB 142, where he defended the 'right to demonstrate and the right to protest on matters of public concern', 'provided that everything is done peaceably and in good order'. Otton J in *Hirst* (1987) was also quoted in support of the same idea. Importantly, the House of Lords in *DPP v Jones* (ibid.) also accepted that the peaceful protest, of 21 people on the grass verge of the A344 at Stonehenge, was not only not an obstruction of the highway, but also not a trespassory assembly under the Criminal Justice and Public Order Act 1994. The English courts seem to be gradually getting into line with the rulings of the European Commission, in *Rassemblement Jurassien et unite Jurassiene v Switzerland* (1979) 17 DR 93 and the European Court of Human Rights, in *Platform Arzte fur das Leben* (1988) 13 EHRR 204, where it was held that there is a *right* to hold meetings in public places.

The *Platform* case also made clear that the State does not merely have a duty to permit peaceful protest, in certain circumstances there may be a duty to protect peaceful protesters from those who would oppose them with violence. Even the English courts have occasionally endorsed this approach and asserted that the authorities should not merely take the easy way out and prevent those with an unpopular message from speaking, for fear of the possible reaction. In *Beatty v Gillbanks* (1882) 9 QBD 308, it was held that the Salvation Army should not be forbidden from marching through Weston-super-Mare, just because they might be opposed by the Skeleton Army. In a modern version of this case, the police were not permitted to stop women preaching from the steps of Wakefield Cathedral just because some of their audience were hostile: *Redmond-Bate v DPP* (1999) 163 JP 789.

It might be apparent from the contrasting cases given above, that the police have many difficult decisions to make. Do they permit free speech or step in to prevent a possible outbreak of public disorder? The English courts have usually been most unwilling to interfere with police discretion. In *R v Chief Constable of Devon and Cornwall ex parte CEGB* [1982] QB 458, even though the Court of Appeal seemed confident that criminal offences were occurring, they were unwilling to instruct the police to act. Similarly, in *R v Chief Constable of Sussex ex parte International Trader's Ferry Ltd* [1999] 1 All ER 129, the House of Lords were unwilling to interfere with the police decision to protect live animal exports from protesters on only two days a week, despite a strong argument that this infringed the free movement of goods under Article 34 of the European Community Treaty. Article 11 of the European Convention on Human Rights explicitly allows for the balancing of conflicting interests and, indeed, the few decisions of the European Court of Human Rights in this area do not seem any more willing to 'overrule' the decisions of the police than the English courts. Perhaps all the English courts need to do is to try and be a bit more consistent and not forget the basic principle that peaceful protest should be permitted.

Question 4

Jennifer has been arrested for allegedly committing an armed robbery. While being taken to the police station, she escapes from police custody and is pursued. She flees into Brian's house where she has a room. Brian refuses to let the police enter his house, but the police overcome his slight resistance and enter anyway. Jennifer is seized by the police in Brian's living room. The police search Jennifer and the living room but do not find anything.

Brian is asked by the police whether they can search Jennifer's rented room and he consents, even though Jennifer objects. While searching her room, the police find documents that seem to indicate her involvement in a financial fraud. The police ask Jennifer about these documents and she explains that her solicitor, Peter, deals with her business affairs and that they will have to ask him about the documents.

The police go to Peter's office with Jennifer and gain entry by claiming that they are delivering office equipment. Peter insists that they need a search warrant, but the police say that they do not as they have just arrested Jennifer. The police search the office and remove all the files relating to Jennifer's business affairs.

Jennifer, Brian and Peter seek your advice on the legality of the police conduct.

Advise Jennifer, Brian and Peter.

 ## Commentary

Earlier in the chapter we have seen that it is accepted that people are allowed to protest and express their views. This has subtly changed from a liberty to a right since the **Human Rights Act 1998** and protest should now be allowed as long as it is not violent. There are, however, other liberties or freedoms that English law has long upheld. One is the idea that people should be secure in their own homes and that the authorities should not interfere with them there. This was expressed as long ago as the early seventeenth century in *Semayne's Case* **(1604) Eliz 908**:

> That the house of everyone is to him as his castle and fortress, as well as for his defence against injury and violence, as for his repose. . .

If a police office or government official wants to gain entry to someone's home or other property, there must be some clear legal authority to permit this. This was the point of the famous case of *Entick v Carrington* **(1765) 19 St Tr 1030**: no official could enter and search the home of Entick, unless the official could clearly point to an Act of Parliament or case that authorised this. Similarly, the law would clearly identify the correct procedure for an official to gain entry as seen in *Semayne's Case* **(1604) Eliz 908**: 'But before he breaks it, he ought to signify the cause of his coming, and to make request to open doors.'

This approach can only be reinforced by the rights guaranteed by the **European Convention on Human Rights**. **Article 1** provides a 'right to respect for his private and family life, his home and his correspondence' and **Article 1 of the First Protocol** concerns the protection of property. As far as personal liberty is concerned, **Article 5** states that 'Everyone has the right to liberty and security of person.'

So when we look at the problem question above, we must be sure that the police actually have the legal power to do what they have done and that they have followed the correct procedures. This can be ascertained by knowledge of the major statute on police powers, the **Police and Criminal**

Evidence Act 1984. This gives the police the power to arrest and search and lays down sometimes quite complicated procedures. There is also a considerable case law on what these powers actually mean in practice. These cases make an answer both much more interesting to write and to read and some have entertaining and interesting facts. Pick your favourite examples, as there is usually more than one case on every point. A convoluted problem like this is best approached line by line and you should try to identify each legal point and be prepared to comment upon it. Is this legal? Which power are the police likely to be using here? Are our facts similar to any reported case? Then gradually you should be able to construct your answer step by step and come to a conclusion.

 ## Answer plan

- Arrest upon reasonable suspicion
- Informing the suspect of their arrest
- S.17 PACE 1984 entry and search
- Consent to search of premises
- S.32 PACE 1984 search of premises where a person is arrested
- S.18 PACE 1984 search of premises occupied and controlled by the person arrested
- S.19 PACE 1984 lawful entry and seizure of evidence of an offence
- Search warrants.

Suggested answer

We must first consider whether Jennifer has been lawfully arrested and then go on to consider the various powers that the police have to enter private premises and to search those premises. Most of those powers of entry and search depend upon whether a person has been arrested, so the first question to ask is whether Jennifer has been lawfully arrested.

No warrant has been issued for the arrest of Jennifer, so we must consider the powers that the police possess to arrest without warrant. Under s. 24 of the Police and Criminal Evidence Act 1984 a police constable may arrest anyone who is guilty of an offence or anyone whom he has reasonable grounds to suspect of being guilty of an offence. Previously, these arrest powers only applied to 'arrestable offences', but they were extended by the Serious Organised Crime and Police Act 2005 to include all offences. 'Suspicion' was defined by Lord Devlin in *Shaaban Bin Hussien v Chong Fook Kam* [1970] AC 942 at 948 as 'a state of conjecture or surmise where proof is lacking . . . I suspect but I cannot prove'. It would seem that the police have reasonable grounds for suspecting Jennifer, for she has escaped from police custody, which is a crime, and allegedly committed armed robbery, for which they could re-arrest her.

Blackstone defined arrest as 'the apprehending or restraining of one's person in order to be forthcoming to answer an alleged or suspected crime' (Blackstone's *Commentaries* p. 289). The old case of *Genner v Sparks* (1705) 6 Mod Rep 173, which also involved the recapture of a fugitive, requires that their must be some touching or seizure of the person. This seems to have occurred. The police must also tell the person that they are under arrest and the reasons for the arrest: s. 28 Police and Criminal Evidence Act 1984 and *Christie v Leachinsky* [1947] AC 573. The explanation must be in simple, non-technical language that the arrested person can understand, as explained in *Taylor v Thames Valley Chief Constable* [2004] 3 All ER 503, where a 10-year-old boy was arrested. It appears that Jennifer has been told nothing, but it appears from the case law that she can be told later. This might be because it was impracticable to tell her at the time, say if she was resisting arrest or trying to escape again: *DPP v Hawkins* [1988] 3 All ER 673. Even if there was no particular reason to delay, if she is told the reasons, for example when she is taken to the police station, then the failure to inform her when first arrested will not make the subsequent police actions unlawful: *Lewis v Chief Constable of South Wales* [1991] 1 All ER 206.

As seen from the Blackstone quotation above, the original purpose of arrest was to secure the suspect so that they could be taken before a court. Nowadays the police often arrest so that they can investigate the offence and question the suspect at the police station. This is perfectly acceptable, according to the House of Lords in *Holgate-Mohammed v Duke* [1984] AC 437.

A more contentious issue is that the police appear to have forced entry to Brian's house, without a warrant and without his permission. Section 17(1) (e) of the Police and Criminal Evidence Act 1984 allows a constable to enter and search for the purpose 'of recapturing a person who is unlawfully at large and whom he is pursuing'. This was possibly allowed by *Genner v Sparks* (1705) 6 Mod Rep 173 mentioned above, but the 1984 Act makes clear that the police can enter Brian's house as long as it is a genuine and continuous pursuit. In *D'Souza v DPP* [1992] 4 All ER 545 a woman was absent without leave from a psychiatric hospital and had returned home. The police could not force entry, but had to obtain a warrant, as they had not pursued her from the hospital. The police here seem to be in pursuit of Jennifer and it does not matter that it is not her house: *Kynaston v DPP* (1987) 84 Cr App R 200. According to s. 117 of the Police and Criminal Evidence Act 1984 the police may use 'reasonable force, if necessary' when exercising their powers under the Act; so pushing their way past Brian, if that is what they did, is not unlawful.

Once they have gained entry the police commence to search the house. Under s. 17(4) of the Police and Criminal Evidence Act 1984 the police may only search 'to the extent that is reasonably required for the purpose for which the power of entry is exercised'. In other words they can search for Jennifer, but for nothing else under this section. They have, however, already found her, so does Brian's consent make their further searching lawful? This is not dealt with in the sections of the Police and Criminal Evidence Act 1984, because it has been clear, at least since the great case of *Entick v Carrington* (1765) 19 St Tr 1030 at 1066, that if the owner or occupier consents to another entering, it cannot be unlawful:

> . . . every invasion of private property, be it ever so minute, is a trespass. No man can set foot upon my ground without my licence, but he is liable to an action though the damage be nothing.

Under the Codes of Practice that accompany the Police and Criminal Evidence Act 1984, the police should obtain Brian's consent in writing. Again, according to the Codes, Brian is unable to consent to the search of a room that is occupied by Jennifer, not him. The fact that the provisions of the Codes have been infringed does not necessarily render the search unlawful. Under s. 67(11) of the Act breach of the Codes of Practice is just something that 'shall be taken into account' in any subsequent proceedings.

Even if there are doubts about the validity of the consent of Brian, the police have other powers to search under the Police and Criminal Evidence Act 1984. Section 32 allows a constable to search the arrested person, but it also allows the police to use s. 32(2)(b) and 'to enter and search any premises in which he was when arrested or immediately before he was arrested for evidence relating to the offence for which he was arrested'. There is some doubt about whether the police can use this power to arrest a person and then, later, return and search the site of arrest (*McLorie v Oxford* [1982] QB 1290), but here the search is contemporaneous. It would seem reasonable for the police to assume that there could be further evidence of an armed robbery at the suspect's home. The permitted search is not unlimited, because s. 32(3) of the Act only allows 'search to the extent that is reasonably required for the purpose of discovering. . . any such evidence'.

In addition the police have powers to search the home of a person that they have arrested, under s. 18 of the Police and Criminal Evidence Act 1984. They can either search when they arrest the person or return later. Entry and search is permitted if the constable 'has reasonable grounds for suspecting that there is on the premises evidence' of that offence or a connected or similar offence. The police cannot use the section to go on a general 'fishing expedition' to search and see whether they can find evidence of an offence, any offence, as illustrated in *Jeffrey v Black* [1978] QB 490. The defendant was arrested for the theft of a sandwich from a public house, but the police searched his house and found illegal drugs. This was an unlawful search as there were no reasonable grounds for the police to suspect that there would be evidence of further sandwich theft at his home. It would seem reasonable, however, to suspect that there could be further evidence of Jennifer's armed robbery at her home. There is a further trap for the unwary police officer in s. 18. They can only 'search premises occupied or controlled' by the arrested person and the recent case of *Khan v Commissioner of Police of the Metropolis* [2008] EWCA Civ 723 stresses that this is actual occupation or control by the arrested person. It is not enough for the police to reasonably suspect that the person lives there, they must actually do so. Fortunately, for the police, Jennifer does.

The police find documents that they suspect indicate involvement in a financial fraud, while they are searching for something else, evidence of an armed robbery. It is legal to seize evidence of a crime, when the police are lawfully on the premises, according to Lord Denning in *Ghani v Jones* [1970] 1 QB 693. This is confirmed by s. 19 of the Police and Criminal Evidence Act 1984, the 'General power of seizure'. When a constable is lawfully on any premises, he may seize anything that he has reasonable grounds for believing is evidence of any offence. It does not have to be evidence of the offence that he is investigating. If the police suspicions are reasonable, they may take Jennifer's documents.

The search of the solicitor's office is illegal. The police should have obtained a search warrant under s. 8 of the Police and Criminal Evidence Act 1984. As indicated by the recent case of *Redknapp v Commissioner of the City of London Police* [2009] All ER 229, the police must follow the correct procedure to apply for the warrant, including practical details such as including the correct address. Jennifer's business records would be held in confidence by the solicitor, so they would be regarded as 'special procedure material' under s. 14 of the Act. The police should apply to a circuit judge, who could issue a Production Order to the solicitor, if the judge agreed that it was likely to be evidence of substantial value to the investigation. A search warrant would only be issued as a last resort, if it seemed that Peter was not likely to comply. Gaining entry to Peter's office by a subterfuge is not necessarily unlawful, because in *R v Longman* [1988] 1 WLR 619 the police pretended to be delivering flowers from Interflora in order to gain entry. In that case, however, the police did actually have a warrant, which they produced upon entry.

Surprisingly, it is not unlawful to search a solicitor's office, but the police are not permitted to search for legally privileged material. This is defined in s. 10 of the Police and Criminal Evidence Act 1984 as legal advice to a client or material connected with legal proceedings. Jennifer's business documents do not seem to be legally privileged and are not protected from search (*R v Crown Court at Northampton ex parte DPP* (1991) 93 Cr App R 376), but the police do need a warrant, which they have not got.

So, in conclusion, Jennifer has little to complain about, as the police had the legal power to search under ss 18 and 32 at the least. Her arrest was probably lawful, though the procedure followed leaves a little bit to be desired. The search of Peter's office was unlawful, as the police needed a search warrant or Peter's permission, which they did not obtain. Peter could make an official complaint about the police or sue them for trespass, as suggested in *Entick v Carrington* (1765) 19 St Tr 1030.

Further reading

Barnett, H. *Constitutional and Administrative Law*, 7th edn (Cavendish, 2008), chs 21 and 22.

Bradley, A. and Ewing, K. *Constitutional and Administrative Law*, 14th edn (Longman, 2007), ch 24 and 21.

Fenwick, H. *Civil Liberties and Human Rights*, 4th edn (Routledge-Cavendish, 2007), ch 8 and ch 11.

10

Freedom of Expression

Introduction

Freedom of speech is one of the most important civil liberties in a democratic society. It enables citizens to say or write what they like. This could include criticism of the government or other powerful institutions and discussion of alternative policies. Without free and open debate it is difficult to see how a democratic system could work.

In English law, freedom of speech is traditionally a civil liberty and not a right so we need to study the various laws that restrict free speech. One can say or write whatever one likes unless there is a law against it. Unfortunately there are a lot of laws that may need to be considered. The main areas would be obscenity, official secrets, breach of confidence and contempt of court. Other relevant laws might be incitement to racial hatred, sedition, incitement to disaffection, incitement to racial and religious hatred and civil and criminal defamation. Different public law courses will have different emphases and may concentrate on only some areas. Read the syllabus and listen to what your lecturers and tutors are telling you! If this does not work, a study of past examination papers should usually give you a clear idea of the areas that are required study.

Different lecturers will often have very different ideas of what should be studied. A traditional concern was the freedom of expression of writers and artists. This is reflected in the 'reform' of the law in the Obscene Publications Act 1959. Other laws would probably be considered such as the common law conspiracy to corrupt public morals, and the statutes regulating cinemas, theatre and videos. A more modern way of looking at this area might be to assume that the battle for artistic freedom was won back in the 1960s and 1970s and that the worry now might be whether there is sufficient control over pornographic material. A topical concern here might be paedophilia and as well as the above laws there might be a consideration of the Protection of Children Act 1978.

Other courses might be interested in the freedom of the press. The Broadcasting Acts, the non-statutory procedures for press complaints, contempt of court and defamation might well be the main focus of study.

Yet again there has been recent concern over the government's control over official information. Here one would look at not just the Official Secrets Acts but also the Public Record Acts, breach of confidence and the Spycatcher trials. The convention of ministerial responsibility can also play a role in controlling the flow of information.

See **Chapter 3,** Prime Minister and Cabinet and the *Scott Report of the Inquiry into the Export of Defence Equipment and Dual-use Goods to Iraq and Related Prosecutions.* When John Major became Prime Minister he announced that he was in favour of open government and a White Paper of this name was issued in 1993 (Cm 2290). This scheme relied on voluntary disclosure, but the Labour government, elected in 1997, promised a legally binding Freedom of Information Act, which was enacted in 2000.

The Human Rights Act 1998 came into force in 2000, meaning that the courts of Britain had to take account of the European Convention on Human Rights, when establishing the meaning of case law and interpreting Acts of Parliament. Article 10 guarantees a right to freedom of expression. Even before 2000, English courts had been considering Article 10, in their attempts to make sense of conflicting case law in the various areas of law that affect freedom of expression. Examples would include *Derbyshire v The Times* [1993] AC 534, which concerned libel and *A-G v Observer, The Times (Spycatcher)* [1990] AC 109, which involved the equitable doctrine of breach of confidence. The general tendency has been to conclude that English case law usually conforms to the demands of Article 10. There has also been a slight change, in favour of liberalising the law to uphold freedom of expression. For example, in the *Derbyshire* case it was concluded that a corporate body, such as a local authority, had no legal personality to sue for libel, free speech being more important. The Human Rights Act has not yet produced major changes in favour of freedom of expression. For example, *The Times* tried to claim that it would be in the public interest, for them to be able to discuss the conduct of politicians and be protected from libel actions. The House of Lords rejected this in *Reynolds v Times Newspapers* [2001] 2 AC 127, but did say that responsible journalism should be protected from libel actions. On the other hand, the courts have developed breach of confidence to protect the private life of celebrities in *Campbell v Mirror Group Newspapers* [2004] 2 AC 457 and *Douglas v Hello!* [2002] 1 FCR 289, among other cases.

The common law offences of blasphemy and blasphemous libel have been criticised for only protecting Christianity and no other religion or for being an unnecessary restraint upon freedom of expression when people follow a variety of religions or no religion at all. Blasphemy was abolished by the Criminal Justice and Immigration Act 2008.

It is unlikely, nowadays, that any constitutional and administrative law course would attempt to cover all of the possible aspects of freedom of expression. So our suggested answers only try to cover the main and, we hope, most likely areas.

Question 1

Humbert, who lives in Alphaville, is interested in computing and child pornography. He obtains from his computer images of young children engaged in sexual activity. These he prints out and exchanges with his friends. He also exchanges DVD recordings dealing with similar subject matter. He is arrested by the police and prosecuted.

In his defence, he wishes to argue that his sexual desires are incurable and that looking at such pictures is beneficial in that it satisfies those desires. He also wishes to argue that some of the computer images are of artistic merit. Eminent psychiatrists and art experts are willing to give evidence on his behalf.

Two days before his trial, the local newspaper, *The Alphaville Record* publishes an article under the headline, 'Hanging is Too Good for Humbert' and reveals that he has previously been convicted for sexual offences. The editor defends publication as in the public interest.

Advise Humbert and the editor of *The Alphaville Record*.

Commentary

This is a fairly typical problem designed to raise most of the main issues on obscenity law. The cases are interesting in themselves and fairly easy to remember. All that is needed is to apply them to the facts. In common with many questions on obscenity the student would also be expected to know about other laws that cover roughly the same area. There are quite a number of them and it is hard to predict which ones would come up in a particular question. So it is best to have a general idea of most of these laws. The examples here are the **Protection of Children Act 1978**, the **Video Recordings Act 1984** and perhaps conspiracy to corrupt public morals.

Another common tactic is to expect students to be aware of fairly obscure changes in the law, here those made in the **Criminal Justice and Public Order Act 1994** will need to be mentioned.

It is hard to make a problem question about obscenity long enough, so it is not unusual to include another area of law in the question. Here it is contempt of court. Again it would be hard to devise a full problem question on contempt. There are only so many points that could be raised.

Answer plan

- Obscenity is a tendency to deprave and corrupt
- Those who are likely to read, hear or see the 'obscene' article
- Expert evidence on artistic merit is allowed
- Offence to possess indecent electronic data
- Freedom of expression can be restricted for the protection of morals
- Contempt is a substantial risk that the course of justice will be impeded or prejudiced
- A discussion in good faith of public affairs is not contempt.

Suggested answer

The first offence that springs to mind is that Humbert might have contravened the Obscene Publications Act 1959. Section 1 makes it an offence to publish an obscene article.

Publishing includes any form of distribution. It is not necessary to show that Humbert did this for gain, for distributing or circulating is enough according to the Act. Even if this was not the case, an 'exchange' might well be held to be for gain. Whether obscene material stored on a computer was an 'article' was open to doubt until the Criminal Justice and Public Order Act 1994 (s. 168 and sch. 9, para. 3) made it clear that the transmission of electronically stored data was covered by the 1959 Act.

The test for obscenity is also set out in s. 1, Obscene Publications Act 1959. It is that the article is obscene 'if its effect. . . is, if taken as a whole, such as to tend to deprave and corrupt persons who are likely, having regard to all relevant circumstances, to read, hear or see' it. This test has eluded precise definition. *R v Secker and Warburg* [1954] 2 All ER 683 stated that the material being merely shocking and disgusting was not enough. The famous, though unreported, case concerning the book, *Lady Chatterley's Lover* in 1960 suggested that it meant 'to make morally bad, to pervert, debase or corrupt morally'. The old case, *R v Hicklin* (1868) LR 3 QB 360 mentioned 'exciting impure or libidinous thoughts'. It is not necessary to show that anyone was actually depraved or corrupted, merely that the material has that tendency.

The statutory definition above also demands that the likely audience is taken into account. If it is children, obscenity is more likely to be proved: *DPP v A & BC Chewing Gum* [1968] 1 QB 519 and *R v Anderson* [1972] 1 QB 304. Here though, although the material concerned children, they are most unlikely to be the 'target' audience. This is likely to be adults. Humbert cannot argue that they are likely already to be paedophiles and so incapable of further corruption. The argument that the 'audience' for pornography is already corrupt has not succeeded: *R v Anderson* [1972] 1 QB 304; *DPP v Whyte* [1972] AC 849.

The vague definition of obscenity may not be a problem. The jury will decide. Expert evidence is not permitted to help them on this issue unless the type of obscene material is outside the normal experience of adults. Expert evidence was allowed upon the effects of cocaine in *R v Skirving* [1985] QB 819 and the effects of horrific pictures upon children in *DPP v A & BC Chewing Gum* (1968). There seems no justification for this type of expert evidence in this case, as the 'target audience' for the material are adults.

Section 4 of the 1959 Act does, however, permit expert evidence upon 'artistic merit' (*R v Anderson*; *Lady Chatterley*). If the material can be shown to be for the 'public good' it is not obscene. The jury decide first whether material is obscene and then, if it is, whether considerations of public good outweigh this and if publication is desirable. More general arguments and evidence that pornographic material has therapeutic effects has never been permitted: *DPP v Jordan* [1977] AC 699 and *A-G's Reference (No. 3 of 1977)* [1978] 3 All ER 1166.

On balance it seems that Humbert's computer images and DVDs will be judged to be obscene. If this is not so, there are other offences that could be considered.

Mere possession of an 'indecent' photograph is an offence under the Protection of Children Act 1978. The prosecution must prove that Humbert had 'knowledge' of what he possesses, but on the facts here that does not seem too difficult: *Atkins v DPP* [2000] 2 All ER 425. Section 84, Criminal Justice and Public Order Act 1994 makes very clear that 'photographs' include both the electronic data and the print-out. There is no defence of public good. Even if he had deleted the images from his computer, if he had the necessary skill to recover them, he would still be guilty: *R v Porter* [2006] 1 WLR 2633. Similarly there is no such defence to the common law offence of 'conspiracy to corrupt public morals': *Shaw v DPP* [1962] AC 220. Paedophile 'rings' have been dealt with under this offence. Lastly it is highly unlikely that Humbert's DVDs have been given a classification under the Video Recordings Act 1984 by the British Board of Film Classification. This is particularly so, since the Board was urged to have 'special regard' to DVDs dealing with 'human sexual activity' in s. 90, Criminal Justice and Public Order Act 1994. It is a criminal offence merely to supply such a video, punishable by imprisonment.

The Human Rights Act 1998 may not help him very much. Under s. 2, a British court must 'take into account' decisions of the European Court of Human Rights. This Court has consistently allowed contracting States a 'margin of appreciation' in the area of obscenity law, because they cannot find an agreed European standard of morals in domestic law of these States. So the Court has refused to say that obscenity laws infringed the Article 10 right to freedom of expression in both *Handysides v UK* (1976) 1 EHRR 737 and *Muller v Switzerland* (1991) 13 EHRR 212.

The Alphaville Record is almost certainly guilty of contempt of court. Under s. 2(2), Contempt of Court Act 1981 there needs to be a 'substantial risk that the course of justice will be seriously impeded or prejudiced'. The publication of previous convictions has long been held to be contempt: *R v Odhams Press* [1957] 1 QB 73. The proceedings are clearly 'active' because Humbert has been arrested (s. 2(3)).

There is a defence under s. 5 that the risk of prejudice is purely incidental to 'a discussion in good faith of public affairs'. A passing mention in a newspaper article about a forthcoming trial might benefit from this section: *A-G v English* [1983] 1 AC 116. Here, though, the main purpose of the article seems to be to discuss Humbert, his trial and his previous convictions. It is a clear contempt. The Contempt of Court Act 1981 was enacted to bring English law into line with the European Convention on Human Rights, following Britain's defeat in *Sunday Times v United Kingdom* (1979) 2 EHRR 245. *R v Sherwood ex parte The Telegraph Group* [2001] I WLR 1983, confirms that contempt laws are necessary to guarantee a fair trial under Article 6.

Indeed, it could be argued that the editor obviously knows about the trial and is deliberately trying to interfere with the administration of justice. This intentional contempt is not covered by the Act (s. 6), but remains as a common law offence: *A-G v Hislop* [1991] 2 WLR 219. It would be treated most seriously by the courts if, as would be likely here, the Attorney-General brought a prosecution against the editor.

In conclusion both Humbert and the editor face conviction. In a strange way the contempt might help Humbert. If convicted, he might be able to appeal successfully on the grounds that the contempt meant that he did not receive a fair trial: *R v Taylor* (1993) 98 Cr App R 361.

Question 2

Jane is a civil servant working for the Ministry of Defence. Because of the nature of her work she had signed the Official Secrets Act on commencing her employment. During the course of her work Jane comes across a document indicating that a British company is selling artillery shells to the government of Fantasia. She knows that this is contrary to British law and contrary to the stated policy of Her Majesty's government. Jane asks a more senior civil servant what she should do. He tells her that the Secretary of State for Defence knows all about it but the matter is to be kept secret.

Jane is still concerned that the law is being broken so she hands over a copy of the document to a journalist who works for the *Sentinel* newspaper. That journalist discovers that there is a DA-notice relating to arms sales to Fantasia. He and his editor decide to publish the document anyway.

The government learns about the proposed publication and wants to stop it. It also wishes to punish the parties responsible.

Advise the government.

 ## Commentary

The problem with this sort of question is that at first glance it might seem unclear which area of constitutional law is relevant. The inspiration for the question is the 'Arms to Iraq' scandal, but it is not about the main concerns there of ministerial accountability and public interest immunity. Reading the rubric carefully, what you are actually asked to do with the facts given, is often helpful. Here it tells you that we are looking at the laws protecting government information.

The Official Secrets Act should immediately spring to mind, but so should breach of confidence, even though it is now some years since the Spycatcher trials. As will be seen from the suggested answer there are a few other bits and pieces of law that come in handy for questions like this.

Although this is a problem question, this sort of area is more often examined by means of an essay. The same material could be 'recycled' to answer an essay. With an essay, though, you would be expected to be critical rather than analytical as with a problem.

Answer plan

- Communicating to an enemy information that is prejudicial to the safety and interests of the State
- Disclosure of defence information that is damaging to British defence
- Disclosure of information relating to international relations that is damaging to British international relations
- Knowing receipt of such information
- The document belongs to the government
- Damages can be recovered for breach of contract
- Breach of confidence can be restrained to protect national security.

Suggested answer

The most obvious avenues for the government to explore are the Official Secrets Acts 1911 and 1989, but there are other possibilities. A civil action, perhaps for breach of confidence, might be possible and as Jane remains a civil servant, she is subject to Civil Service discipline.

Jane has signed the Official Secrets Act. This is a common procedure, but has no legal effect. All it does is warn her that she is in the sort of job that may be subject to the Act. Despite the reforms of 1989, s. 1 of the Official Secrets Act 1911 remains in force. Breach of this is a serious offence and can be committed by communicating to an enemy information that may be 'prejudicial to the safety and interests of the State'. Jane might well argue that she has not communicated to an enemy and that her actions are not 'prejudicial to the safety and interests of the State'. *Chandler v DPP* [1964] AC 763 indicates that only the government can decide what is in the interests of the State. In *R v Ponting* [1985] Crim LR 318 Clive Ponting, another civil servant, tried to argue that he was helping the State by revealing to an MP information that ministers were hiding from Parliament. This is the 'whistle-blower' argument: he had a duty to expose wrongdoing. In *Ponting* the court ruled that this argument was unacceptable, for, as in *Chandler*, only the government of the day could rule on what was 'in the interests of the State'. Despite the ruling the jury acquitted Ponting. For this reason, it is unlikely that the government would use s. 1 against Jane or the journalist, who would also be liable.

The old s. 2 of the 1911 Act was replaced by the Official Secrets Act 1989. Geoffrey Robertson QC described it in *Freedom, the Individual and the Law* (1993) (p. 168) as replacing 'a blunderbuss with an armalite rifle'. The Act is meant to focus only on those areas where the Crown is genuinely concerned with the revelation of official information. Section 1 warns Crown servants, such as Jane, that she must not reveal information acquired during her work if it relates to the security or intelligence services. Her revelation would not seem to affect security or intelligence, but it might affect defence. Under s. 2 it is an offence to disclose 'defence' information. 'Defence', as defined in s. 2(4)(b), includes 'weapons' but only those used by the Armed Forces of the Crown. Foreign Armed Forces are not included. Maybe it is possible that foreign weapon sales come under subsection (d), the more general 'defence policy'. Not only this but the prosecution must prove that disclosure of information is 'damaging' to British defence. It is difficult to see how this could be so. Damage to British interests abroad is also mentioned in s. 2 and might be easier to prove on our facts. There is also a 'did not know' defence in s. 2(3) of the Act, which was considered in *R v Keogh* [2007] 1 WLR 1500 together with a similar defence in s. 3(4). Read literally, the subsections seem to reverse the burden of proof and require Jane to prove that she did not know that it was defence information and did not know that it was damaging to reveal it. The Court of Appeal held that this was incompatible with the presumption of innocence in Article 6 of the European Convention on Human Rights. It would be up to the prosecution to prove that Jane knew that it was defence information and that it would be damaging to reveal it. Another government possibility is s. 3 of the Act, which protects information relating to 'international relations' in a similar way. Conceivably arms sales to a foreign country might well be connected to foreign policy matters. Again the prosecution would have to prove that Jane knew that the information was damaging to international relations.

Chandler v DPP (1964) suggests that the courts would accept the government's view upon what was 'defence', 'international relations', or 'the interests of the United Kingdom abroad'. It was hoped that the courts would take a more liberal line under the 1989 Act and allow defendants, such as Jane, to put forward their own evidence on what was damaging to the country's defence or international relations. In *R v Shayler* [2003] 1 AC 247, however, the defendant claimed that he had tried to reveal the wrongdoings of the security services and that this was in the public and national interest. He also argued that the Official Secrets Act 1989 was incompatible with Article 10 of the European Convention of Human Rights, because it infringed his right to freedom of expression. The House of Lords did not agree. They followed decisions of the European Court of Human Rights, where the needs of 'national security' were deemed to outweigh freedom of expression: *Engel v Netherlands (No. 1)* (1976) 1 EHRR 647 and *Klass v Germany* (1978) 2 EHRR 214.

Shayler's 'whistle-blower' argument also fell on stony ground. *R v Ponting* [1985] Crim LR 318 had stated that a civil servant, concerned about wrongdoing, should report their worries to their superiors, not the press. The House of Lords suggested that Shayler should have told his Secretary of State. A minister may authorise the disclosure of 'secrets' under s. 7 of the 1989 Act. It seems, on these precedents, that Jane's best hope would be to use *R v Keogh* [2007] 1 WLR 1500 and argue a defence that she did not know that the information that she revealed would be damaging, but instead hoped that her revelation of wrongdoing would be for the benefit of the country.

The journalist too, commits an offence if he knowingly receives the information and knowingly passes it on (s. 5). This the *Sentinel* newspaper seems determined to do. It is necessary, however, for the information to contravene the foregoing provisions of the Act for this to be an offence. As we have seen, it is by no means clear that it is 'defence' or 'international relations' information. The journalist also has a 'not damaging' defence.

Under s. 8 it is a specific offence for a Crown servant like Jane to retain the actual document 'contrary to her official duty'. Again, though, for the offence to be committed it has to relate to 'defence' or 'international relations'.

The government has other measures that it could utilise against Jane. The 'Defence Advisory notice' is just a non-statutory warning issued by a committee of members of the media, civil servants and the military, known as the Defence, Press and Broadcasting Advisory Committee. It advises the media not to publish information relating to certain military and intelligence matters. It is not an offence to ignore the notice, but it acts as a warning that publication might infringe the law. Civil injunctions can be sought to prevent breach of the Official Secrets Act, as occurred in the Zircon Affair of 1986–7. As such an injunction would probably be issued ex parte, the government might be successful in obtaining it. The court would await the full trial before looking into the finer legal points.

There is possibly a very simple way to recover the document. The document and copies of it are personal property that belong to the government. It could simply sue in tort for its return. This occurred in a rather similar case to our facts, *Secretary of State for Defence v Guardian Newspapers* [1984] Ch 156. Sarah Tisdall, a civil servant, had handed a document about cruise missiles to *The Guardian* newspaper. Section 10 of the Contempt of Court Act 1981 allows a journalist to protect his sources, but not if it is an issue of national security. This might well be such an issue and the document's return would be ordered. Although it is in the discretion of the court, journalists are usually ordered to reveal their sources: *Ashworth Security Hospital v Mirror Group Newspaper Ltd* [2004] 4 All ER 1.

Jane, as a civil servant, would be subject to dismissal for breach of contract. If the newspaper paid her, the fee could be recovered as damages according to *A-G v Blake* [2001] 1 AC 268.

The most flexible remedy that the government has, is to seek an injunction for breach of confidence. It is clear that Jane has an obligation of confidence as a civil servant. The government would need to show that it was in the public interest to prevent disclosure: *A-G v The Observer, The Times (Spycatcher)* [1990] 1 AC 109. Damage to the security services was the reason for non-disclosure in that case. Here, though, Jane, wishes to reveal breaches of the law. It is permissible to reveal criminal wrongdoing, even if it is a breach of confidence: *Cork v McVicar* (1984) Times, 31 October. The court did not extend this approach to the revelation of government wrongdoing in *Attorney-General v The Observer, The Times* [1990] AC 109. A civil servant, such as Jane, should report their worries to their superiors and not the press.

It is possible though, that the entry into force of the Human Rights Act 1998 might help Jane. Decisions of the European Court of Human Rights have emphasised the importance of freedom of expression. Although the Court found the law on breach of confidence acceptable in *Observer v UK* (1991) 14 EHRR 153, they thought that the 'Spycatcher' injunction should have been lifted earlier, as the material was already in the public domain. Now, under s. 12 of the Human Rights Act 1998, the courts of the UK must have special regard to freedom of expression. In *Attorney-General v The Times* [2001] 1 WLR 885 the newspaper was about to publish extracts from a book by Tomlinson, a former MI6 officer. The court allowed this as the material had already been published elsewhere. It was up to the government to prove that there was a need to restrict freedom of expression 'in the interests of national security'. The newspaper did not have to prove that the material was already in the public domain, the government had to prove that it was not.

Jane's problem is that her material is not already in the public domain. I would suggest that the court is more likely to follow the approach in *Shayler* (above) and issue an injunction to protect national security. The *Sentinel* would also be injuncted and all other newspapers that could reasonably be expected to know about the injunction would also be bound as happened when *Punch* magazine published some of the *Shayler* material in *Attorney-General v Punch Ltd* [2003] 1 All ER 289. So, in conclusion, Jane risks conviction under the Official Secrets Act 1989, damages for breach of contract and an injunction forbidding her disclosures. The Human Rights Act 1998 does not seem to have allayed the courts' fears about endangering national security.

Question 3

In a democracy, people should have information about the workings of government. Without it, they cannot call their representatives to account and make informed use of their rights as citizens and electors.

(Cm 7285 White Paper on reform of the Official Secrets Act 1911)

Consider whether a Freedom of Information Act would give people more information about the workings of government.

Commentary

The 1997 Labour government promised a Freedom of Information Act in their election manifesto. The authors of this book have long memories and they can recall that the previous Labour government of 1974–79 also considered such legislation. That is the origin of the quotation above, but, as usual in constitutional and administrative law, it is not necessary to be familiar with the source of a quotation in order to answer. If you read the question it is perfectly straightforward; would a Freedom of Information Act be a good thing?

There was a long-running campaign to introduce such an Act, and the **Freedom of Information Act 2000** finally became law after making very slow progress through Parliament. It was not until late in 2005 that it finally came fully into force. Campaigners for freedom of information want more rights of access to information than any government, of any political persuasion, is likely to concede. The Act has been much criticised, particularly because of the large number of exemptions to the right of information contained within it and, also, because of the considerable powers that the government has retained to decide what those exemptions should be. Therein lies valuable material for your essay! The suggested answer below is slightly more ambitious, in that it attempts to set a Freedom of Information Act in the context of the various powers that the government has to control the flow of information. Here you could show your knowledge of legislation such as the **Official Secrets Acts**, which you might have revised or studied anyway. Another possibility would be to try and compare the British Act with similar legislation in other countries. That would, however, require a reasonably detailed knowledge of that foreign legislation.

Answer plan

- The **Public Records Acts** allow the release of some government documents
- The **Official Secrets Act 1911** prevents the release of information for a purpose prejudicial to the safety and interests of the State
- The **Official Secrets Act 1989** protects information relating to security and intelligence, defence, international relations and criminal investigations
- Breach of confidence protects government information
- A voluntary Code of Practice promoted the release of government information
- The **Freedom of Information Act 2000** requires public authorities to publish information
- The public may request information from a public authority
- But there are many exemptions
- Government ministers have a strong role in exempting information
- Appeal to the Information Commissioner.

Suggested answer

The Home Office's 1999 consultation paper on freedom of information starts by stating that:

> Freedom of information is an essential component of the government's programme to modernise British politics. This programme of constitutional reform aims to involve people more closely in the decisions which affect their lives.

While this may be true, the government did not plan to repeal the laws that successive governments had used to control the release of government information.

The Public Records Act 1958 allows public access to some historical government documents. Each government department decides upon which of its files needs preserving for historical reasons. Normally these are released after 30 years and contain much interesting material, such as the minutes of Cabinet meetings. However some material is never released, such as security and intelligence, civil and home defence, atomic energy and the personnel records of civil servants. Other material is retained for periods in excess of 30 years. For instance information on the award of honours is kept back for 60 years and information on law and order for 100 years. Decisions on retention were taken by the Lord Chancellor, but at least the Freedom of Information Act replaces that with its general statutory scheme for access, complete with an appeal mechanism and an Information Commissioner.

The Official Secrets Act 1911 can always be used in a serious case, for s. 1 remains and makes it a serious offence to obtain or communicate any document or information 'for a purpose prejudicial to the safety or interests of the State'. *R v Ponting* [1985] Crim LR 318 held, in the case of a whistle-blowing civil servant, who wanted to reveal documents about a controversial military act to an MP, that only the government could decide what was in 'the safety or interests of the State'. The Official Secrets Act 1989 was a reform, but the crucial areas of information, that a government would wish to keep secret, are still protected by criminal sanction. These are security and intelligence, defence, international relations and criminal investigations. The Defence Advisory Notice, which warns journalists not to investigate certain areas, for fear of prosecution, also still exists, as does the practice of 'signing' the Official Secrets Act, which serves a similar warning function for individuals.

Failing this, a government could always use the civil remedy of breach of confidence to restrain, by injunction, government employees, ex-employees and those they pass the information to, such as newspapers and publishers, from betraying confidences. The most spectacular example of this was the protracted litigation against the ex-security agent Peter Wright's book *Spycatcher* in the late 1980s and early 1990s, culminating in the House of Lords' decision *A-G v Guardian (No. 2)* [1990] 1 AC 109, where the injunctions were only lifted because the information was, by now, so well known that to continue them would be pointless. Governments have not tired of pursuing such actions for in *A-G v Blake* [2001] 1 AC 268, an ex-member of the Secret Intelligence Service had been sued for breaching his contractual obligation, not to reveal what he had learnt from his employment. The House of Lords decided that Blake would have to account (i.e. restore) the profits made from the book, that he published about his career.

Legal proceedings against Blake actually began in 1991, under the previous Conservative government of John Major. At the same time he was proclaiming his belief in 'open government'. This started with the release of hitherto secret information, such as the names and composition of the various cabinet committees, the guidelines for ministerial behaviour 'Questions of Procedure for Ministers' (now known as the Ministerial Code) and some details about M15 and M16. Later on a Code of Practice was introduced that, for instance, required government to routinely release far more information than previously. A Code of Practice was chosen, rather than a legally binding system, because the government claimed that they did not want to damage the convention-based system of ministerial responsibility, under which ministers voluntarily release information in parliamentary statements, answers to MPs' questions etc. (See **Chapter 3.**) The more cynical might think that the government preferred a system where the courts would not be able to order them to release information. Under the Code, an applicant might make a 'reasonable request for information' although a charge reflecting 'actual costs' could be made. Unlike, say, the US Freedom of Information Act 1966, copies of the actual document themselves would not be released, just the information that they contained. If the request was refused there was an appeal mechanism, first to the department concerned, then to an MP and finally to the Parliamentary Commissioner for Administration. As is common with such systems in other countries, there were a great number of categories of information exempt from disclosure, ranging from defence to commercial confidences.

In the year 2000, a Freedom of Information Act was enacted to replace this voluntary Code of Practice. Although this made requests for information enforceable in court and there were some improvements in access to information, the problem of numerous exemptions still remains.

First, the government wanted to promote a 'change of culture within the public sector' and encouraged all 'public authorities' to voluntarily publish far more information. Public authority is broadly defined, to mean any body or office exercising a public function and includes those providing services of that nature to the public authority. There is a list of over 400 public authorities in the Freedom of Information Act and all must draw up a publication scheme. This includes things like schools admission criteria and how priorities on hospital waiting lists are determined, which are matters of concern to the general public, not just to those interested in politics.

Otherwise any person can request information from a public authority. The public authority has a duty to confirm or deny whether they hold the information or not. If they do they must provide it, although a small fee may be charged. The applicant may even express a preference about whether they want the information to be provided as a copy of a document, a digest or summary or whether they just want to inspect it. There are a number of grounds upon which the public authority can refuse to supply the information, such as that it is already available, about to be published, would be too expensive or the request is 'vexatious', e.g. the applicant has made repeated requests for the same information.

The main criticism of the Act is that there are a large number of exempted categories of information where there is no duty to disclose. Apart from this obvious criticism, the different exemptions are differently defined, which may cause confusion amongst the public. There are categories of information that are absolutely exempt from disclosure such as that relating to security organisations, court records, personal data, information obtained in confidence, and information whose disclosure is forbidden by statute, European Community obligation or would be in contempt of court. There is a longer list of information categories where it has to be decided whether the public interest requires disclosure or withholding of the information. Defence, international relations, the economy, public investigations, law enforcement, the formulation of government policy, the award of honours, and communications with the Queen are just some of the 'public interest' exempt category.

Another problem is the strong government role in these exemptions, when the government is the very organisation that may be trying to conceal information. Government ministers certificate whether information has been supplied by a security or intelligence agency and whether it is a threat to national security. Communications between government ministers, cabinet communications and advice from civil servants on policy formulation are all exempted information. What is more, a government minister can also give an opinion that information should be withheld because it could prejudice the convention of collective responsibility, inhibit the free and frank provision of advice or prejudice public affairs. The courts of Scotland have held, in *Scottish Ministers v Scottish Information Commission* [2007] SC 330 that this does not allow ministers to say that all documents containing advice to ministers should be withheld. The Information Commissioner was entitled to examine individual documents to assess whether they could safely be released. Lastly, and most controversially, a Secretary of State can add to the list of exempt information, merely by using delegated legislation. This could even be retrospective, so a government confronted with an unwelcome request for information could, presumably, change the law so that they did not have to release the information. Parliament would, however, have to agree to this delegated legislation, as the Act requires the affirmative resolution procedure.

Fortunately, the Freedom of Information Act comes complete with a fairly robust enforcement system. First, the public authority needs to provide an internal complaint procedure. Then the applicant can apply to the 'Information Commissioner', an independent official created by the Act. Either the applicant or the public authority has an appeal to an Information Tribunal, with further appeals on a point of law to the High Court and then upwards to the Court of Appeal and House of Lords, if necessary. It may be noted that the Tribunal can only question a minister's national security certificate on a judicial review basis. In *R (Secretary of State for the Home Department) v Information Commissioner* [2006] All ER (D) 328 the court held that it could investigate whether there really was a national security reason for refusing information, under the similar provisions of the Data Protection Act 1998, where an individual may request data held about them. This Information Commissioner will also have pretty impressive enforcement powers and she will be able to investigate, obtain search warrants and order the release of information. The penalty for defying her or lying to her could be proceedings in the High Court for contempt of court.

When compared to freedom of information legislation in other countries, such as the US Freedom of Information Act 1966, or the Australian or Swedish equivalents, the same problem of exemptions occurs. The British Act, in comparison, does seem to have rather a lot of exemptions and they are rather widely drawn. The government also seems to have undue power to widen the scope of these exemptions. A strong Information Commissioner would help to counteract this and it is to be hoped, in the post-Human Rights Act 1998 era, that courts dealing with the inevitable appeals will interpret the Act in a way that promotes freedom of information. There are some small signs that that they are trying to do so.

Question 4

Is there a right of privacy in English law?
  Discuss.

 Commentary

It is very hard to define exactly what privacy is and how a legal right to privacy should be defined. Many sorts of activities could be covered by a right to privacy and there could be many possible infringements of that right by the State, the media, powerful business interests or, maybe, other people. Historically, English law does not have a specific right of privacy, but the tort of trespass and the equitable doctrine of breach of confidence both give some protection to specific aspects of privacy. In contrast, the **European Convention on Human Rights** clearly does grant a right to a 'private life' in **Article 8.1**:

Everyone has the right to respect for his private and family life, his home and his correspondence.

The **European Convention** is now enforceable in UK courts under the **Human Rights Act 1998**. The European Court of Human Rights has made many decisions on what can be covered by **Article 8**, and, under **s. 2 of the Human Rights Act 1998**, UK courts are required to take such decisions into account. A change of sex was held to be a matter concerned with a person's private life in *Goodwin v UK* **(2002) 35 EHRR 44**, it was not acceptable to criminalise homosexuality in *Dudgeon v UK* **(1981) 4 EHRR 523**, telephone tapping was a breach of human rights in *Halford v UK* **(1997) 24 EHRR 523**, and the placing of a bugging device in a private house was unacceptable in *Khan v UK* **(2001) 31 EHRR 1016**.

The major concern has, however, been media intrusions into the private lives of famous and not so famous people. The UK courts have been able to adapt the old law of breach of confidence to meet some of those concerns, reinforced by the **European Convention on Human Rights**. There is a steady stream of new cases, usually involving celebrities, and so they even make the mainstream news, not just the pages of legal journals. That makes this an interesting subject to write about.

A comprehensive survey of the law is not possible in such a relatively short essay, so the key to a good answer is a good structure and some clear arguments, backed up by some good examples from the case law.

 ## Answer plan

- Trespass does not include a right of privacy
- Breach of confidence
- Breach of confidence depends upon a confidential relationship
- The public interest must also be considered
- There is no confidence in iniquity
- **Article 8 ECHR**—right of respect for private life
- **Article 10 ECHR**—freedom of expression
- The private life of public figures may be protected
- Private life may be revealed if it is a legitimate subject of public debate
- Should there be a more extensive right of privacy?

Suggested answer

Historically, no right of privacy has been recognised in English law, unlike the situation in other European countries such as France or Germany, where the protection of privacy is a recognised part of the law. In England, privacy did not become accepted as a recognised tort nor has there been legislation on the subject, despite the recommendations of the Younger Committee on Privacy in 1972 (Cmnd 5012) and the Calcutt committee in 1990 (Cm 1102).

Although unauthorised entry to someone's house has long been recognised as a trespass in famous cases like *Entick v Carrington* (1765) 19 St Tr 1030, the courts felt unable to extend trespass to cover other intrusions into a person's home or private life. In *Malone v Metropolitan Police Commissioner* [1979] Ch 344, Megarry VC was unable to grant a remedy to Malone, whose telephone had been tapped by the Metropolitan Police, but thought that the matter needed legislation. Similarly, there was nothing unlawful about taking aerial photographs of a person's house, without their permission, in *Bernstein v Skyviews Ltd* [1978] 1 QB 479. It is not possible to trespass by flying over someone's land. Even as late as 2004, the courts declined to recognise a right of privacy when visitors to a prisoner sued after being strip searched: *Wainwright v Home Office* [2004] 2 AC 406.

Yet the courts were not completely without the means to deal with some of the grosser intrusions into a person's private life. In *Kaye v Robertson* [1991] FSR 62, a well-known actor was lying injured in a hospital bed after an accident, when journalists photographed him and published the pictures without his permission. The courts stopped this, on the slightly dubious grounds that this was a malicious falsehood. A better legal doctrine to use would have been the old equitable doctrine of breach of confidence.

The Court of Chancery decided in *Prince Albert v Strange* (1849) 1 Mac & G 25 that Strange could not publish etchings that Prince Albert had made of members of his immediate family. Prince Albert had not given permission for any publication and Strange had obtained copies from an employee of the printer, who had been entrusted with the printing. To publish them would be a breach of confidence. Many years later, this precedent was followed in the notorious case of *Argyll v Argyll* [1967] Ch 302, where the Duke and Duchess of Argyll were divorcing and the Duke sold a story, with intimate details of their married life, to the *People* newspaper. Publication could be restrained, because this was information from a confidential relationship, marriage.

The concept of the confidential relationship was developed in *Attorney-General v Guardian Newspapers (No. 2)* [1990] 1 AC 109, where Peter Wright, a retired intelligence services officer, published a book, *Spycatcher*, revealing what he had allegedly done during his working life. The government tried to stop publication of the book and newspaper reports of what it contained, by suing for breach of confidence. Lord Keith, at 255, held that:

> The law has long recognised that an obligation of confidence can arise out of particular relationships. Examples are the relationships of doctor and patient, priest and penitent, solicitor and client, banker and customer. The obligation may be an express or implied term in a contract, but it may also exist independently of any contract on the basis of an independent equitable principle of confidence.

Third parties, outside the relationship of confidence, could also be restrained from revealing the confidential information. The public interest also had to be taken into account. Here it was not in the public interest for government secrets to be revealed, particularly as it might encourage other intelligence officers to follow Wright's example. By the time this case came to court, however, the book had been widely distributed and Wright's allegations were well known. There was little point in continuing injunctions against the newspapers, forbidding them to reveal what Wright claimed. The injunction remained against Wright.

It could be in the public interest to reveal confidential information, which was an argument unsuccessfully raised by Wright, but accepted in other cases. It was held that there was 'no confidence in iniquity' in *Woodward v Hutchins* [1971] 1 WLR 760, where the *Daily Mirror* published details of the private life of the singer, Tom Jones, revealed by a former employee. Jones had courted publicity in the past, so he could not complain about unwelcome publicity now. It would be in the public interest to reveal a crime, as in *Cork v McVicar* (1984) Times, 31 October, where McVicar taped private conversations with Cork, a retired police officer, which seemed to provide evidence of police corruption. The *Daily Express* was free to publish. Similarly it was acceptable for the police to publish the photograph of a suspect in *Hellewell v Chief Constable of Derbyshire* [1995] 1 WLR 804.

The confidential relationship that is being protected is not always well defined in all the cases. In *Prince of Wales v Jim Regan* (1981) Times, 7 May, telephone conversations between the Prince of Wales and his fiancée, Lady Diana Spencer, were intercepted, but publication was forbidden. Presumably, engagement was the relationship, but in *Francome v Mirror Group Newspapers Ltd* [1984] 2 All ER 408, the court disapproved of a journalist tapping a famous jockey's telephone when there was no relationship.

It seemed that some judges, at least, were willing to extend the protection given by breach of confidence, and this process was accelerated by the European Commission on Human Rights in *Spencer v United Kingdom* (1998) 25 EHRR CD 105. Earl Spencer complained about newspaper reports relating to his marriage. He lost, but the Commission did say that there was a remedy in UK law for breach of Article 8, the right to respect for private life and that was breach of confidence. So since the coming into force of the Human Rights Act 1998 there has been an increase in court actions attempting to protect confidential information and a person's privacy, as Lord Woolf CJ remarked in *A v B plc and Another* [2003] QB 195. There a married professional footballer was having sexual relationships with two other women, who had sold their stories to a national newspaper. He wanted to stop publication, but failed on the grounds that the court set great store in protecting the confidentiality of marriage and other permanent relationships, but far less value in protecting the confidentiality of this sort of liaison. The court had to consider not just the right to a private life, which was protected by Article 8, but also the newspaper's right to freedom of expression, which was guaranteed by Article 10, as A was a public figure. This balancing of interests was familiar from the equitable origins of breach of confidence, as Lord Woolf CJ explained at p. 202.

> The court is able to achieve this by absorbing the rights which articles 8 and 10 protect into the long-established action for breach of confidence.

In *Douglas v Hello! Ltd* [2001] QB 967, Michael Douglas and Catherine Zeta Jones had sold exclusive rights to their wedding photographs to *Hello!* magazine and wanted to stop a rival magazine publishing surreptitious photographs taken by a wedding guest. They failed, because they had not imposed an obligation of confidentiality on all the people at the wedding. Naomi Campbell gained a partial victory in *Campbell v Mirror Group Newspapers* [2004] 2 AC 457, where a newspaper had revealed that she was receiving treatment for drug addiction. This was acceptable, but publishing photographs of her leaving the place of treatment was not. Lord Nicholls had some important things to say about the development of the right of privacy. Although s. 6 of the Human Rights Act says only that 'public authorities' can be sued for breaching human rights, this type of action can be brought between individuals and between individuals and a non-governmental body such as a newspaper. He also wanted to abandon the use of the term 'duty of confidence' and the insistence that only 'confidential' information could be protected. He preferred to refer to it as 'private' information and stated at p. 465: 'The essence of the tort is better encapsulated now as misuse of private information.'

Article 10 can be outweighed by more important and fundamental rights. In *Venables v News Group Newspapers* [2001] Fam 430, the court ordered all the media never to reveal the new identities or whereabouts of the child murderers, Venables and Thompson, who were about to be released from prison. Freedom of expression and the public interest in uncovering crime were outweighed by the possible threat to the lives and safety of the two young men, protected by Article 2, the right to life, and Article 3, freedom from inhuman and degrading treatment.

The 'public interest' is not at all the same thing as the public being interested in something, as the court held in *HRH Prince of Wales v Associated Newspapers Ltd* [2008] Ch 57. An employee of Prince Charles gave the Prince's diaries to a newspaper, which was a breach of the employee's contract. Although there was some public interest in the diaries, the Prince was a public figure and the diaries criticised the leaders of China, which might be seen as a matter of political debate; the extreme confidentiality of a person's private diaries outweighed this.

The law continues to evolve. According to the European Court of Human Rights, it is not permissible to publish photographs of the private life of a public figure unless it contributes to political debate. In *Von Hannover v Germany* (2005) 40 EHRR 1, Princess Caroline of Monaco successfully complained that German newspapers should not publish photographs of her with her husband and children, when engaged in their private life. The State has an obligation to protect the private life of individuals from other individuals. Sometimes it is permissible to look at the private life of public figures if it relates to a political debate, but that was not the situation here.

This case has been reflected and further developed in decisions in the UK courts. In *Murray v Express Group Newspapers* [2008] HRLR 33, the Court of Appeal suggested that taking a photograph, without permission, of the young child of J. K. Rowling on an Edinburgh street was a breach of the child's 'reasonable expectation of privacy'. Similarly, in *Mosley v News Group Newspapers* [2008] EWHC 1777, the *News of the World* was condemned for publishing a story, photographs and a video of the head of motor racing's Formula 1 engaged in an orgy with five prostitutes. He was a public figure, but his sexual preferences were private and did not relate to his work. The newspaper had alleged that 'F1 Boss has sick Nazi orgy with 5 hookers', which Eady J had thought might make this a matter of public interest and legitimate free expression. Mosley was the son of a well-known Fascist leader and an orgy with a Nazi theme would cast doubt on his fitness to run a public organisation; but the 'Nazi' allegations were untrue. We can see, from these two cases, that the right of privacy does not now depend upon any confidential relationship existing and that the idea of only marriage deserving privacy has been abandoned.

So there does now seem to be a right of privacy, but the granting of this right is highly discretionary and depends upon many factors. We can see that the law has changed. Revelations about the private sexual lives of the famous were allowed in *Woodward v Hutchins* [1971] 1 WLR 760 and *A v B plc and Another* [2003] QB 195, but not in *Mosley v News Group Newspapers* [2008] EWHC 1777. *Mosley* has proved unpopular with those who run newspapers, who claim that it will prevent the legitimate investigation of the private lives of public figures. The media claim that they need to do this in order to show whether these people are fit to hold public office. The cynical might say that the newspapers are just worried about their profits, but there may be something in the argument that free expression requires that newspapers should be able to investigate the rich and powerful, without being intimidated by the threat of costly court actions. The right of privacy is still very limited and only seems to have been developed to deal with the excesses of the tabloid press. Would a right of privacy extend, say, to State intrusions into the lives of less affluent people and of what would that right consist? From the decision in *Wainwright v Home Office* [2004] 2 AC 406, considered earlier, it does not seem that the right extends so far.

Further reading

Bradley, A. and Ewing, K. *Constitutional and Administrative Law*, 14th edn (Longman, 2007), ch 23 and ch 13F.

Barnett, H. *Constitutional and Administrative Law*, 7th edn (Routledge-Cavendish, 2008).

Fenwick, H. *Civil Liberties and Human Rights,* 4th edn (Routledge-Cavendish, 2007), chs 5–7.

Administrative Law: Judicial Review

Introduction

This chapter covers one of the most important growth areas of the law. Some courses have found it impossible to include it within the general constitutional law course and have hived it off into a separate administrative law or public law course. These questions are designed to cover all the aspects likely to be included in a general, rather than a specialised course.

This subject lends itself particularly well to problem questions, and is for that reason popular with examiners seeking to give a more legal slant to what might otherwise be an excessively political subject. Students will need to demonstrate their legal skills in identifying and applying the appropriate case law.

The diagram opposite provides a template for answering problem questions on judicial review. It is most unlikely that any one question will raise all the issues identified, or all the grounds of review. Questions 2, 3 and 4 of this chapter are typical in raising a limited number of issues. But examination questions, unlike seminar questions, do not come with a convenient heading identifying the topic, such as 'questions on natural justice'. So, if you are not sure which issues are being raised, working through the questions on the diagram will help. It will also ensure that you do not miss out on the extra marks that may be available for, e.g. discussing the applicant's locus standi, or identifying the appropriate remedy.

Question 1

The twentieth century saw both the decline of administrative law to virtual extinction, and its revival and development to unprecedented heights.

Discuss. Why has the development of administrative law been so erratic?

Commentary

The basis of the answer to this question will be a description of the way administrative law, particularly judicial review, has developed over the century, illustrated with the appropriate cases. What will make the answer a good one will be the discussion of the reasons for its erratic progress. There are no cut and dried answers on this; the student's answer will be judged on the way the arguments are presented and the evidence marshalled in support.

Answer plan

- Historical prerogative and other remedies
- Initial development of ultra vires and natural justice
- Decline in review during and after the Second World War
- Alternatives proposed
- Revival from 1960s.

Suggested answer

The history of English administrative law can be traced back through many centuries. The prerogative writs of certiorari, prohibition and mandamus were originally developed in the Middle Ages, but first came to prominence with the growth of a more effective administrative system under the Tudors. The seventeenth century sees the first precedents concerning the rules of natural justice (*Baggs Case* (1615) 11 Co Rep 93b) and the doctrine of ultra vires (*Hetley v Boyer* (1614) Cro Jac 336).

It was during the nineteenth century that something approaching a system of administrative law was established, in the wake of the Victorian reforms of central and local government, and official intervention in such areas as health, factory conditions and sanitation. The courts were able to use the old prerogative remedies against the new administrative authorities, and to develop and refine the concepts of natural justice and ultra vires, in cases like *Cooper v Wandsworth Board of Works* (1863) 14 CB (NS) 180. Maitland pointed out in 1888 that half the reported cases in the Queen's Bench Division dealt with aspects of administrative law. New remedies also became available; in *Dyson v Attorney-General* [1911] 1 KB 410, the Court of Appeal confirmed that a declaration could be granted to a person who wished to establish the unlawfulness of administrative action. By the beginning of the twentieth century, it seemed that English law was well on the way to developing a comprehensive and effective system of administrative law.

But during the next 50 years, this promising development was halted; in some respects the law went into reverse. One of the main factors was a conceptual problem about judicial and administrative decisions. Until the nineteenth century reforms, much local administration was conducted through the justices of the peace, and it was natural to describe their power as jurisdiction and their decisions as judicial, whether they were convicting a thief or allocating poor relief. The availability of the prerogative remedies of certiorari and prohibition were also described as being dependent on the decision challenged being judicial. This presented no problems as long as the courts were willing to define decisions as judicial whenever they affected individual rights. But, during the 1920s and 1930s, the courts started to distinguish between judicial and administrative decisions more strictly, confining the definition of judicial decisions to those where Parliament had imposed some kind of judicialised procedure. As a consequence, the rules of natural justice were no longer applied to decisions affecting individual rights where these were classified as administrative: see *R v Metropolitan Police Commissioner ex parte Parker* [1953] 1 WLR 1150.

Over the same period, the courts showed some antipathy to the very idea of administrative law, perhaps under the influence of Dicey, who was critical of the French idea of a special body of rules governing the conduct of the administration, assuming that it would give them too much protection. The term '*droit administratif*' was used almost as a term of abuse! Perhaps, as a further effect of this, academic lawyers paid little heed to the subject, and it was not taught except as a minor part of constitutional law.

What was perhaps most unfortunate in these developments was that the courts abdicated their responsibility for protecting the rights of the individual at the very time when the government's activities put those rights most at risk. A notorious example is the case of *Liversidge v Anderson* [1942] AC 206, where the Secretary of State had the power to detain persons without trial if he had reasonable cause to believe them to be of hostile origin or associations, a power justifiable enough in wartime. But the House of Lords, with the honourable exception of Lord Atkin, held that the reasonableness of the Secretary of State's belief was not reviewable, turning an objective power into a wholly subjective one. A similarly unfortunate ruling was made in *Duncan v Cammel Laird* [1942] AC 624, when the House of Lords held that the Crown had an absolute and unreviewable privilege to withhold documents in litigation, if ministers felt it was in the public interest to do so.

The courts' attitude was not surprising in wartime, but even after the war, the courts remained very reluctant to interfere in the work of the administration in any way. In *Franklin v Minister of Town and Country Planning* [1948] AC 87, the House of Lords refused to apply the rule against bias to an administrative decision taken by a minister, even where Parliament had imposed a quasi-judicial process. In *Smith v East Elloe RDC* [1956] AC 736, the House of Lords accepted as effective a clause excluding judicial review, even where bad faith was alleged. Perhaps the most likely explanation for this lies in the effect of the doctrine of precedent. It will always be difficult to convince a court that the recent precedents should be disregarded and an ancient ruling preferred. A rare example of such a decision was *R v Northumberland Compensation Appeal Tribunal ex parte Shaw* [1952] 1 KB 338, where the Court of Appeal revived the doctrine of error of law on the face of the record after a century of disuse, as a means of controlling the increasing numbers of statutory tribunals.

Overall, anyone surveying the condition of administrative law in the early 1960s would have found a depressing sight. Natural justice was restricted, discretionary power not subject to judicial control, and remedies constrained by ancient rules and obscurities. As a consequence, few applicants considered the risks of litigation to be worthwhile, causing the law to fall yet further into decline. It was generally assumed that the law could not offer a means of controlling the administration, and attention turned to other methods, such as the reform of tribunals and inquiries after the Franks Committee report in 1957, and the introduction of an Ombudsman. Some even advocated the importation of the French system of *droit administratif,* and the establishment of an English *Conseil d'Etat.*

But, to the surprise of many, the English courts showed themselves to be capable of reviving this moribund area of law. In *Ridge v Baldwin* [1964] AC 40, the House of Lords attacked the dichotomy of judicial and administrative decisions, restoring the rule that decisions affecting the rights of subjects were subject to natural justice, even if Parliament was silent on the need for a hearing. This was followed by a stream of cases, extending the right to a fair hearing even into areas that had always been characterised as administrative. Other precedents were reversed. In *Conway v Rimmer* [1968] AC 910, the House of Lords removed the Crown's power to withhold documents in litigation, replacing it with the power of the court to grant public interest immunity. In *Anisminic v Foreign Compensation Commission* [1969] 2 AC 147, the House of Lords found a way of defeating the express exclusion clause that had been held effective in *Smith v East Elloe RDC* (1956), and in so doing extended the courts' powers to review errors of law. In *Padfield v Minister of Agriculture* [1968] AC 997, the House of Lords rejected the idea of the unfettered and unreviewable administrative discretion.

Why did the courts change the law so radically and so unexpectedly?

One important factor was certainly a change in judicial personnel, with judges used to Diceyan orthodoxy being replaced by others with a less restricted outlook. One of the most influential was Lord Reid, who came to the House of Lords from Scotland, where administrative law had never fallen to such a low ebb. Lord Denning also played a significant part, as he did in so many branches of the law. Some credit is also due to academic lawyers, such as S. A. de Smith and Sir William Wade, whose publications and research into administrative law established it as an important academic subject. It is possible that the courts may have felt that, if the law was not reformed, they would lose out to other methods of redress, such as the Parliamentary Commissioner for Administration, who was introduced in 1967. Such statutory reforms also demonstrated that governments were willing to contemplate improved methods of redress, and the courts would not be risking political controversy if they joined in.

Once the process of revival began, there was no shortage of litigants seeking redress for what would once have been inescapable injustices. Within a few years, a new body of precedents had been built up, and cases decided between 1910 and 1960 are almost always viewed with suspicion. To consolidate this new law, procedural reforms were introduced on the advice of the Law Commission: see the Supreme Court Act 1981, s. 31.

The overall effect has been a huge expansion in the role of judicial review, which now shares with criminal justice the highest profile and the most media attention. From October 2000, its importance was recognised by the formal establishment of the Administrative Court as a specialised section of the Queen's Bench Division. Few other branches of the law can show such dramatic changes. It is to be hoped that the courts will maintain their role of protecting individual rights against abuse at the hands of the administration, as they have during the last 40 years.

Question 2

Under the (imaginary) Radiation Protection Act 1993, any person wishing to use radioactive materials must obtain a licence from the Radiation Protection Agency (RPA). On receipt of an application, the RPA must consult any organisation that it considers to be representative of those affected, and must publish notice of the application in the national and local press, and in any other way it considers desirable. The RPA must allow three months for the submission of comments and objections, which should include the name and address of the sender. After considering all representations submitted to it, and giving the applicant a hearing, the RPA may grant or refuse a licence.

The Sulphurous Chemical plc applied for a licence to use radioactive materials in its factory in Coketown. The RPA published notice of the application in three national and two local newspapers, and put up a small notice in the Coketown public library. The RPA wrote to the Coketown Borough Council and the Cokeshire County Council asking for comments. It received a reply only from the Coketown Borough Council. The RPA made no attempt to consult the National Union of Chemical Workers, which represented the majority of Sulphurous Chemical's employees.

The RPA received many objections, including several from an unknown and unidentified group calling itself the Green Anti-Nuclear Faction; the RPA threw these away. A petition signed by 25,000 inhabitants of Coketown was presented the day after the three month submission period had expired, but the RPA refused to accept it.

After completing its consideration and giving Sulphurous Chemical a hearing, the RPA granted the licence.

Consider the validity of the licence.

Commentary

This question is concerned with judicial review, primarily though not exclusively with procedural ultra vires. The student will need to identify and explain the general principle involved, the distinction between mandatory and directory procedural requirements. It is then simplest for the student to work through the problem point by point. Although some issues raised in this type of question may bear a sufficient resemblance to decided cases to be straightforward, others will require the student to argue by analogy. Where issues are debatable, the student will be assessed on the quality of the argument, whichever conclusion is reached. Refer back to the diagram on p. 177 for advice.

Answer plan

- Distinguish mandatory and directory conditions
- Notice of application
- Consulting representative organisations
- Challenge by judicial review
- Locus standi.

Suggested answer

The validity of this licence can be challenged by judicial review, because, as laid down in *O'Reilly v Mackman* [1983] 2 AC 237, it concerns the activities of a public body in matters relating to public law. The grounds of challenge mostly concern procedural defects in the way the RPA dealt with the application.

In dealing with procedural defects, the courts have to balance the need to ensure that statutory procedural safeguards are carefully observed against the risk that trivial procedural defects are used as a pretext by objectors seeking to halt or delay an unpopular scheme. To do this the courts have generally drawn a distinction between mandatory and directory procedural requirements. A mandatory requirement is one that is regarded as so essential that failure to observe it justifies treating the decision reached as invalid. A directory require-ment is one whose non-observance will not invalidate the decision. In *London & Clydeside Estates v Aberdeen District Council* [1980] 1 WLR 182, Lord Hailsham LC suggested that these two categories should not be regarded as the only two alternatives, but as the extremes of a range of possibilities. An example of a more subtle approach can be found in *Coney v Choyce* [1975] 1 WLR 422, where various detailed publication requirements were only partially complied with. The court held that it was mandatory that there be substantial compli-ance with the requirement of publication, but that the exact details were merely directory.

It is possible for statute to specify the precise consequences of failure to comply with procedural requirements, but in practice this rarely occurs. It is therefore left to the courts to decide retrospectively whether the failure has invalidated the decision. This area of the law is criticised as uncertain, but some guidance may be obtained from decided cases.

The RPA is required by the Act to publish notice of the application 'in the national and local press'. They published it in three national and two local newspapers. In *Bradbury v Enfield London Borough Council* [1967] 1 WLR 1311, the court held that giving notice was to be construed as a mandatory requirement as it was essential for the protection of the rights of the individual citizen. But in that case there was a complete failure to give notice. In *Coney v Choyce* substantial compliance was held to be sufficient. It could be argued here that there has been substantial compliance. The size of the petition is evidence that there was widespread awareness of the application. In *Coney v Choyce* it was considered material that all those affected had become aware of the proposal in spite of the defects in the publication. The RPA is given a discretion to publicise the application 'in any other way it considers desirable'. It could be argued that one small notice in the library is hardly sufficient. But any challenge would have to be on the ground of 'Wednesbury' unreasonableness: see *Associated Provincial Picture Houses v Wednesbury Corporation* [1948] 1 KB 223. It is unlikely that the courts would consider this to be beyond the limits of a reasonable exercise of discretion.

The RPA is required to consult 'organisations that it considers to be representative of those affected'. Consultation is generally held to be a mandatory requirement, as it is a means of protecting the interests of those affected: see *R v Secretary of State for the Environment ex parte Association of Metropolitan Authorities* [1986] 1 WLR 1. The consultation of the Coketown Borough Council seems to have been satisfactory. But in *Agricultural Training Board v Aylesbury Mushrooms Ltd* [1972] 1 WLR 190, sending a letter that went astray, and failing to make further enquiries was held not to amount to adequate consultation. If the RPA has made no attempt to follow up its letter to the Cokeshire County Council and check that it indeed has no comment to make, it will be considered to have broken a mandatory requirement. As this is a licence application to use radioactive materials, in fairness the RPA should disclose the scientific information, on which their decision is based, to the groups consulted: *R v Health Secretary ex parte US Tobacco International Inc* [1992] QB 353 and *R (Eisai) v National Institute for Health and Clinical Excellence* [2008] EWCA Civ 438.

The RPA's failure to consult the National Union of Chemical Workers could be challenged as an unreasonable use of discretion, as in *Secretary of State for Education v Metropolitan Borough of Tameside* [1977] AC 1014; no reasonable authority could have failed to consider the Union representative of those affected.

The RPA is required to consider 'all representations submitted to it', but it throws away the objections from the Green Anti-Nuclear Faction. The only possible justification for this is the provision in the Act that objections should include the name and address of the sender. This requirement could be classed as mandatory if it is essential for the conduct of the administration. In *Chapman v Earl* [1968] 1 WLR 1315, the failure of a tenant to indicate the proposed rent in an application to a rent tribunal was held to be a breach of a mandatory requirement. However, requirements imposed merely for the convenience of the administration are likely to be classified as directory only. In *Jackson Developments v Hall* [1951] 2 KB 488, the requirement that the tenant supply the landlord's name to a rent tribunal was held to be directory. In this problem, the objectors' failure to identify themselves hardly seems of sufficient importance to be treated as breach of a mandatory requirement. Their objections should therefore have been considered.

The petition is rejected because it is submitted one day late. Time limits will be held to be mandatory where they are essential in establishing legal rights and obligations. In *Howard v Secretary of State for the Environment* [1975] QB 235, the statutory time limit of 42 days for appealing against an enforcement notice was held to be mandatory, because it determined the legal powers of the local authority. But if no such compelling reasons exist, time limits will be treated as directory. In *James v Minister of Housing and Local Government* [1966] 1 WLR 135, a local authority was held to be entitled to make a planning decision after three months, though regulations imposed a limit of two months. In this problem, as the RPA will be spending some time considering the application, there seems no reason to treat the time limit for receipt of representations as mandatory.

An application for judicial review to challenge the validity of the licence under the Supreme Court Act 1981, s. 31 and Part 54 of the Civil Procedure Rules could be made by any person with locus standi, that is, with a sufficient interest in the matter. Cokeshire County Council and the National Union of Chemical Workers would clearly have a sufficient interest, as would members of the Green Anti-Nuclear Faction, if willing to identify themselves. In *R v Secretary of State for the Environment ex parte Greenpeace* [1994] 4 All ER 352, Greenpeace was held to have locus standi, as a pressure group with local members, to challenge the licensing of the THORP nuclear plant. It could further be argued that any of the inhabitants of Coketown who had signed the petition would have locus standi. In *R v Inland Revenue Commissioners ex parte National Federation of Self-Employed & Small Businesses* [1982] AC 617, Lord Diplock referred to the desirability of 'a single public-minded taxpayer' being able to challenge the validity of unlawful administrative action.

The most appropriate remedies in this case would be a quashing order to quash the licence, or a declaration that it was invalid. It would, however, be open to Sulphurous Chemical plc to make a further application for a licence.

Question 3

Under the (imaginary) Social Services Act 2000, all residential homes for the elderly must be licensed by the local authority. Unsatisfactory homes will be refused a licence and closed down, but there is a right to appeal against the refusal of a licence to an Appeal Tribunal.

Mrs Danvers applied to the Cokeshire County Council for a licence for the Manderley Home. The application was referred to the Social Services Committee, which instructed Rebecca, one of its employees, to investigate the suitability of the Home. Rebecca visited the Home, posing as someone looking for accommodation for an elderly relative. After completing her researches, Rebecca produced a report recommending that a licence be refused, because the kitchens and bathrooms were not cleaned properly and few of the staff had the appropriate professional qualifications.

The Committee considered the report and then invited Mrs Danvers to a meeting to discuss her application. She came to the meeting accompanied by her husband, a solicitor, but he was asked to wait outside. At the meeting, she was handed a copy of Rebecca's report and asked to comment on it. She asked for an adjournment so she could consult her husband, but the Committee refused. She denied the allegations in the report and invited the members of the Committee to visit the Home and talk to the residents. The Committee declined to do so and, after deliberating in private, refused the licence.

Mrs Danvers appealed to the Tribunal, which gave her a hearing, but refused to hear evidence from the staff of the Home or allow her to cross-examine Rebecca, who gave evidence in person. The Tribunal confirmed the original decision. Mrs Danvers has now discovered that the wife of the Chair of the Committee is a member of the board of a charity that campaigns for better care for the elderly.

Advise Mrs Danvers.

Commentary

This problem raises a number of issues relating to judicial review, principally concerning natural justice. Such a problem may appear at first sight rather long and daunting, but if you have a reasonable understanding of the issues it is actually quite straightforward. It is best tackled as advised earlier by working systematically through the facts of the problem, picking up each issue as it arises, explaining the law on that point, citing the relevant authority and then applying the law to the problem. You may, if you wish, introduce your answer by a few general remarks on the topic, though this answer does not. What you should not do is to attempt to answer this, or any other problem, by writing an essay. It is the ability of the student to select from the material they have learnt just those points that are relevant that marks out the competent student.

Answer plan

- Challenge by judicial review
- Has she a right to a fair hearing
- Notice of charges

- Legal representation
- Evidence
- Real possibility of bias.

Suggested answer

As Mrs Danvers has exhausted the statutory procedure, she will have to use judicial review if she wishes to challenge the refusal of a licence. Both the Council Committee and Tribunal are clearly public bodies and her grounds of challenge derive from public law, making judicial review the appropriate procedure to use. She must apply to the Administrative Court *ex parte* for permission to make an application for judicial review promptly and in any event within three months of the Tribunal's decision. As the person directly affected by the decision she has locus standi.

It appears that Mrs Danvers will have grounds for arguing that there has been a breach of the rules of natural justice, but she must first establish that she was entitled to a fair hearing. In *Ridge v Baldwin* [1964] AC 40 it was held that natural justice applied whenever a decision affected the rights of the individual, and it was made clear in *Re HK* [1967] 2 QB 617 that this applied even if the decision was of an administrative nature. By imposing a requirement that a licence must be obtained for an activity that could previously have been carried on without restriction, the law is affecting individual rights and so a fair hearing must be given. This was applied in *R v Gaming Board ex parte Benaim* [1970] 2 QB 417 to the grant of gaming licences and is clearly applicable here.

At what stage in the procedure is Mrs Danvers entitled to be heard? There is no general right to be heard during preliminary investigative or preparatory processes. In *Pearlberg v Varty* [1972] 1 WLR 534, it was held that there was no right to a hearing by the Inland Revenue as they prepared a taxpayer's assessment; he would be heard at the proper time before the relevant tribunal. It is therefore acceptable for Cokeshire County Council to conduct a covert investigation. Nor is there an objection to the matter being referred to a committee, as the Local Government Act 1972 specifically authorises this form of delegation. But, before any decision is made about the licence, Mrs Danvers must be given an opportunity to state her case. For this it is necessary that she be informed of the matters that are causing concern, otherwise she cannot offer an effective defence. In *Fairmount Investments v Secretary of State for the Environment* [1976] 1 WLR 1255, a compulsory purchase decision was held to be invalid because the inspector had based his decision on defects in the building that he had noticed but had not mentioned to the parties. Here Mrs Danvers is not shown Rebecca's report in advance or even informed of its contents. The Committee could argue that she was shown the report at the hearing, but this did not allow her any time to prepare a defence. In *R v Thames Magistrates' Court ex parte Polemis* [1974] 1 WLR 1371, it was held that it was a breach of the rules of natural justice to serve a summons on a defendant in the morning and try him that afternoon as he had no chance to prepare a defence. It therefore appears that there has been a breach of the rules of natural justice.

Mrs Danvers was refused permission to be accompanied by or to consult her husband, who was presumably also her legal adviser. It appears, from *R v Maze Prison Visitors ex parte Hone* [1988] AC 379, that there is no absolute right to legal or other representation. But in *R v Home Secretary ex parte Tarrant* [1985] QB 251, the court held that an adjudicatory body must consider in each case whether to permit legal representation, and that an unreasonable refusal could invalidate the proceedings. Mrs Danvers would find it difficult to argue that she should have been represented at the hearing, but will certainly be able to show that the refusal to adjourn the hearing to allow her to read the report and seek advice was a breach of natural justice.

The Committee is obliged to hear all relevant evidence: see *R v Hull Prison Visitors ex parte St Germain (No. 2)* [1979] 1 WLR 1401. It could be argued that they should have visited the Home and spoken to the residents, but in cases such as *Osgood v Nelson* (1872) LR HL 636, it has been held to be acceptable for a subordinate to collect evidence for submission to those who decide, as was done here.

The breach of natural justice committed by the Committee will render its decision invalid, and it can be argued that as a matter of logic no subsequent procedures can cure that initial invalidity. But the courts have accepted that where an appeal takes the form of a full rehearing, it can make up for any defects in the initial process: see *Calvin v Carr* [1980] AC 574 and *Lloyd v McMahon* [1987] 1 AC 625. This is however dependant on the appeal itself being conducted fairly, which is open to question in Mrs Danvers' case.

The Tribunal refused to hear evidence from the staff of the Home. This seems to be a clear breach of the obligation to hear all relevant evidence discussed above, as the qualifications of the staff seem to be one of the principal issues of concern. The refusal to allow Mrs Danvers to cross-examine Rebecca is more problematical. In *Bushell v Secretary of State for the Environment* [1981] AC 75, the House of Lords held that, at a public inquiry into the route of a proposed motorway, the inspector was entitled to refuse to allow witnesses to be cross-examined, as this would lead to excessive judicialisation of what was basically an administrative decision. In this problem, however, the Tribunal can properly be described as a fully judicial body and it might be considered that as Rebecca gave her evidence in person, cross-examination should have been allowed.

The final substantive issue is the allegation that one member of the Tribunal was biased. It is clear that the presence of one biased person is enough to invalidate a decision. A breach of natural justice could involve several forms of bias, which are conveniently subdivided into 'actual bias' and 'apparent bias' according to the House of Lords in *R v Abdroikov* [2008] 1 All ER 315. Actual bias leads to automatic disqualification and includes: a financial interest in the decision, as in *Dimes v Grand Junction Canal Co* (1852) 3 HLC 759; the decision makers have already decided the matter before the hearing, as in *Eszias v North Glamorgan NHS Trust* [2007] 4 All ER 940; or direct association with a party to the case, as in *Ex parte Pinochet* [1999] 1 All ER 577. The last two seem the more likely on the facts here, but neither seems strong enough to invalidate the decision of the Tribunal. For other, more indirect, forms of 'apparent bias', the courts have formulated various tests, such as looking for a 'real likelihood' or 'reasonable suspicion' of bias. In *Porter v Magill* [2001] UKHL 67, [2002] 1 All ER 465, the House of Lords formulated a general test for bias as follows:

> whether the fair-minded and informed observer, having considered the facts, would conclude that there was a real possibility that the Tribunal was biased.

This was confirmed as the correct approach in the more recent House of Lords case of *R v Abdroikov* [2008] 1 All ER 315.

Can it be argued that there is such a real possibility here? It is doubtful; the Tribunal's very existence is in order to improve the care of the elderly and there is nothing in the background of the Chair of the Tribunal to indicate any connection with or prejudice against Mrs Danvers.

If Mrs Danvers is successful in establishing grounds for judicial review, as seems likely, the most appropriate remedy would be a quashing order to quash the decisions of the Committee and Tribunal, though a declaration would also be a possibility. She could in addition ask for a mandatory order to compel them to reconsider her application. The award of remedies is at the discretion of the court, but there seems no reason why the court should decline to give redress. However, the court's decision will not necessarily mean that Mrs Danvers will obtain the licence she seeks. That decision will be made by the Committee and Tribunal and will be based, as it should be, on the suitability of the Home she runs.

Question 4

As a result of local elections, the Radical Party has taken control of the Coketown District Council. It has implemented the following changes and wishes to know whether there could be any legal challenge to them. It also wishes to know who could make such a challenge and by what legal process.

(a) To revoke, with immediate effect, the licences given to Able (A), Baker (B) and Charlie (C) to sell ice creams from their vans in council owned parks.

(b) To refuse to give any more discretionary grants for the insulation of homes.

(c) To save money by closing the three old people's homes that it runs and instead paying privately-run old people's homes to house these old people.

(d) To increase the pay of its lowest paid workers to 20% more than the statutory minimum wage.

(e) To pay a famous conceptual artist £100,000 to drape the Town Hall in multi-coloured fabric.

Commentary

This question raises a variety of issues relating to judicial review and must be tackled by identifying the material relevant to each part of the problem. It will be appropriate to introduce the answer by dealing with those issues that are clearly common to all parts of the question. But there is no need to write an essay on judicial review before tackling the problems and little credit will be given for doing so. The good student will look separately at each part of the problem, identify one or two relevant grounds and support them with references to cases. Putting in far-fetched suggestions, such as challenging a perfectly sensible decision on the grounds of irrationality, is likely to make the examiner think you do not really understand the law. Note also that the question specifically asks about locus standi and process, and it will be appropriate as part of this to suggest which remedy or remedies should be sought.

Answer plan

- Public body, public law, judicial review
- Breach of natural justice
- Proportionality
- Fettering discretion
- Legitimate expectation
- Misuse of discretion
- Unreasonableness.

Suggested answer

Because the Council is a public body, its decisions can be challenged by way of judicial review. Any person who has a sufficient interest will be able to bring a case on the grounds characterised by Lord Diplock as illegality, irrationality and procedural impropriety. Such a person must apply to the Administrative Court for permission to make an application for judicial review within the three-month time limit. If permission is granted, the case will proceed to a full hearing.

(a) No information is given about the grounds on which the Council has acted, but it is clear from the facts given that the way the decision was made is open to challenge. A, B and C, as licence holders, have rights and under the general principle laid down in *Ridge v Baldwin* [1964] AC 40, decisions affecting the rights of individuals must be made in accordance with the rules of natural justice. Indeed it was specifically held in *R v Wear Valley DC ex parte Binks* [1985] 2 All ER 699 that contractual as well as statutory licences were protected. It therefore appears that if the revocation of the licences was not preceded by an opportunity for A, B and C to state their cases, it can be challenged. It has been held, however, that in situations of extreme urgency a decision can be made before any hearing is given. In *R v Secretary of State for Transport ex parte Pegasus* [1989] 2 All ER 481, it was held that an air charter company's licence could be revoked with immediate effect because of fears over public safety. If the Council's decision in this problem was provoked by, for example, fears that the ice cream posed a threat to public health, there would be no breach of natural justice, provided a proper hearing was given at a later stage. Nowadays, the court might also consider the issue of proportionality, when a person's livelihood is at stake. 'Proportionality' has been defined by Bradley and Ewing's *Constitutional and Administrative Law*, 14th edn (2007) at p. 737:

> In outline, if action to achieve a lawful objective is taken in a situation where it will restrict a fundamental right, the effect on the right must not be disproportionate to the public purpose sought to be achieved.

So Coketown DC would have to prove that there really was a public health problem and that there was no other way of dealing with it, short of shutting down the businesses of A, B and C. In an early case, *R v Barnsley MBC ex parte Hook* [1976] 1 WLR 1052, Lord Denning MR quashed the council's decision to revoke the licence of a market trader, who had urinated in the street. The punishment was out of all proportion to the crime. A, B and C clearly have locus standi as the persons directly affected by the decision and are likely to seek either a quashing order to quash the Council's decision or a declaration that it is invalid.

(b) The Council appears to have a discretion to make these grants. It is entitled to adopt general policies to guide it in allocating such grants, but that does not permit it to adopt a rule and refuse to depart from it. In *R v London County Council ex parte Corrie* [1918] 1 KB 68, the Council was held to have acted ultra vires in adopting a rule against the sale of pamphlets in parks and refusing even to consider making an exception to it. In *A-G ex rel Tilley v Wandsworth LBC* [1981] 1 WLR 854, the court declared invalid a council's decision never to use a statutory power to rehouse homeless families with children.

There is, however, nothing unlawful in the adoption of a policy, provided that consideration is given to each individual case. In *British Oxygen v Board of Trade* [1971] AC 610, a decision to refuse the applicant an investment grant, in accordance with a stated policy, was held to be valid, because consideration had been given to the individual application. The easiest way to demonstrate that individual cases are considered is to offer applicants an opportunity to state their case either orally or in writing. The Council would therefore be well advised to adopt a procedure that shows its willingness to consider applications; it can then lawfully reject any applications that it does not feel justify a departure from its policy.

If the Council does not do so, its decision could be challenged by anyone who has applied for a grant and been rejected. Such an applicant could ask for a declaration that the Council was acting unlawfully or a mandatory order to compel them to consider the application again. It will remain within the Council's discretion, however, whether any particular grant is made or not.

(c) This situation seems to resemble *R v North Devon Health Authority ex parte Coughlan* [2001] QB 213. In 1993, North Devon moved Coughlan and other geriatric patients into a new home and assured them that this could be their home for life. However, in 1998, North Devon decided to close the home and move the residents into local authority care. The court held that North Devon could not go back on its promise to the residents as they now had a 'legitimate expectation' that they could stay and it would be an abuse of power to break the promise. This case seems to do justice, but as a precedent it has caused problems for public authorities, who often need to change their policies, particularly if the financial situation changes. *R (Bibi) v Newham Borough Council* [2002] 1 WLR 237 is a comparable case, where Newham had told some refugees that it would place them in permanent, secure accommodation within 18 months. The Council had thought that they were legally obliged to do this, but when a House of Lords decision held that this was not so, Newham continued just to provide temporary accommodation. The refugees claimed that they had been promised permanent accommodation and the court agreed that the Council had created a legitimate expectation. The court did not, however, order the Council to provide permanent accommodation, because that would be a court assuming the power of the executive. Instead, the problem would be referred back to the Council for it to determine how best to keep their promise of permanent, secure accommodation. In contrast, our facts do not reveal that Coketown DC have made any specific promises to any of the residents of the old people's homes. This would seem to be an important element of legitimate expectation, as it was held in *R (Niazi) v Secretary of State for the Home Department* [2008] EWCA Civ 755 that there either has to be a distinct promise to a specific person or group that an existing policy would be maintained, or that the policy affected a specific person or group and it was reasonable for that person or group to expect that policy to continue. Coketown have made no promises that the old people's homes would remain open, so if there was a challenge to the closure by one or more of the residents, it is likely that it would fail.

(d) The Council will have a discretion over the rates of pay it adopts and this discretion must be exercised on the basis of relevant considerations and to achieve proper purposes. In examining this problem, it is clear that the Council must take into account its fiduciary duty to its rate and tax payers, as laid down in *Roberts v Hopwood* [1925] AC 578 and *Bromley LBC v Greater London Council* [1982] 1 AC 768. In *Roberts v Hopwood* excessively generous wages were found to breach that principle. The radical Poplar Borough Council had ignored such relevant considerations as the cost of living and the rates of pay agreed by collective bargaining with the trade unions. If it could be shown here that the Council had made an arbitrary decision to increase the wages, its decision might be open to challenge. If, on the other hand, the increase was part of a negotiated wage settlement, or a response to an acute shortage of workers, no objection could be made.

This decision could be challenged by a council tax payer by way of judicial review. The courts have generally accepted the locus standi of those who pay local taxes to challenge councils' activities: see *Barrs v Bethell* [1982] Ch 294. The most appropriate remedy would be a declaration.

(e) This final decision could be challenged on two grounds. First, as in the previous problem, it could be said to be a breach of the Council's fiduciary duty to its tax payers. Secondly, it could be suggested that it is unreasonable or irrational, within the strict test laid down by Lord Greene in *Associated Provincial Picture Houses v Wednesbury Corporation* [1948] 1 KB 223: 'something so absurd that no sensible person could ever dream that it lay within the powers of the authority'. It could well be argued that this scheme is an absurd extravagance, though it is possible to envisage circumstances that justify it. Many local authorities, for example, spent considerable sums on celebrating the millennium, without legal objection. There are a number of older cases that have upheld expenditure on public celebrations as lawful. *Attorney-General v Corporation of Blackburn* (1887) 57 LT 385 is one such case, where £700 was spent on lighting the streets, fireworks and music to celebrate the Jubilee of Queen Victoria. It was held reasonable to enhance the life of Blackburn with this celebration. Challenges based on pure unreasonableness are rarely successful, because the test is so strong, but the challenge might be successful in this case, as a lot of money has been spent and there seems to be no particular public event being celebrated.

Any council tax payer would have locus standi to challenge this decision. There are several possible remedies; a quashing order to quash the decision; a declaration that it would be unlawful; or an injunction to stop the scheme going ahead.

Question 5

The divorce between public and private law, proclaimed by Lord Diplock in *O'Reilly v Mackman* [1983] 2 AC 237, has not been a happy addition to English administrative law. It has caused problems for litigants, without aiding the development of a coherent system of judicial review. Discuss.

Commentary

This question deals with the complex issue of the division between public law and private law procedures. The student will need to explain the background to this development, and then examine *O'Reilly v Mackman* itself in some detail. The ensuing problems and how the courts have dealt with them should then be discussed. A good answer might make some reference to other legal traditions and should certainly offer suggestions as to whether the law should be reformed and, if so, how.

Answer plan

- After reform of remedies, abuse of process to use private law remedies
- If judicial review is appropriate, it must be used
- What is a public body
- What is a matter of public law
- How has the distinction developed?

Suggested answer

In the civil law tradition, the distinction between public and private law is the primary and fundamental classification of law. It is traceable back to the jurist Ulpian, writing in AD200, and is among the first rules mentioned in Justinian's *Institutes*; to this day it forms one of the first lessons for the student of civil law. But in English law, which developed incrementally and without a theoretical framework, the distinction between public and private law was almost unknown. Principles such as ultra vires and natural justice were applied indifferently to public and private bodies and, with the exception of the rules limiting the liability of the Crown, the same laws of tort, contract and property applied to public and private bodies. Indeed, Dicey's analysis of the rule of law depended heavily on the absence of any division. He praised the English use of private law as a means of controlling the activities of the government, and compared it favourably with the strictly separated French system of *droit administratif*.

The only area where the distinction between public and private law was important was in relation to remedies. The prerogative remedies of certiorari, prohibition and mandamus were available only against public bodies, defined by Atkin LJ in *R v Electricity Commissioners* [1924] 1 KB 171 at 205 as 'any body of persons having legal authority to determine questions affecting the rights of subjects'. But the private law remedies of injunction, declaration and damages were equally available against public and private bodies, with the exception of the immunity of the Crown from injunctions, preserved by the Crown Proceedings Act 1947, s. 21(1)(a). Litigants against public bodies therefore had a choice of remedies, but unfortunately could not combine remedies from the two groups in the same proceedings, until the introduction of the application for judicial review in 1978.

This new procedure adopted many features from the prerogative remedies, such as the need to obtain leave to make an application, and the short time limit, now set at three months. All applications for certiorari, mandamus and prohibition had to use this new procedure. Applications for injunction, declaration and damages could also use it where the case concerned matters for which the prerogative remedies were available and appropriate. In effect, if an injunction or declaration was sought against a public body, on grounds arising from public law, the new judicial review procedure was available. But the new rules did not use any conceptual terms such as 'public law'. If there was any legal principle underlying the changes, it was not openly expressed.

What was left uncertain was the boundary between those claims for injunction and declaration where judicial review procedure should be used and those where the normal High Court procedure was still applicable. Did it matter which procedure was used? The Law Commission had specifically addressed this issue and had recommended that the new procedure should not be exclusive. But when the issue came before the House of Lords, a stricter rule was adopted.

O'Reilly v Mackman [1983] 2 AC 237 concerned various prisoners who wished to challenge decisions taken by prison Boards of Visitors on grounds of breach of the rules of natural justice. Judicial review would clearly have been the appropriate procedure to have used, but instead they started actions by writ in the High Court for declarations, the time limit for judicial review having long since expired. The defendants successfully claimed that the actions should be struck out as an abuse of process. Lord Diplock's justification for this decision was as follows. In the days before the reform of remedies, it was justifiable for applicants to use ordinary High Court procedure rather than the prerogative orders, because of such procedural defects as the absence of discovery and the virtual impossibility of cross-examination of witnesses. But these procedures were now available under the reformed application for judicial review. On the other side, judicial review contained safeguards against the 'groundless, unmeritorious or tardy harassment' of public authorities and applicants should not be allowed to evade these. It was therefore generally contrary to public policy and an abuse of process, for an applicant to begin an action by writ that should have been brought by judicial review. If the case concerned a public body and an infringement of public law rights, judicial review must normally be used, though Lord Diplock conceded that there might be exceptions.

It therefore became essential for the first time for an applicant to identify whether the case was suitable for judicial review or action by writ. This presented two difficulties. First, judicial review is only available against public bodies, not private bodies; they do not have 'legal authority' merely rights and duties under contract. Trade unions, private employers and sporting bodies have all been held not to be subject to judicial review, though it has taken substantial litigation to establish this in some cases: see *R v Chief Rabbi ex parte Wachman* [1992] 1 WLR 1036 and *R v Jockey Club ex parte Massingberd-Mundy* [1993] 2 All ER 207. But problems arise because of the lack of any conceptual distinction between public and private bodies embodied in English law. The court found it very difficult to decide, in *Scott v National Trust* [1998] 2 All ER 705, whether the National Trust, a charity created and given a privileged status by Parliament, was a public or private body, but came down in favour of it being a public body because it was a charity of great importance and its purposes were of high public importance. Nevertheless, judicial review was denied, because there was a specific statutory procedure for monitoring charities under the Charities Act 1993. The issue of public/private was most fully addressed in *R v Panel on Takeovers and Mergers ex parte Datafin* [1987] QB 815, and the result was pragmatic rather than theoretically based. The Panel, one of the self-regulatory bodies of the City of London's financial markets, was held to be subject to judicial review, in spite of having no legal authority or even existence! The court pointed out that it was performing a function that, if it did not perform, would have had to be performed by a public body set up for the purpose. If the Panel were held not to be subject to judicial review, its decisions could be arbitrary or unfair and no redress would be available. Subsequent decisions on bodies such as the Advertising Standards Authority, LAUTRO, and university visitors have confirmed the impression that the courts define a body as public in order to subject it to judicial review, rather than subjecting it to judicial review because it is public. In the absence of a specific precedent, it is difficult to tell whether a body without a clearly defined status will be treated as public or private.

The second problem is identifying which issues are regarded as public rather than private law, again in the absence of a theoretical framework. In *O'Reilly v Mackman* itself the case was clear; the prisoners' complaint was of breach of the rules of natural justice by a statutory tribunal to which they were subjected by statute, public law in all respects. On the other hand, the rights of public employees in their work derive ultimately from the private law of contract, so judicial review is not appropriate: see *R v East Berkshire Health Authority ex parte Walsh* [1985] QB 152. But many cases can be characterised as either public or private depending on the perspective the parties choose to adopt. The GCHQ case, *Council of Civil Service Unions v Minister for the Civil Service* [1985] AC 374, was brought as a public law case, by judicial review; in this perspective it concerned a breach of the rules of natural justice by the government in the exercise of a discretionary power. But it could have been treated as a private law matter relating to the contractual right of government employees to belong to a trade union. Conversely, in *Gillick v West Norfolk Area Health Authority* [1986] AC 112, the plaintiff brought a private law action complaining that the advice given to doctors infringed her rights as a mother, but the case could have been defined more easily as a public law challenge to the legal validity of the advice.

Particular problems arise where liability in tort or contract is alleged to arise as a consequence of the validity or invalidity on public law grounds of some administrative decision. In *Cocks v Thanet DC* [1983] 2 AC 286, a case decided at the same time as *O'Reilly v Mackman*, the House of Lords attempted to split up a claim for damages for failure to rehouse a homeless family. If the claim was that the decision that they were not eligible for rehousing was invalid, that was a matter of public law; if it was a claim that the council, having decided they were eligible, had failed to rehouse them, that was a matter of private law. This makes choosing the right procedure very difficult.

The difficulties of attempting to draw the distinctions that the decision in *O'Reilly v Mackman* rendered necessary soon led the courts to develop the possibility of exceptions to the rule. In *Davy v Spelthorne Borough Council* [1984] AC 262, the plaintiff was allowed to proceed with a private law action for damages, even though it depended on establishing the invalidity of a council decision. In *Wandsworth LBC v Winder* [1985] AC 461, the defendant was allowed to resist an eviction order by arguing that a rent demand was ultra vires and void. It becomes clear that, provided the ultimate form of the action is suitable for an action begun by writ, the involvement of public law issues does not matter. In *Roy v Kensington Family Practitioner Committee* [1992] 1 AC 624, the plaintiff was allowed to bring a private law action based on the claim that the decision to deprive him of certain payments was invalid and this was followed in *Trustees of Denis Rye Pension Fund v Sheffield City Council* [1998] 1 WLR 840.

A particular problem concerns the relationship between judicial review and the criminal law. It had long been accepted that the invalidity of a by-law could be subject to collateral challenge by being raised as a defence to a prosecution. But it was not clear whether this was affected by the decision in *O'Reilly v Mackman*. In some cases it was suggested that whether collateral challenge was allowed depended on the particular ground of invalidity, some grounds only being challengeable by judicial review. However, in *Boddington v British Transport Police* [1998] 2 WLR 639, the House of Lords restored the rule that any ground of invalidity could be pleaded as a defence to a criminal charge of breaking a by-law.

As the law has developed, it appears that the courts are unwilling to reject any claim on the basis that the plaintiff has chosen the wrong procedure, unless the procedure chosen is clearly inappropriate. In *Mercury Communications v Director-General of Telecommunications* [1996] 1 All ER 575, the House of Lords rejected the assertion that a challenge to the validity of the defendant's ruling in a dispute between Mercury and British Telecom could only be sought by judicial review. The court stated that, as the limits of public and private law were not worked out, the procedural rules should be applied flexibly. In *British Steel plc v Customs and Excise* [1997] 2 All ER 366, the plaintiffs were allowed to claim repayment of taxes by a private law action in restitution. In 1998, the introduction of the Woolf reforms to civil procedure rules created the opportunity for some of the problems caused by *O'Reilly v Mackman* to be reduced. In *Clark v University of Lincolnshire and Humberside* [2000] 1 WLR 1988, Lord Woolf pointed out that under the new rules the differences between public and private procedure were much reduced. The judge's powers of case management ensure that even in private law procedure a case can be stopped, so that the courts could and should be flexible about allowing cases to proceed by either procedure, unless it was clearly an abuse of process. A further effect of the new rules was that at last it became possible for a case wrongly begun by private law procedure to be transferred into the judicial review system; transfer the other way had always been possible.

So what remains of the ruling in *O'Reilly v Mackman*? It is still unclear, sometimes, whether applying for judicial review or suing in contract or tort is the most appropriate procedure. Lloyd's of London, who deal in insurance, could not be judicially reviewed in *R (Julian West) v Lloyd's of London* [2004] 3 All ER 251, because it performed no public function. West had contracts with Lloyd's and should pursue contractual remedies. In contrast, a pupil attending a private, fee-paying school, could judicially review that school when expelled, because their place at the school was paid for by government funds: *R v Governors of Haberdashers' Aske's Hatcham College Trust ex parte J* (1994) Times, 19 October. But litigants who choose one of two possible and appropriate procedures are unlikely now to have their claim rejected.

The problems thrown up by the decision in *O'Reilly v Mackman* can all be traced back to the absence of any conceptual distinction between public and private law in the English legal tradition. It has proved almost as difficult to incorporate the distinction into English law as it would be to incorporate the distinction between common law and equity into a civil law system.

The decision in *O'Reilly v Mackman* can now been seen as an unfortunate development from which the law has only just recovered.

Question 6

What are the main procedural difficulties facing someone who wishes to make an application for judicial review? Should any of the rules in this area be reformed?

Commentary

This is a straightforward question, requiring the student to examine just the procedural aspects of judicial review, not the substantive law. There is scope for differences of emphasis about what is included; the selection made here covers the principal issues, but other issues could properly be included. What will make for a good answer is the assessment of the law and discussion of whether reform is needed. This answer concludes with a defence of the present law, but it would be just as acceptable to conclude with criticism and calls for changes.

Answer plan

- The public/private divide
- Applying for permission to sue
- Time limit
- Locus standi.

Suggested answer

From the earliest times, when the courts developed the prerogative writs, there have been special procedures for obtaining judicial review, which have differed from those used in ordinary civil proceedings. Generally such procedures have made it more difficult to seek judicial review, because they have been imposed to protect public authorities. Whether the retention of special procedures can be justified has been widely debated. Some changes to the rules have been made, but other aspects remain problematic.

An applicant who is thinking of seeking judicial review must first of all be sure that judicial review is the appropriate procedure to use. The defendant must be a public body, not a private body. But because the conceptual difference between public and private is not a traditional part of English law, this rule may be difficult to apply, and litigants have failed through using the wrong procedure. The courts have little difficulty in identifying as private those bodies whose legal authority derives only from contract, such as trade unions and sporting bodies: see *R v Disciplinary Committee of the Jockey Club ex parte Aga Khan* [1993] 1 WLR 909. But where bodies of uncertain status perform a public function, the courts tend to classify them as public, in order to subject them to judicial review, as in *R v Panel on Takeovers and Mergers ex parte Datafin* [1987] QB 815. The applicant must also show that the case concerns issues of public, not private law, though in recent cases the courts have taken a more flexible view on this matter. It is in any case possible for a case wrongly commenced by an application for judicial review to be transferred for hearing as an ordinary civil case. Since the reform of the civil procedure rules in 1998, it is also possible for cases begun by writ to be transferred into the judicial review procedure.

Having decided to use judicial review, applicants are faced with one of the main procedural hurdles. They cannot commence proceedings as of right, but must apply for permission (formerly leave). The defendant public authority will be informed, and then a judge in chambers will consider the papers and decide whether to grant permission. If the judge is minded to refuse, the request will be considered in open court, and the applicant can appeal against a refusal to the Court of Appeal. Why is permission needed? The justification offered is that attempts are made to seek judicial review in cases that are plainly hopeless, sometimes as a publicity stunt or as a last desperate throw of the dice. There would be a great waste of resources if public authorities had to defend all such cases at a full hearing. Instead, these cases are filtered out at the permission stage, and this also saves the applicant unnecessary expense. The counter-argument is that it is wrong in principle that litigation should need the permission of the court. In no other branch of the law is permission needed. An action against a public authority in tort or contract can be commenced as of right. Frivolous or vexatious claims are deterred sufficiently by the risk of liability for costs. Although every applicant with an arguable case should be granted permission, there is a danger that someone with a good case may be unable even to start proceedings. There have been cases where an applicant, having initially been refused permission, went on to win the case on its merits.

When the Law Commission examined this issue in 1994 it recommended that the permission stage should be retained as the only means of preventing a flood of hopeless cases. Many writers have criticised this finding, but public authorities are happy with it. Provided that judges are generous in their initial assessment of cases, the current law can be defended.

The next problem for the applicant is the time limit. Application must be made promptly and in any event within three months of the decision being challenged. This is a much shorter time limit than applies in normal civil proceedings, but it is justified by the need for the legal position of public authorities to be firmly settled at the earliest opportunity. Short time limits are normal in administrative law. Under Article 230 of the EU Treaty, the limit for challenging the actions of European Union institutions is only two months, a period adopted from French administrative law. The courts do have the power to extend the period for a good reason; in *R v Stratford on Avon DC ex parte Jackson* [1985] 1 WLR 1319, the applicant justified his delay by showing that he was waiting for a decision from the Legal Aid Board. But the court will not allow a belated application if this would cause administrative difficulties. In *R v Dairy Produce Quota Tribunal ex parte Caswell* [1990] 2 AC 738, the court refused to allow a challenge after two years to the way milk quotas had been allocated to farmers, as there would have been enormous problems in trying to undo previous allocations. It seems reasonable to expect applicants to be prompt and no change to this rule seems necessary.

The final issue that may cause problems for applicants is locus standi. When the Application for Judicial Review was introduced, locus standi was deliberately described in words without a previous legal meaning, as a 'sufficient interest' in the matter. The meaning of this expression was discussed by the House of Lords in *R v Inland Revenue Commissioners ex parte National Federation of Self-Employed and Small Businesses* [1982] AC 617. The applicants wished to challenge the validity of an agreement between the IRC and Fleet Street casual workers about past and future payments of tax. Although the challenge failed on the facts, the House of Lords felt that only 'busybodies, cranks and other mischief makers' should be regarded as not having locus standi to seek judicial review of the actions of public authorities. Pressure groups and even 'a single public-spirited taxpayer' should be allowed to bring such cases, in order to ensure that the rule of law applies.

The effect of this decision was a general liberalisation of the rules of locus standi. The 'single public-spirited taxpayer' has brought actions for judicial review. In *R v HM Treasury ex parte Smedley* [1985] 1 QB 657, a taxpayer challenged, albeit unsuccessfully, the UK's payment of certain sums to the European Community. The locus standi of pressure groups has been generally accepted, though in *R v Secretary of State for the Environment ex parte Rose Theatre Trust* [1990] 1 QB 504, the judge refused to allow a pressure group formed specifically for the purpose of saving the Rose Theatre to challenge the government's decision. Other cases have been more generous. Most striking was the decision in *R v Foreign Secretary ex parte World Development Movement* [1995] 1 WLR 386. The applicants were a respected voluntary organisation whose interest in challenging the use of UK aid to fund the Pergau Dam in Malaysia was purely moral. But, as the court said, if WDM did not have locus standi, no one would be able to challenge the decision, except people living in a remote area of Malaysia whose opportunity to take legal action in the English High Court is limited. It seems therefore that locus standi will not cause a problem to genuine applicants and no change to the law on this point is needed.

In conclusion, it can be argued that, although there are practical problems in bringing any type of legal action, the special rules relating to judicial review do not act as too great a hindrance to litigants. The need to obtain permission is the most contentious issue but even this can be defended. It would be a great problem for those seeking judicial review if frivolous or vexatious cases filled the courts and caused delay to genuine applicants.

Question 7

The (imaginary) Protection of Airfields Act 2005 empowers the Secretary of State to make regulations, in the form of a statutory instrument, 'in order to protect and maintain the security of airfields used by the Royal Air Force'. The Act provides that, before drafting such regulations the Secretary of State 'shall consult organisations and groups appearing to him to be representative of those who may be affected by the regulations'. It is further provided that before the regulations become law the draft statutory instrument must be approved by the House of Commons under the affirmative resolution procedure.

In 2008 the Secretary of State for Defence made SI 1688, the RAF Crookwaters Protection Regulations, under which it is an offence, punishable with a maximum fine of £200, for anyone to go within one mile of the perimeter fence of RAF Crookwaters. The Secretary of State only consults the RAF and the regulations are not laid before the House of Commons.

Alan is a farmer, whose fields border on RAF Crookwaters. He has been threatened with prosecution if he enters any of his fields that are within a mile of the airfield. He has never heard of these regulations and nor has the National Farmers Union as the regulations have not yet been published.

Advise Alan.

Commentary

Delegated legislation can seem a somewhat dry topic and most law students probably think that Acts of Parliament are more important. In fact, most modern law making is done by way of delegated legislation and there can be 10,000 or more new pages of it every year. Governments prefer to make delegated legislation, because it is less time-consuming than passing a new Act of Parliament and new laws can be passed almost instantaneously. Similarly, some delegated legislation is very technical and detailed and would just clog up parliamentary time with draft laws that few of the MPs understand anyway. Most modern Acts only lay out the general principles with the details to be filled in later by means of statutory instrument. Critics see this as undemocratic, in that Parliament should make the law, not ministers and civil servants. Some suspect that governments could be tempted to hide controversial new laws in delegated legislation, which does not attract as much publicity as an Act of Parliament. Therefore the courts might be persuaded to judicially review delegated legislation, particularly if the court considers the legislation fundamentally unfair: see *R (C) v Secretary of State for Justice* [2008] EWCA Civ 882 in the Suggested Answer as an example.

Problem questions on delegated legislation will usually focus on the main grounds that the courts have used to overturn ultra vires legislation. Knowledge of just a few cases should enable you to answer most questions of this type.

Agricultural, Horticultural and Forestry Training Board v Aylesbury Mushrooms (1972) shows that lack of consultation can mean that the delegated legislation is void and of no effect. It is as though that legislation never existed.

Council of Civil Service Unions v Minister for the Civil Service [1985] AC 374 is always a good case on judicial review, generally, as it sets out the main grounds in a clear way, but it also shows that a failure to consult can make legislation void.

No taxation without legislation raises a major constitutional theme, linking back to the **Bill of Rights 1689** and is nicely illustrated by *Attorney-General v Wiltshire United Dairies Ltd* (1921) 37 TLR 884.

Human Rights are an important new element in this area, particularly since the **Human Rights Act 1998**. An Act of Parliament is still valid, even if it is incompatible with the human rights protected by the Act, but delegated legislation can be held void by the courts if it is contrary to human rights.

Lastly, the defence that a statutory instrument has not been published always makes a nice little point in problems of this kind, as illustrated by *Simmonds v Newell* **[1953] 1 WLR 826.**

 ## Answer plan

- Judicial review of a statutory instrument
- A matter of public law
- Procedural impropriety—lack of consultation
- Procedural impropriety—lack of parliamentary approval
- Illegality—criminal penalty must be authorised by the Act
- Illegality—regulations must be within the purpose of the Act
- Irrationality
- Breach of human rights
- Failure to publish the regulations may provide a defence
- Collateral challenge.

Suggested answer

It seems that Alan's livelihood is threatened by the RAF Crookwaters Protection Regulations, yet he faces prosecution for allegedly infringing them. It is not possible for him to challenge the fairness and legality of the Protection of Airfields Act 2005. Due to the doctrine of the supremacy of Parliament, it is not possible for the courts to even begin to question the legal authority of an Act of Parliament: *Pickin v BRB* [1974] AC 765.

There is nothing, however, to stop Alan seeking to challenge the legal validity of the statutory instrument. This could be done by seeking a judicial review. The Secretary of State for Defence is a government minister and he has made delegated legislation, so the Secretary of State is clearly a public body exercising a public law power. So, according to *R v City Panel on Takeovers and Mergers ex parte Datafin Ltd* [1987] QB 817, the matter is susceptible to judicial review. All types of delegated legislation can be judicially reviewed under the three main grounds of illegality, irrationality and procedural impropriety: *Council of Civil Service Unions v Minister for the Civil Service* [1985] AC 374.

For Alan to succeed in a judicial review on the grounds of procedural impropriety, he would need to show that the Secretary of State for Defence has failed to follow the correct procedure when making the RAF Crookwaters Protection Regulations. The correct procedure is laid down in the parent Act, the Protection of Airfields Act 2005, and requires that before making the regulations, the Secretary of State consults those who may be affected by the regulations. Such consultation requirements are common in Acts of Parliament that allow ministers to make delegated legislation and, despite the wording, 'appearing to him', that seems to allow the Secretary of State to consult whoever he chooses, the courts have held that a minister does not have complete discretion on this matter. There was a similar statutory consultation requirement in *Agricultural, Horticultural and Forestry Training Board v Aylesbury Mushrooms* [1972] 1 WLR 190 and the court held that, although the minister had a discretion on whom to consult, he must exercise that discretion reasonably and in good faith. In the *Aylesbury Mushrooms Case*, just sending a letter and sending a copy of the draft regulation, which did not arrive, was not proper consultation. Similarly, allowing insufficient time for the consulted body to study the proposals before replying, does not amount to genuine consultation: *R v Secretary of State for Social Services ex parte Association of Metropolitan Authorities* [1986] 1 WLR 1. Here, the Secretary of State for Defence has not consulted at all, except for the RAF, who would presumably agree to the Regulations anyway. There may be an expectation of consultation, particularly as Alan is so personally affected by the Regulations. The courts have certainly held that, where there has been a previous practice of consultation, it should continue and not to consult is a breach of natural justice: *Council of Civil Service Unions v Minister for the Civil Service* [1985] AC 374. If the court agrees that there is a procedural impropriety, then the Regulations are ultra vires and of no legal effect.

It also seems, from the facts, that the affirmative resolution by the House of Commons has not taken place. This, too, is a statutory requirement, but there is little case law on the matter. Older cases, such as *Bailey v Williamson* (1873) LR 8 QB 118, suggest that this might only be a directory requirement and not mandatory, but where an affirmative resolution is required it would seem logical to argue that the resolution must be granted by Parliament or the Regulations will be null and void and of no effect: *R v Department of Health and Social Security, ex parte Camden LBC* (1986) Times, 5 March.

Illegality, as grounds of judicial review, means that the court will closely inspect the wording of the delegated legislation and the parent Act and decide whether the delegated legislation goes beyond what is permitted under the Act. If the delegated legislation allows the authorities to charge a fee or levy a fine, this must be clearly permitted under the parent Act. In *Attorney-General v Wiltshire United Dairies Ltd* (1921) 37 TLR 884, the Food Controller charged a duty of 2d per gallon on milk imported from another county. This was not legal as the Defence Regulations did not authorise charging citizens money. Similarly the tax authorities could not charge extra taxes that were not statutorily authorised: *Commissioners of Custom and Excise v Cure and Deeley* [1962] 1 QB 340. So the Secretary of

State for Defence will have to show that the Protection of Airfields Act 2005 does allow fines to be imposed for breach of a statutory instrument.

The court will also try to interpret the Protection of Airfields Act 2005, to see whether it allows the restriction of the citizen's freedom of movement. In *R (Spath Holme Ltd) v Secretary of State for the Environment* [2001] 2 AC 349, the Environment Secretary made the Rent Acts (Maximum Fair Rent) Order 1999, under the authority of the Landlord and Tenant Act 1985, restricting rent increases for tenants. A landlord, Spath Holme, sought a judicial review to quash the Order, on the grounds that the Act only allowed restrictions on rent increases to control inflation within the economy, not to prevent hardship for poor tenants. The House of Lords disagreed and held that the overall purpose of the 1985 Act was to regulate the relationship between landlord and tenant and to protect tenants form the hardship of increased rents. A statute called the Protection of Airfields Act would suggest that it would allow the government to take reasonable measures to protect the security of an airfield.

However, is a complete ban on anyone approaching within a mile of the airfield reasonable? Judicial review is also permitted on the grounds that a measure is irrational. This was defined by Lord Diplock in *Council of Civil Service Unions v Minister for the Civil Service* [1985] AC 374 at 410 as 'a decision so outrageous in its defiance of logic or of accepted moral standards that no sensible person who had applied his mind to the question to be decided could have arrived at it'. It is fairly unusual for the courts to overturn delegated legislation on the grounds that it is irrational, because the decision on how to exercise the statutory power generally turns on political and economic considerations, which are better evaluated by the minister and Parliament than the courts: *R (Javed) v Home Secretary* [2001] 3 WLR 323. It is much more likely, however, that the court will hold the delegated legislation to be irrational if it infringes human rights. In the *Javed* case the Home Secretary had the power to make statutory instruments designating safe countries, to which asylum-seekers could be returned. The Court of Appeal disagreed with the Home Secretary's assessment that Pakistan was a safe country to which to return women and Ahmadis (a religious minority) and overturned the Order. This was despite the fact that Parliament had actually approved the Order, as required, by affirmative resolution. So Alan's case seems stronger as there has been no parliamentary approval on our facts, so the court would not fear that they were obstructing the wishes of the democratically elected Parliament. In a recent case, *R (C) v Secretary of State for Justice* [2008] EWCA Civ 882, the Court of Appeal overturned a statutory instrument that allowed for the physical restraint of children held in privately run secure training centres, partly on the grounds that Articles 3 and 8 of the European Convention on Human Rights had been infringed. Article 3 prohibits inhuman and degrading treatment and Article 8 protects a person's private life. But have any of Alan's human rights actually been infringed? His farm is also likely to be his home and restricting access to it would be a breach of Article 8, respect for his home, and Article 1 of the First Protocol, the right to peaceful enjoyment of his possessions. The Secretary of State would have to show that there really was a security reason for stopping him from using his farm.

So it seems that Alan would have a good case for a successful judicial review of the RAF Crookwaters Protection Regulations on a number of grounds, but he might not want to take this course of action. Judicial review cases are heard in the High Court in London, and this would make it expensive and maybe inconvenient for Alan. He could, instead, just wait to be prosecuted in his local magistrates' court and then there are two defences that he could use.

A huge volume of delegated legislation is enacted each year and there are sometimes delays in publishing it, particularly if the statutory instrument is lengthy. Therefore there is a defence in s. 3(2) of the Statutory Instruments Act 1946 to a prosecution for breach of a statutory instrument if it has not been published. This would give Alan a defence to a prosecution as we are told that the RAF Crookwaters Protection Regulations have not been published: *Simmonds v Newell* [1953] 1 WLR 826. This defence will not, however, be available if the government has taken reasonable steps to bring the contents of the statutory instrument to the attention of the public or to the persons affected by it, as seen in *R v Sheer Metalcraft* [1954] 1 QB 586. As neither Alan, who is directly affected by them, nor the National Farmers Union, who represent other farmers, have heard of these new regulations it would seem that the government has not taken reasonable steps to publicise the Regulations. So the non-publication defence is still available to Alan.

There is another defence that Alan could use if he is taken to court, which is sometimes known as a collateral challenge. He, or more likely, his lawyers, would argue that if the Regulations are ultra vires, then they are void and of no effect and therefore he cannot be prosecuted under them. This was permitted in *DPP v Hutchinson* [1990] 2 AC 783, where some 'Greenham Common' women succeeded in their defence to a prosecution for breaking a by-law not to enter RAF Greenham Common, by showing that the parent Act stated that the Secretary of State could not make a by-law 'to take away or prejudice any rights of common'. This was what is known as substantive ultra vires, which we classified as illegality and irrationality and it was thought, at first, that collateral challenge did not allow a defence based on procedural ultra vires, which we classified as procedural impropriety. The House of Lords ruled in *Boddington v British Transport Police* [1998] 2 All ER 203 that the magistrates' court had jurisdiction to rule on both substantive and procedural ultra vires.

So in conclusion this is probably Alan's best option: carry on using his fields, wait to be prosecuted and then argue that the RAF Crookwaters Protection Regulations are ultra vires.

Further reading

Bradley, A. and Ewing, K. *Constitutional and Administrative Law*, 14th edn (Longman, 2007), chs 30 and 31.

Cane, P. *Introduction to Administrative Law*, 4th edn (OUP, 2004), chs 1–6.

Turpin, C. and Tomkins, A. *British Government and the Constitution*, 6th edn (Cambridge, 2007), ch 10.

Barnett, H. *Constitutional and Administrative Law* 7th edn (Routledge-Cavendish, 2008), ch 25 and ch 26.

DELEGATED LEGISLATION

Bradley, A. and Ewing, K. *Constitutional and Administrative Law*, 14th edn (Longman, 2007), ch 28.

Craig, P. *Administrative Law* 6th edn (Sweet and Maxwell, 2008), ch 22.

Public Authority Proceedings

Introduction

The topics dealt with in this chapter are more likely to be included in an administrative law course than in a general constitutional law course, with the exception of public interest immunity, which is of such constitutional interest that it may be included where the other aspects are not. Students will need to be guided by their own examiners and syllabus.

Examples of both essay and problem questions are included. Good answers will require the student to show skills of legal analysis and application. A student who has studied or is studying tort or contract need not be afraid to bring that extra knowledge into the answer. The law may be divided into discrete subjects for the purpose of teaching and examining, but in reality it is an undivided whole.

Question 1

The Home Office decided, as part of its policy of reducing the prison population, to establish hostels where long-term prisoners could spend the last year of their sentences, being gradually rehabilitated into the outside world. One of these hostels was established in Coketown. It was a converted house in a residential area, occupied by eight prisoners, who went out to work during the day, but were otherwise supervised by a warden and his staff.

Consider the liability of the Home Office in the following situations.

(a) White, Black and Gray, who live in the same street as the hostel, consider that it has reduced the amenity and value of their homes. They consider that the hostel should have been established somewhere else.

(b) Brown, who lives next door to the hostel, thinks that the choice of site for the hostel was made because he is a prominent campaigner against Home Office policies: he suspects that there is evidence of this hidden in Home Office files.

(c) The Home Office decided that prisoners convicted of violent crimes could if considered suitable, be sent to the hostel. Reg had been sentenced to 15 years for attempted murder and, because he had behaved impeccably throughout his time in prison, was due for release next year. He was sent to the hostel, obtained a job, and apparently settled in well. But last week, on the way home from work, he went to the pub, got drunk, and punched Green, the landlord. The previous week, Reg had threatened Green.

 ## Commentary

This question raises various issues relating to the liability of public authorities. It is important for students to deal both with the general rules applicable to all public authorities and with the special rules governing the liability of the Crown. The student will not be expected to examine issues of tortious liability in as great depth as would be appropriate in a tort examination, but should concentrate on those aspects peculiar to public authorities. The question also touches on public interest immunity.

 ## Answer plan

- Nuisance, subject to statutory authority
- Breach of **Article 8 ECHR**
- Misfeasance in public office
- Public interest immunity
- Liability in negligence for policy and operation
- Breach of **Article 2 ECHR**.

Suggested answer

(a) White, Black and Gray will have to prove that the hostel constitutes an actionable nuisance if they wish to obtain redress. Under the Crown Proceedings Act 1947, s. 2, the Crown is subject to the same liabilities as any other person in respect of torts committed by its servants or agents, and torts arising from its ownership, occupation or control of property. But there are circumstances in which a body may be able to plead that it has statutory authority. If a statute specifically authorises some activity that will inevitably result in the commission of a nuisance, no action will lie. In *Allen v Gulf Oil Refinery Ltd* [1981] AC 1001, the defendants obtained a private Act of Parliament authorising them to construct a refinery on a particular site, from which some nuisance would inevitably result. They were held to be immune from action, unless they negligently operated the refinery in such a way as to increase the nuisance beyond what was inevitable.

But this defence does not operate where the authorisation is general and the nuisance not inevitable. In *Metropolitan Asylum District v Hill* (1881) 6 App Cas 193, the plaintiff had statutory authority to build hospitals, and chose to build one in a place where it would cause a nuisance. As it would have been possible to exercise the statutory power without causing a nuisance, no defence of statutory authority existed.

In this problem, it appears that the choice of site was in the hands of the Home Office. It can be argued that the hostel could have been established anywhere, including places where it would not have constituted a nuisance.

In contrast, Thames Water escaped liability for nuisance, when their sewers overflowed and flooded the property of Marcic: *Marcic v Thames Water Utilities Ltd* [2004] 2 AC 42. The sewers were properly maintained, but the volume of sewerage had increased since the sewers were built. The House of Lords held that there was no liability for nuisance, particularly as there was a detailed statutory scheme for making complaints, which Marcic had not used. There is no statutory scheme under which White, Black and Gray can complain but, as in *Marcic v Thames*, the court would probably say that the wider interests of the population, in having criminals rehabilitated, outweighed the interests of White, Black and Gray. Marcic also claimed that Thames Water had infringed his right of respect for his home under Article 8 of the European Convention of Human Rights. The House of Lords rejected his claim and applied *Hatton v UK* (2003) 37 EHRR 28, a decision of the European Court of Human Rights concerning aircraft noise at Heathrow Airport. In these types of claim the interests of the householder had to be weighed against the wider interests of society. It could not be said that the statutory scheme for regulating sewage failed to keep a balance between the interests of Marcic and the interests of everyone else in having their sewers emptied. Following *Marcic v Thames*, it seems less likely that the interference, which the hostel causes to surrounding property, is sufficient to amount to nuisance. If it did, White, Black and Gray will be able to sue for damages. They will not, however, be able to obtain an injunction against the Crown to order the closure of the hostel. By the Crown Proceedings Act 1947, s. 21, no injunction may be awarded against the Crown, though a declaration may be awarded instead.

(b) Brown is alleging that the choice of site for the hostel was made maliciously. This would constitute grounds for judicial review, the decision being made for an improper purpose or even in bad faith. Such proceedings would be an appropriate way of getting the decision quashed but would not lead to the award of any compensation to Brown unless he can demonstrate the existence of some established form of liability.

To make a decision that subsequently proves to be unlawful does not in itself give rise to any liability. In *Dunlop v Woollahra Municipal Council* [1982] AC 158, the Privy Council refused to impose any liability on a local authority whose decision, based on a misunderstanding of their legal powers, was later held to be ultra vires.

Brown may be able to recover damages for the tort of misfeasance in a public office, which is designed to provide redress for the victims of malicious abuses of public power. The elements of this tort were set out in *Three Rivers DC v Bank of England* [2000] 3 All ER 1. The House of Lords held that liability exists where a public official, exercising power as such, either does something intended to injure a person, or does something knowing that it is unlawful and that it will probably injure the plaintiff. Brown's claim is based on the first form of this tort, intentional or targeted malice. An example is *Roncarelli v Duplessis* (1959) 16 DLR (2d) 689, where the defendant ordered the revocation of the plaintiff's liquor licence, because he had annoyed the authorities by his lawful activities in support of an unpopular religious sect. The defendant knew the revocation was unlawful, but chose it as a good way to make the plaintiff suffer. According to *Watkins v Home Secretary* [2006] 2 All ER 353, Brown would also have to prove that the opening of the hostel had caused him material damage, in the sense of financial loss or physical or mental injury.

Brown would have to prove that the decision was in fact made with the deliberate intention of causing him injury and had caused him financial loss, perhaps the decline in value of his house, in order to recover damages. His difficulty will be to obtain proof.

Any attempt by Brown to obtain the documents that he thinks will reveal misfeasance may be met by a claim for public interest immunity from the Home Office. Such a claim may be based on the contents of the particular document, or on the assertion that that class of document needs, in the public interest, to be kept secret. As was made clear in *R v Chief Constable of the West Midlands Police ex parte Wiley* [1994] 3 All ER 420, if the Home Office does not think that the public interest would be harmed by revealing these documents, there is no obligation on it to claim public interest immunity.

The case of *Conway v Rimmer* [1968] AC 910 established that the decision on disclosure or otherwise rests with the court, not the government. The court has to balance two aspects of the public interest; on the one hand, the public interest in secrecy and confidentiality, and, on the other hand, the public interest in the fair administration of justice. Where necessary, the court may inspect the documents to help it decide whether disclosure should be ordered.

The Home Office may have two possible grounds for arguing that these documents should be kept secret. One is that the security of the hostel, its inmates and neighbours might be compromised if the documents were revealed. This does not appear to be very plausible, though security would generally be taken as a reasonable ground to use as a basis for secrecy. The other ground might be the confidentiality of Civil Service advice to ministers. It has been asserted in various cases that the candour of public officials, and hence their usefulness to ministers might be impaired if they knew their words might be revealed in later litigation. But the courts have shown themselves very unsympathetic to such claims, refusing to believe that officials, whose advice will in any case be preserved on file, will be frightened by the remote possibility of later litigation into failing to do their job properly. In *Williams v Home Office* [1981] 1 All ER 1151, this argument concerning candour was rejected and documents relating to penal policy revealed. In that case, inspection of the documents revealed them to be essential to the plaintiff's case, so that the court had no difficulty in holding that the public interest in the fair administration of justice prevailed.

In this problem, it may well be that the court will find it necessary to inspect the documents to discover whether they are necessary to Brown's case, because, if unnecessary, they need not be disclosed. In *Burmah Oil Co. v Bank of England* [1980] AC 1090, where sensitive papers were concerned, the court inspected them before deciding that their evidential value to the plaintiff was so limited as not to outweigh the genuine claim to confidentiality put forward by the Attorney-General. Brown is therefore in the hands of the court, which must perform the difficult task of balancing the two aspects of the public interest.

(c) The Home Office's liability to Green would have to be based on the claim that it has been in some way negligent. The basic principles governing the liability of public authorities in negligence have been laid down by the House of Lords in the cases of *X v Bedfordshire CC* [1995] 2 AC 633 and *Phelps v London Borough of Hillingdon* [2000] 4 All ER 504. Some policy decisions may be regarded by the courts as non-justiciable in public law terms and they can then give rise to no duty of care to any individual. But for other decisions, it is sufficient to establish liability using the ordinary tort principles laid down in *Caparo Industries v Dickman* [1990] 2 AC 605.

Applying these principles to Green's case, it is difficult to see how he could succeed in any claim based on the policy decision to create such a hostel. The choice of appropriate penal policies is one that the Home Office has to make and, in the absence of some extreme irrationality, the courts will not intervene in such a decision. Green might attempt to assert that the Home Office was negligent in choosing Reg for admission to the hostel. Such negligence would have to be established on ordinary tort principles, and this might prove difficult. It is not clear whether the court would find it fair, just and reasonable to impose a duty of care. In *Hill v Chief Constable of West Yorkshire* [1989] AC 53, the court held that the police owed no duty of care to members of the public in respect of the investigation and prevention of crime. Even if Green had warned the Home Office about the previous threat from Reg, it seems unlikely that there would be any liability for negligence, according to *Van Colle v Chief Constable of Hertfordshire Police*,

Smith v Chief Constable of Sussex Police [2008] 3 All ER 977. Smith had warned the police that his former partner, Jeffrey, had threatened to kill him and Jeffrey eventually succeeded in seriously injuring him. The House of Lords declined to hold that the police had any duty of care to protect victims and witnesses of crime. To impose such a duty would be contrary to public policy, as it would make the police fearful of legal action and cause them to perform their duties in a defensive manner, which would be detrimental to the whole of society. Although there was no cause of action in negligence, the House endorsed the principle, laid down by the European Court of Human Rights, in *Osman v UK* (1998) 29 EHRR 245. The police could be liable for a breach of the right to life under Article 2 of the European Convention of Human Rights, if they knew, or ought to have known at the time, of the existence of a real and immediate risk to the life of the claimant and then failed to take reasonable steps to prevent it. Reg's threat does not seem to be serious or persistent and there is no evidence that Green reported it to the Home Office. In *Van Colle*, only Lord Bingham was willing to extend the *Osman* principle to cover not just threats to life, but threats of serious injury, so Green would not seem to have a human rights case either.

Green will have a much stronger case if he can show that the warden and staff were under instruction to keep the inmates under supervision and had failed to do so. In *Home Office v Dorset Yacht Co* [1970] AC 1004, the Home Office were held to be vicariously liable for the negligence of prison officers, who had failed to keep a party of borstal boys under supervision as they had been instructed to. But if, as seems to be the case here, the whole reason for the inmates' stay in the hostel is that they are not under constant supervision, no negligence on the part of the warden and staff can be shown. It would therefore appear that Green may be unable to establish any liability on the part of the Home Office, in which case he will be left with the right to sue the probably impecunious Reg only.

Question 2

How far is it true to say that the Crown, when involved in litigation, is in the same position as any other litigant before the English courts? Are any further reforms to proceedings involving the Crown necessary?

 ## Commentary

This question covers a fairly wide range of issues relating to Crown proceedings and the student will need to be careful to pick up issues that may not all have been covered under that heading.

Clearly, the **Crown Proceedings Act** will form the core of the answer, but there are still areas where common law rules remain applicable. There are further areas where other changes to the law have had an incidental effect upon the Crown, such as Crown service, which has been affected by the development of statutory rights for workers. The **Human Rights Act 1998**, which binds the Crown, is also beginning to extend the liability of the Crown.

Answer plan

- 'The king can do no wrong'
- Normal tort liability
- Liability to Armed Forces
- Crown service
- Contractual liability
- Procedural immunities.

Suggested answer

Until 1947, the Crown enjoyed substantial immunities from liability in English law, and benefited from various procedural advantages in litigation. These derived from historical developments. The impossibility of subjecting the king to the jurisdiction of his own courts produced the paradoxical saying that 'the king could do no wrong'; because there was no remedy for those wrongs, they did not legally exist. But an immunity that originally attached to the person of the Monarch also applied if he exercised his powers through his servants and ministers. Though the individual servant might be personally liable, the Crown remained immune. When, through the development of parliamentary government, the exercise of the Crown's power was controlled by a government, the immunity remained intact. It was therefore impossible to sue the Crown in tort, and possible to sue in contract and restitution only with the permission of the Crown, if the Attorney-General granted his fiat to a petition of right.

It was, however, possible, in appropriate cases, for the victim of a tort to sue the individual Crown servant responsible. Dicey indeed regarded this as a powerful demonstration of the rule of law, as it forced the individual to accept responsibility for his or her own actions, rather than being able to hide behind some official immunity. But as a means of ensuring adequate compensation for the victim it was seriously defective, until the Crown developed the practice of standing behind its servants and paying any damages awarded against them. Even this did not help in those circumstances where tortious liability attached to the Crown itself, perhaps as employer or landowner, and not to any individual Crown servant. The cases of *Adams v Naylor* [1946] AC 543 and *Royster v Cavey* [1947] KB 204 showed that the courts were no longer willing to co-operate in evading the effects of Crown immunity by making findings of liability against nominated defendants who were not personally liable. Statutory reform, which had been under discussion for some years, was finally introduced.

The Crown Proceedings Act 1947, s. 2 subjects the Crown to the same liabilities in tort as a person of full age and capacity in the following respects. Most importantly, it is vicariously liable for torts committed by its servants or agents; by s. 6, Crown servants are defined as those directly or indirectly appointed by the Crown and paid out of the Consolidated Fund or other Treasury-controlled moneys. To avoid any suggestion of Crown interference in the judicial system, no such liability exists in respect of those acting in a judicial capacity. The only significant limitation on this form of liability, s. 2(1), gives the Crown the right to plead any defence that the servant could have pleaded. This includes not only the ordinary tort defences but defences like Act of State, which had developed to limit the liability of Crown servants. But as the case of *Nissan v Attorney-General* [1970] AC 179 showed, this defence is very limited in scope and, in recent cases involving UK military activity abroad, the Crown has chosen not to plead Act of State as a defence: *R (Al Skeini) v Secretary of State for Defence* [2007] 3 WLR 33 and *Bici v Ministry of Defence* [2004] EWHC 786 (QB).

The other forms of tortious liability imposed by s. 2 are employers' liability to employees and liability arising from the ownership or occupation of property.

The Crown is also subjected to liability for breach of statutory duty, but this is subject to two limitations. First, the statutory duty must also be binding on persons other than the Crown. The Crown Proceedings Act is concerned only to extend the ordinary forms of tort liability to the Crown, not to create new forms of liability to which only the Crown could be subject. Secondly, by a common law rule expressly preserved by s. 40(2)(f), the Crown is not bound by statutes unless the statute so provides, expressly or by necessary implication. This rule has been the subject of stringent criticism, as making it far too easy for the Crown to evade liabilities and obligations to which it should be subject, but was confirmed by the House of Lords in *Lord Advocate v Dumbarton Council* [1990] 2 AC 580. Most modern Acts of Parliament now expressly state that they apply to the Crown, as seen in s. 22(5) of the Human Rights Act 1998.

There remain some specific limitations on the liability of the Crown in tort. Under s. 40(2) the Act only applies to liabilities arising in the UK. No action could therefore be brought, for example, in respect of a nuisance committed by the British Army in Berlin; *Trawnik v Lennox* [1985] 1 WLR 532. This seems an undesirable rule as the doctrine of state immunity may well prevent any action being brought in the foreign state either. A major problem arose as a result of s. 10, which exempted the Crown from liability for injuries caused to one member of the Armed Forces by the negligence of another, if the injury was classed as pensionable. After sustained criticism of this rule, the Crown Proceedings (Armed Forces) Act 1987 repealed s. 10. The repeal, however, did not have retrospective effect. In *Matthews v Ministry of Defence* [2003] 1 All ER 689, it was argued that the continuing exemption for pre-1987 injuries was a breach of the right to a fair trial under Article 6 of the European Convention on Human Rights. But the House of Lords held that this was a substantive bar to action, not a procedural one, so Article 6 did not apply. In the 1987 Act, the Crown reserved the right to revive its immunity in case of war or emergency, but in recent conflicts it has not done so. It has in any case been held in *Mulcahy v Ministry of Defence* [1996] 2 All ER 758 that in battle conditions no soldier owes a duty of care to his fellow soldiers, nor does the Crown, as employer, owe any duty of care to military personnel in active combat. This so-called 'combat immunity' does not extend to policing and peacekeeping operations. So in *Bici v Ministry of Defence* [2004] EWHC 789 (QB), the Ministry of Defence was vicariously liable for soldiers, who negligently shot Albanian civilians during an operation in Kosovo.

There may also be liability under the Human Rights Act 1998, for infringing Article 2, the right to life. The European Convention of Human Rights applies when foreign territory is under the control of UK forces and so it covered the killing of an Iraqi civilian, while held in British custody in Iraq: *R (Al Skeini) v Secretary of State for Defence* [2007] 3 WLR 33. There is no reason why other Articles of the Convention could not apply as well as seen in *R (Al-Jedda) v Secretary of State for Defence* [2008] 2 WLR 1. Human rights could also protect the soldiers themselves, not just civilians, wherever the soldiers might be in the world. It could cover issues such as the provision of defective equipment to soldiers, that endangered the life of the soldier as held in *Smith v Assistant Deputy Coroner for Oxfordshire* [2008] 3 WLR 1284.

The final issue in relation to tort liability is the provision in s. 40(1) which excludes the possibility of any action in tort against the Monarch in his or her personal capacity. Although this could be criticised, it is perhaps an appropriate way of preserving the Monarch's dignity. It is in any case difficult to imagine any circumstances in which the Monarch would have the opportunity to commit torts in person—perhaps a bite from a royal corgi? In any such case compensation would no doubt be paid ex gratia.

Turning to liability in contract, the Crown Proceedings Act 1947, s. 1 simply states that actions that could formerly have been brought by petition of right can now be brought as of right. Actions in contract against the Crown are now therefore straightforward, with the exception of actions against the Monarch in person that would have to use the old petition of right procedure.

The only area of contractual liability that has given rise to any substantial amount of litigation is the law of Crown service. At common law, Crown servants, both civil and military, were employed at the pleasure of the Crown and could therefore be dismissed at any moment, regardless of any terms in the contract; see *Dunn v R* [1896] 1 QB 116. This rule remains in the case of military personnel, whose engagement is not contractual at all; see *Mitchell v R* (1890), noted at [1896] 1 QB 121. But for civil servants, the law has been transformed by the extension to them of most of the statutory provisions governing employment. Civil servants are now entitled to redundancy payments, to compensation for unfair dismissal and to protection from racial and sexual discrimination. Although their common law rights remain limited, these are in general insignificant compared with statutory rights. Some categories of Crown servants continue to be governed by special rules, such as prison officers who are subject to strict disciplinary codes. The Crown's treatment of its employees has given rise to some disputes, such as the *GCHQ case* [1985] AC 374, but on the whole its behaviour compares satisfactorily with that of most large employers. It is planned to place the Civil Service on a statutory basis in the Constitutional Renewal Bill 2008, which would further regularise the position of Crown employees.

As far as other contractual litigation is concerned, few cases ever come to court. The Crown prefers to settle disputes by negotiation or arbitration, especially where sensitive matters, such as defence procurement, are involved. The Crown's freedom of contract is now constrained by the EU rules on public procurement. These are intended to ensure that there is a single Europe-wide market in the supply of goods and services to states, rather than preference being given to national contractors. There have been suggestions in some cases that the Crown may be entitled to certain immunities in contract, but the Crown does not seem to assert these. Most sweeping was the suggestion in *Rederiaktiebolaget Amphitrite v R* [1921] 3 KB 500 that the Crown cannot by contract fetter its future freedom of action in matters affecting the welfare of the State. Taken literally, this would entitle the Crown to break any contract it has entered into, but it is doubtful that such a wide proposition can be supported. Indeed, it can be argued that in the case itself there was no actual contract, so the remarks were merely obiter. The Crown has in any case sufficiently wide statutory powers, especially in emergencies, to make such a common law doctrine unnecessary.

Another limitation on the contractual power of the Crown was suggested by the case of *Churchward v R* (1865) LR 1 QB 173, where a contract was awarded to Churchward on condition that moneys were voted by Parliament. When Parliament voted against the payment, the contract necessarily fell. It was argued that this made all government contracts dependent on money being voted by Parliament, but this was refuted by the Australian case of *Attorney-General of New South Wales v Bardolph* (1934) 52 CLR 455, where the State was held liable even in the absence of a specific vote of money, provided that the contract was a proper one and was covered by a general vote of funds. It remains possible, under the doctrine of parliamentary supremacy, for Parliament to forbid payments under a contract, and that would be legally effective. It is not, however, the practice of the Crown to bankrupt its contractors by refusing to pay its debts.

The Crown Proceedings Act preserves certain procedural immunities. By s. 25(1) awards of damages against the Crown cannot be enforced by the usual machinery of execution or attachment but this is no real problem. The Crown will always be able to pay damages awarded against it and, on the rare occasions when it does not wish to do so, as in *Burmah Oil v Lord Advocate* [1965] AC 75, it will procure the passage of legislation to reverse the decision. More serious is the provision in s. 21(1) that the courts cannot grant an injunction, specific performance or an order for the delivery up of land against the Crown. It was long thought that this would prevent the award of an injunction against a Crown servant acting in his or her official capacity. But in *M v Home Office* [1994] 1 AC 377 the House of Lords, acting under the influence of European Community law, held that the Act did not preclude the grant of an injunction against a particular Crown servant, even a government minister. So although the Crown is not subject to this coercive remedy, its servants who carry out its tasks are so subject. This case demonstrates the willingness of the courts to restrict the immunities and privileges of the Crown, which is further illustrated by the historic decision in *Conway v Rimmer* [1968] AC 910, which removed the Crown's absolute right to withhold evidence.

The remedy of declaration has always been available against the Crown as a final remedy. But no such thing as an interim declaration existed; see *International General Electric Co. v Commissioners of Customs and Excise* [1962] Ch 784. Recent reforms to the Civil Procedure Rules have, however, authorised the courts to award interim declarations in interlocutory proceedings, a valuable reform.

Such immunities as do survive do not seem to cause too many problems for litigants, particularly as the Crown does not seek to rely on the more extreme privileges suggested in the cases. But there needs to be continuing vigilance to ensure that the rule of law is observed and the Crown subjected to the proper degree of liability.

Question 3

To what extent has English law developed special rules to govern the liability in negligence of public authorities? Do you consider the law on this subject to be satisfactory?

Commentary

This question raises an issue that has given rise to a good deal of litigation and a lot of debate among academic lawyers. There are many different opinions as to what the law should be. As usual, it does not matter so much what opinion you express as how well you express it. Some students may be studying or have studied tort, and so would be able to give a more sophisticated discussion of the tort issues involved than is given here. It is important to remember that, though the law is divided into separate topics for teaching purposes, it is not divided in reality.

Answer plan

- One law of tort for all
- Relevance of public law principles
- Imposing a duty of care
- Finding negligence
- Liability for breach of human rights
- Liability for omissions.

Suggested answer

Because English law did not traditionally distinguish between public and private law, the ordinary principles of tort liability were developed to apply to public and private bodies alike. In *Mersey Docks and Harbour Board Trustees v Gibbs* (1866) LR 1 HL 93, it was held that public bodies enjoyed no inherent immunity from liability in negligence. The only exception related to the Crown, which was immune from tortious liability until the Crown Proceedings Act 1947. The Act expressly made the Crown liable 'as if it were a private person' so confirming the general principle that there is just one law of tort.

There are few problems in applying the law where the activities alleged to have been conducted negligently are of a type common to both public and private bodies. Liability for careless driving, dangerous premises or unsafe working practices is the same for public and private defendants. But difficulties may arise where the claim arises out of the exercise by a public authority of statutory powers of a type that private individuals do not have. Complaints about the exercise of such powers are principally dealt with by judicial review. This may provide adequate redress where the authority's action can be halted or reversed, by remedies such as injunction or quashing orders. But to claim compensation it is necessary to establish liability in tort. In *Dunlop v Woollahra Municipal Council* [1982] AC 158, the plaintiff established that the Council's decision was ultra vires and had it quashed, but he was unable to obtain any compensation, because he could not establish any form of tort liability.

What then is the relationship between judicial review and tort liability? Is it necessary to prove breaches of both laws or is tort liability alone sufficient? These questions have been addressed by the House of Lords in several cases, but their judgments have not always been consistent. In *Anns v Merton LBC* [1978] AC 728, the court drew a distinction between claims based on the negligent operation of statutory powers, for which tort liability alone needed to be proved, and claims based on policy decisions made by the public authority. In this situation, it would be necessary to prove that the policy decision was unlawful in public law terms before there could be any question of going on to establish liability in tort. This decision provided a rough test but was rendered problematic by the difficulty of deciding where the line between policy and operation could be drawn in practice.

The House of Lords returned to the problem in *X v Bedfordshire CC* [1995] 2 AC 633, a group of cases in which public authorities were alleged to have been negligent in the exercise of their child care and education powers. Rather than applying the *Anns v Merton LBC* distinction between policy and operation, the court held that some policy decisions, such as how to allocate limited resources, are regarded as non-justiciable in the context of judicial review. Cases like *R v Secretary of State for the Environment ex parte Nottinghamshire CC* [1986] 2 AC 240 had established that the courts would not be willing to challenge the political judgments of public authorities in such areas. That being so, the House of Lords felt that such policy decisions could not give rise to a duty of care to any individual. This decision must be correct, as it is inevitable that decisions on the allocation of what are always limited resources must mean that some individuals do not receive benefits or services that they might otherwise have received. Legal action by one disappointed claimant could only be satisfied by creating another dissatisfied claimant who would have an equally valid claim.

For claims falling outside this non-justiciable area, whether regarded as policy or operational, the House of Lords felt that there was no need to invoke principles of public law. Rather, the cases should be dealt with on the basis of the normal principles of tort liability laid down in *Caparo Industries v Dickman* [1990] 2 AC 605. These principles require the court to start by deciding whether it is just and reasonable to impose a duty of care. Public authorities were keen to argue that for policy reasons it would not be just and reasonable to impose any duty of care on them when exercising their statutory responsibilities, so that cases could be disposed of at an early stage and litigants deterred from pursuing actions against them. The courts were initially sympathetic to this view. In *Hill v Chief Constable of West Yorkshire* [1989] AC 53, the House of Lords held that the police owed no duty of care to members of the public in respect of the prevention and investigation of crime; any other decision would have lead to resources being taken away from policing and given to the victims of crime, probably creating more victims in consequence. The decision in *Hill v Chief Constable of West Yorkshire* [1989] AC 53 has been confirmed in two subsequent House of Lords cases, *Brooks v Commissioner of Police of the Metropolis* [2005] 2 All ER 489 and *Van Colle v Chief Constable of Hertfordshire Police* [2008] 3 All ER 977. The latter case extended the ruling in *Hill*, in that the police still owed no individual duty of care, even if an individual alerted them to threats from a third party against that individual. Similarly, in those of the *X v Bedfordshire CC* cases that concerned the immensely difficult question whether or not to take a child into care on suspicion of abuse, the court held that it would not be just and reasonable to impose a duty of care on social service departments, as such decisions are normally taken after discussion with all the agencies concerned.

As a result of these precedents, it became common for public authorities to apply to strike out claims in these areas before the facts were established. In *Osman v United Kingdom* (1998) 29 EHRR 245, the European Court of Human Rights ruled that striking out a claim in this way was a breach of Article 6 of the European Convention on Human Rights. This decision was widely criticised as revealing a misunderstanding of the legal process. But the European Court of Human Rights revisited the issue in *Z v United Kingdom* [2001] 2 FLR 612, a case brought by one of the unsuccessful claimants in *X v Bedfordshire CC*. This time the Court held that to strike out a claim after considering whether it is just and reasonable to impose a duty of care is not a breach of Article 6, as that very consideration is the fair trial to which the individual is entitled.

Although there may not be any liability in negligence, that does not prevent there from being liability for the breach of human rights themselves. The European Court of Human Rights held that there was a breach of Article 2, the right to life, in *Osman v UK* (1998) 29 EHRR 245 and a breach of Article 3, freedom from torture and inhuman and degrading treatment, in *Z v UK* (2002) 34 EHRR 3. The English courts have declined to develop and change the tort of negligence, to take into account the additional Convention rights, despite the spirited dissent of Lord Bingham in *Van Colle v Chief Constable of Hertfordshire Police* [2008] 3 All ER 977. According to that case it is possible to bring an action for breach of a human right, when it is not possible to bring a claim in negligence.

There have been many cases in which the courts have found it just and reasonable to impose a duty of care, especially where the claim is based on the failure of a public authority to put into effect the decisions it had made. In *X v Bedfordshire CC* itself, the court imposed a duty of care on education authorities that had taken responsibility for dealing with pupils' problems but had failed to do so. Similarly, in *Barrett v Enfield LBC* [1999] 3 All ER 193, the court imposed a duty of care on an authority that, having rightly decided that a child needed to be taken into care, failed to ensure that he was properly cared for. But the court emphasised how difficult it was for them to deal with these cases when only the preliminary issue of whether to impose a duty of care was before them, and none of the facts were established.

The House of Lords returned to this question in *Phelps v London Borough of Hillingdon* [2000] 4 All ER 504, a group of cases alleging that education authorities had failed to identify and deal with pupils' problems, such as dyslexia. The local authorities had argued that policy considerations, such as the complexity of any litigation and the danger of a flood of vexatious claims, should preclude the imposition of a duty of care. But the House of Lords held that a duty of care should be held to exist; genuine claims should not be rejected out of hand. Instead, the court felt that policy considerations would only be material at the later stage of deciding whether the duty of care had been breached, and this would only be done once the facts had been established by evidence.

This decision makes it far more likely that cases will go forward to trial, but it does not necessarily mean that claimants will be successful. The courts are well aware that public authorities make attractive defendants; they have plenty of money and will not evade the payment of any damages awarded against them. But the courts do not wish to impose excessive financial burdens on public authorities, and have emphasised that negligence must be proved to the high standard of professional negligence laid down in *Bolam v Friern Hospital Management Committee* [1957] 1 WLR 582.

Although all the above cases were dealt with using just tort principles, it seems to be possible that, in limited circumstances, public law principles may remain relevant in establishing liability. An example is the case of *Stovin v Wise* [1996] AC 923, where the local authority had a statutory power to remove obstructions adjoining the highway, but had not removed the obstruction in question, for reasons that were perfectly acceptable in public law terms. The House of Lords held that no liability could arise unless the failure to remove the obstruction was unlawful in public law terms, which it was not. If the danger created by the obstruction were so great as to make the failure to remove it unlawful or unreasonable in public law terms, tortious liability would have been properly imposed. But as the authority was entitled to do nothing, its omissions could not create liability. In any situation where an authority has a positive duty to act, however, only tort principles will be applicable.

In conclusion, the courts face difficult problems in dealing with actions in negligence against public authorities. There is constant pressure from litigants who choose to sue public authorities even in situations where someone else (with less money) is primarily liable. One thinks of the borstal boys in *Home Office v Dorset Yacht Co* [1970] AC 1004, the negligent builder in *Anns v Merton LBC* [1978] AC 728 or the careless driver in *Stovin v Wise* [1996] AC 923. Recent cases show the courts trying to steer a careful course between offering the victims of negligence appropriate compensation, and keeping vexatious claims out of court. The law in this area is likely to show further development.

Question 4

Consider the following situations in the light of the doctrine of public interest immunity.

(a) Smith was employed by Proton plc in their factory making nuclear warheads for Britain's missile defence system. He was killed in an explosion in the factory. His widow wishes to establish that the defective design of the warheads, or of the system for making them, caused the explosion, and so recover damages from Proton plc.

(b) A charity wishes to seek judicial review of the Home Office's plan to lock up young offenders in secure training centres. It believes that civil servants in the Home Office research department advised the Home Secretary that the scheme would make the offenders more delinquent, not less. The Home Office says all advice to ministers is confidential.

(c) Farmer Giles was shocked to receive a visit from animal welfare inspectors from the RSPCA, who said they had been informed that he was keeping veal calves in illegal crates. This accusation was wholly untrue. When Giles tried to discover the source of the accusation, the RSPCA said that it was their policy never to reveal the identity of their informants, in order to encourage people to inform them of cases of cruelty to animals.

 ## Commentary

As the question makes clear, its principal concern is the doctrine of public interest immunity. It is therefore appropriate to begin with a brief introductory paragraph explaining what public interest immunity is and how it developed, though it would be wrong in such a problem question to write a detailed history. In each part of the question, the student needs to identify briefly the subject matter of the litigation and the parties to it, but the bulk of the answer should be devoted to PII. Because it is a matter for the discretion of the court whether the claim to PII is upheld in any case, the student will be assessed not on the correctness or otherwise of the final conclusion, but on the quality of the arguments deployed, and the depth of knowledge of decided cases.

 ## Answer plan

- Court to decide claims to PII
- Public interest in secrecy
- Public interest in fair litigation
- Claims to PII from any source.

Suggested answer

The doctrine of public interest immunity (PII) is intended to ensure that documents are not revealed in the course of litigation if it is not in the public interest that they should be revealed. Originally such a claim could only be made by the Crown and was therefore known as Crown Privilege. In *Duncan v Cammell Laird* [1942] AC 624, the House of Lords laid down the unfortunate rule that any claim made by the Crown had to be accepted by the courts, but in *Conway v Rimmer* [1968] AC 910, this rule was reversed, and the courts themselves took the responsibility of assessing whether or not it would be in the public interest for the documents to be disclosed.

(a) In this problem, Mrs Smith will be suing her late husband's employers, Proton plc, for negligence in failing to provide him with a safe system of work. She will therefore need the plans of the warheads and of the manufacturing system in order to identify the defects that gave rise to the explosion. But the Ministry of Defence is certainly going to claim that it would be against the public interest for these plans to be disclosed. That claim may be made in spite of the fact that the ministry is not a party to the case. Because of the adversarial nature of English legal proceedings, disclosing the documents means revealing them to the parties, their solicitors and barristers as well as to the judge. The possibility of hearing the case in camera does not eliminate the danger of the documents getting into the wrong hands.

In *Conway v Rimmer* (1986), the House of Lords laid down that, in deciding whether documents should be disclosed or not, two aspects of the public interest had to be balanced. Firstly, there was a public interest in ensuring that no harm was done to the national interest by disclosing documents that should be kept secret. But secondly, there was a public interest in ensuring that the conduct of litigation was not frustrated. The court distinguished between claims based on the contents of the particular documents and those based merely on the class to which the documents belonged. Contents claims would generally be much stronger than class claims. As a consequence of the Scott Inquiry into the Matrix Churchill affair, the government announced that it would no longer make class claims, but only claims based on the contents of particular documents. At the same time, in *R v Chief Constable of the West Midlands Police ex parte Wiley* [1995] 1 AC 274 the House of Lords showed little enthusiasm for the idea that whole classes of documents should be kept secret or that the holder of a class of documents was legally obliged to claim public interest immunity. If necessary, the court could inspect the documents to identify the strengths of the arguments for and against disclosure.

Applying these principles to the case of Mrs Smith, it seems very probable that her chances of establishing liability will be almost completely dependent on access to the documents, which, if they do reveal design flaws, will virtually prove her case by themselves. The litigation will be frustrated if she cannot gain access to them. But the arguments against disclosure are particularly powerful. The PII claim will be based on the contents of the documents themselves, and it is hardly possible to dispute an assertion that it would pose a grave threat to national security if the plans of the nuclear deterrent fell into the wrong hands, or if designs indicating how to build a nuclear warhead came into the possession of terrorists. Inspection of the documents is not likely to be necessary to convince the court that these are genuine state secrets. Comparison may be made with *Duncan v Cammell Laird* (1942) where the Admiralty was clearly justified in wishing to keep secret the plans of its latest submarine.

There is no doubt that the courts do have the power to order the disclosure even of documents as sensitive as these in the interest of justice, but it is doubtful whether they would do so in this case.

(b) The charity's appliction for judicial review may be based on the unreasonableness of the Home Office's decision or on the failure to take relevant considerations into account. Under the principle laid down in *Conway v Rimmer* (1968) it will be for the court to decide whether the public interest in confidentiality or the public interest in the fair conduct of litigation should prevail.

It appears that the Home Office's objection to the disclosure of documents in this case is based not on the contents of the particular documents, but on the claim that documents containing advice to ministers are a class that need to be kept confidential. The justification for this claim has been explained as the danger that officials might be deterred from being completely candid in their advice to ministers if they knew that such information might one day be revealed to the world through its use in litigation. But the courts have generally been unsympathetic to such assertions. In *Conway v Rimmer* (1968) such an argument was advanced in respect of the reports prepared by police officers on the conduct of a probationer, but the court rejected it. They pointed out that any such report would be protected by qualified privilege, so the official would have nothing to fear provided the report was honest. This point was also raised in *Williams v Home Office* [1981] 1 All ER 1151, where the court ordered the Home Office to disclose various documents including advice to ministers on the development of penal policy, rejecting the argument that the candour of public servants might be hindered by the remote chance of later disclosure in litigation. It would therefore appear that, unless some other, stronger argument for non-disclosure is presented to the court, the court may feel that the case for secrecy has not been made out.

Turning to the other side of the balance, the court will need to be satisfied that the disclosure of the documents is necessary for the fair conduct of the litigation. In *Air Canada v Secretary of State for Trade* [1983] 2 AC 394, this was interpreted as meaning that the applicants must show that it is very likely that the documents sought do contain material supportive of their case; applicants cannot embark on 'fishing' expeditions by demanding any document whether or not they have any grounds for thinking it material evidence. But once the applicants have passed this threshold, it may well be appropriate for the court to inspect the documents, because if they do not in fact assist the applicants' case, there is no need to order disclosure.

In this problem, the applicants seem to have good grounds for suggesting that the documents from the research department will assist their case, by demonstrating that relevant considerations were ignored. The court may feel that this is sufficient to justify an order for disclosure, given the weakness of the opposing case, or may feel it better to inspect the documents before coming to a conclusion. Only if the documents fail to support the applicants' case at all is it likely that disclosure will be refused.

(c) Before *Conway v Rimmer*, the term Crown privilege demonstrated clearly that claims for non-disclosure could be made only by the Crown. But in *Rogers v Home Secretary* [1973] AC 388, the claim was made by the Gaming Board which, though a public body, was not a government department. The House of Lords stated that claims based on the public interest could be made by any interested party, not just the Crown. This was applied in *D v NSPCC* [1978] AC 171, where the defendant, a charitable voluntary organisation, with a recognised status in the protection of children, was held able to claim PII in respect of certain confidential information. It would therefore be open to the RSPCA to raise an issue of PII in this case.

The basis of their claim is the need to offer complete confidentiality to informants who might otherwise be reluctant to contact them. Such claims have been accepted by the courts as being in the public interest. The case of *Rogers v Home Secretary* [1973] AC 388 concerned confidential information supplied to the Gaming Board about an applicant for a gaming licence. The court accepted that, in the sometimes murky world of gaming, informants needed to be given an absolute guarantee of confidentiality. In *D v NSPCC* [1978] AC 171 the charity was held to be justified in claiming that confidentiality served the vital function of encouraging people to report suspected child abuse. *R v Chief Constable of the West Midlands Police ex parte Wiley* [1995] 1 AC 274 also accepted that the identity of a police informer should be kept secret.

Whether the court would feel that the same justification applied in the case of cruelty to animals is not clear. But such activity can be criminal and the RSPCA is active in prosecution, so it seems that they could assert a public interest in the enforcement of the law. To obtain information about such organised cruelty as cock-fighting or badger-baiting might well require promises of complete confidentiality for informers.

To set against this is the public interest in the fair conduct of litigation. Clearly Giles will be unable to bring proceedings for defamation against the informant if he cannot discover who the informant was, and this may seem unfair, particularly as the defamation may even have been malicious. But the court may feel, as they did in *D v NSPCC* [1978] AC 171 that this is a price worth paying for the better protection of the vulnerable.

Further reading

Bradley, A. and Ewing, K. *Constitutional and Administrative Law*, 14th edn (Longman, 2007), ch 32.

Cane, P. *Introduction to Administrative Law*, 4th edn (OUP, 2004), chs 10, 11, 12 and 14.

Harlow, C. *Compensation and Government Torts* (Sweet and Maxwell, 1982).

Craig, P. *Administrative Law* 6th edn (Sweet and Maxwell, 2008), ch 28 and ch 29.

INDEX